Very Thai
Everyday Popular Culture

Very Thai

Everyday Popular Culture

Philip Cornwel-Smith
photographs: John Goss
& Philip Cornwel-Smith

RIVER
BOOKS

First edition published in Thailand in 2005 by
River Books Co., Ltd.
396 Maharaj Road, Tatien, Bangkok 10200
Tel 66 2 6221900, 2254963, 2246686
Fax. 66 2 2253861
E-mail: riverps@ksc.th.com
www.riverbooksbk.com

Reprinted 2005, 2006, 2008, 2009

British Library Cataloguing-in-Publication Data.
A catalogue record for this book is available
from the British Library

ISBN: 978-974-9863-67-1

Publisher: Narisa Chakrabongse
Editor: Alex Kerr
Design: Holger Jacobs at Mind Design, London
Production Supervision: Paisarn Piemmettawat

Printed and bound in Thailand by
Bangkok Printing Co., Ltd.

front papers: **Day-Glo Thai idylls
on velvet at a Sukhumvit Road
souvenir stall.**

page 1: **A pop icon of Thailand,
the *tuk-tuk* literally carries the
country's name.** *PCS*

page 2: **Typically Thai colours
on umbrellas and deckchairs at
Bang Saen beach resort.**

this page: **Modern gestures – the
wai gets the plastic McDonald's
treatment** (*JG*), **while a school-
boy in military crewcut does the
'handsome sign' that countless
Thais love to adopt when posing
for photographs** (*PCS*).

endpapers: **Saffron plasticware
and lucky-hued scarves in the
spiritual aisle of Tesco-Lotus
hypermarket.** (*PCS*)

cover portraits: **Philip Cornwel-
Smith** (*JG*); **John Goss** (*AR*).

Contents

Preface
by Alex Kerr

This is the book I wish I'd had when I first came to Thailand. A hundred things which had intrigued me for decades became clear on reading it. Such as where the statue of the beckoning lady came from, or why the alphabet always appears with pictures. Another hundred things, to my great embarrassment, I had hardly even noticed, but these turned out to be among the most interesting. Such as the condiments containers and little pink napkins set out on café tables, or the organisation of motorcycle boys at the mouths of *soi*.

Thailand seems an informal, free-wheeling place, even at times chaotic. But the more time you spend here you realise that the there's an internal logic and symbolism invisibly ordering everything. One of my Ten Laws of Thai life is: "There is always a Thai way to do it." Somewhere, inside an item of molded plastic, or submerged in the glossy pages of a *hi-so* magazine, the inner structure is there to be found.

This book begins to get at that inner structure, at deeply ingrained attitudes towards life. In popular culture, these are embellished with fantasy, redesigned for convenience, and finished off with a feeling of *sanuk*. Thus Hindu goddesses end up as beauty queens, court etiquette asserts itself at the whisky serving table, boat prows transform into the painted bonnets of trucks, and the sparkle of temple walls, in the form of electric light bulbs, drapes itself over trees and avenues.

I feel like a godfather to this book. I was there when many of the photos were taken, edited the text, and saw the book grow and transform. Both John and Philip in their separate ways began collecting photographs and ideas years before the idea of the book arose. In his photos, John has the knack of capturing Thai things as we really encounter them, on the street. With Philip, what struck me in the process was his incredible curiosity and persistence. We would be speeding along a highway and he would suddenly insist that the car stop – so that he could investigate a roadside shack where they made trash bins out of used tyres.

Philip would grill an expert for hours about what society women's hairdos had to do with fashions in the 19th century court. If he heard about a temple fair, or a medium's convention, or a new comedy hall, or a *luuk thung* song event – Philip was off to see it. Only someone with great curiosity – and energy to match – could have written this book.

In the process Philip ended up taking an entirely new approach to Thai pop culture. My mathematics teacher in high school used to jump on the table and shout at us:

"The secret of life is to look deeply into simple things!" This is what Philip Cornwel-Smith has done. *Very Thai* looks at the little things, the details of daily life that Thais and Western commentators usually pass by, but in these very details lie the mystery and magic of what it is to be Thai.

The chapters link the past to the present, Thailand to the outside world. They hint at the delicate connections between the zany and wonderful, and often beautiful forms that Thai pop culture takes. Unlike most writing about Thai culture, it's not a book about the past, but a book about now. At the same time, *Very Thai* is a precious documentary of many customs that are dying away, or transmuting as Thailand loses a bit of its 'Thainess' and blends into world mass culture. It's a snapshot of a moment in time.

A book seemingly about trivia and trifles, *Very Thai* is about Thailand's very soul. As such it has a truly transformative power. I know that I can never look the same way again at a motorcycle boy's jacket, a potted plant, fairy lights, a little pink napkin, a blue pipe, or the number nine.

above: **Many homes and shops install shrines to King Rama V and King Rama VI, as seen in Chelsea hair salon, Bangkok.** *PCS*

left: **A bus painted in the colours of the Thai flag.**

Introduction
What makes something very Thai?

Coffee-table books and advertisements like to present an Amazing Thailand™ of dancers and temples, elephants and floating markets, with lots and lots of fruit carving. While these marvels of official Thainess do exist, you often have to look for them. Though sometimes the elephants go looking for you, while they wander city streets for a living. Most of the time, what residents and visitors experience is the unsung popular culture. Everyday things, being the public's choice, are no less Thai and do frequently amaze.

Dayglo paintings of village huts zoom by on mini-buses. Overloaded broom carts bristle like a roadside art installation. Vendors sell multi-bladed knuckle-dusters off souvenir stalls. Rubber tyres get recycled into lotus ponds. Arresting all the senses, popular culture goes way beyond entertainment. It embraces practical folk arts, updated traditions and pop culture, a product of mass media, commercialisation and the urban street. *Very Thai* celebrates the miscellany of Thai life, whether folk or formal, pop or ethnic, homegrown or imported.

Unselfconscious consumers rarely consider streetlife as culture, a term reserved for refined arts and national prestige. Modernising Thailand often treats anything 'street' as undeveloped, low-brow or kitsch. Public and official comments tend to gloss over the reality of local lifestyles, especially when they touch on taboos like sex, gambling or magic. Yet while different classes in the rigid hierarchy socialise in separate worlds, most Thais live in mixed neighbourhoods, and display more tastes in common than they'd probably care to admit. Individuals of higher rank may also delight in ordinary activities like markets, streetfood or soap operas.

When presenting itself to foreigners, however, Thailand prefers to impress with grand sights, staged spectaculars and souvenirised crafts. And no holiday brochure is complete without concrete infrastructure: bridges, dams, malls. What impresses foreigners may be something else. Many travellers and expatriates avoid the contrived and pursue the authentic.

Fortunately, Thailand rewards the 'flaneur' – the wandering seeker of experience, open to impressions. Each step yields surprises for eyes, ears and nose, but precious few explanations. Guidebooks leave people wondering about the country's alternative sights: "Why is society women's hair so huge?" "How come napkins are tiny and pink?" "Where do so many ladyboys come from?" "What made Thai cat tails bent?" "Was that shop really called Porn Gems?" Stumped onlookers reach for the catch-all description "it's, well... very *Thai*".

left: **Styles clash at every turn in contemporary Thailand. Florid traditional décor at Wat Suan Plu gets dwarfed by a vast backdrop of curved balcony balustrades on the neo-classical skyscraper State Tower, which is topped by a huge gilded dome on the 65th floor.**

top: **Lost in Translation. Shops offer every imaginable service to** *farang* **from 'marriage for alien' to 'detectives', as hidden under an expressway at Sukhumvit 'Soi Zero' in Bangkok.** PCS

above: **The national shoe in all its colourful glory, artfully displayed at Cape Promthep, Phuket.** PCS

This book gets its name from tracking down that elusive 'very Thainess'. For over a decade, while editing guidebooks on Thailand and *Bangkok Metro* magazine, I've repeatedly been asked to unravel curiosities. The pictures shot by John Goss also begged questions. So I sought to research the first overview of Thai popular culture. Naturally, there's much more to say and many phenomena confound generalisation, especially given the regional diversity. This is a partial view drawn from an expatriate's experiences. Later books might reach other conclusions. Thais will have their own insights.

Information in Thailand continues to be guarded by seniors and issued bit-by-bit to initiates. Getting it is like a video game treasure hunt; you reach the next levels by sifting clues and acquiring keys to overcome barriers. Never subject to colonial standardisation, Thailand keeps its ancient ways, imbued with Buddhism, hierarchy, spirit beliefs. Indirectness avoids confrontation, leaving much unfathomable to Western reasoning, so asking questions is very *un*-Thai. Thais disarmingly respond "*mai pen rai*" – the answer is "never mind". The biggest booby-trap is 'face'. It relates more to self-image than to what others actually perceive and losing face – either yours or someone else's – means 'game over'.

Anthropologists call this situation 'bricolage' – the way that an animist society arranges the objects of life into a self-contained logic that bewilders outsiders. The science of bricolage 'reads' objects as signs. So in looking at lots of cultural objects, this book hopes to signpost the domestic, ritual and social lifestyle of the average Thai.

That average Thai is increasingly urban or suburban. Bangkok may be as untypical of Thailand as any capital is of its country. But being the focus of almost every national activity and over half its wealth, Bangkok imposes its ways and tastes on the remotest provincial outpost. In return, rural migrants bring the village to town, where traditional etiquette infuses corporate PR.

In that unplanned collision of values, delicate classical Thainess has taken on a harder, commodified edge. Many wood carvings turn out to be cast in resin. Garlands swing from the car mirror in moulded plastic. Monk supplies fill an aisle in the supermarket. Other traditions end up utterly disguised: lucky car plates are numerology in action, beauty queens embody deities. The status-aware middle classes tend to distance themselves furthest from old ways. Bourgeois pop veers towards fashionable, processed modernity – think TV, celebrity, golf, cute. This leads to a Warhol-like obsession with brands, whether imported, adapted or pirated.

"Pop is always a copy," says Gilda Cordero-Fernando, a Filipina connoisseur of the genre. "It's different from 'folk', which is rural, traditional, communal and a lot more innocent. It's different from ethnic, which is also all the above but comes from the minority groups. Folk and ethnic often become pop. Some ethnic/pop things climb up the social ladder and become elite. Some elite things get too popular, slide down and become pop. Pop therefore also means out-of-date and not-quite-in-synch."

All this applies to Thais. Long nails on men dropped from high class to low class, while boutiques promote fishermen's pants into must-haves. Ethnic remedies, while maligned if steeped in liquor, get upgraded at the spa. Technology may prompt such a shift: trucks take their decor from boats; Western instruments turned languid folk songs into dynamic *luuk thung* music.

This process is driven by the ingrained principle of emulating the master of any art. This tradition – found in dance, boxing and general education – seems to recur in revering the masters of global commerce. The elite feel compelled to adopt the styles of developed countries, which in turn get copied by the Thai masses: Greco-Roman architecture, Frenchified furniture, ornate gates, premium whisky. But just as a pupil can't help tweaking his master's template, with imports something always gets lost – or found – in translation.

Making imports Thai is actually an old tradition. Handicrafts with Japanese *manga* motifs aren't betraying Thai heritage, just repeating earlier moments when Hindu iconography or Western costume reflected the prevailing taste. While all nationalities absorb outside influences, Thais have retained their distinctiveness and independence despite living at a crossroads of cultures: Chinese, Indian, Western, Japanese, Khmer, Burmese, Malay, and indigenous tribes. The customisation of imports is key to that elusive, immutable Thainess, since the essence lies not in invention, but transformation.

"Eclectic borrowing, temporisation, adaptive skill, and pragmatism are the very flavour of the Thai cultural genius," Siamologist Niels Mulder believes. "They trust their own ways; meanwhile they are not shy to incorporate whatever is perceived as useful or attractive." Bling-bling plays a role, but in usually in service of practical, social or spiritual ends. The *tuk-tuk*, which originated in Japan, becomes Thai when restyled using flashing lights and the flared lines of auspicious motifs. You could say Thai things have less to do with things than with an attitude towards them: an aesthetic, a palette, a line, all conveyed with a blend of serenity and fun. Anything, given time enough to steep here, can end up very Thai.

There's actually an official definition of Thai culture: *watthanatham*. The World War II military regime of Phibunsongkhram defined it as "qualities which indicated and promoted social prosperity, orderliness, national unity and development, and morality of the people." Coined in an era of nation-building, under Japanese and European influences of the 1930s, it enforces a fixed, centralised vision of a state culture from the top down.

Popular culture, by contrast, is the incremental result of decisions by diverse, ordinary people – a continual reinvention of the moment. Welling up from below without plan or policy, pop proves more responsive to that 'development', whether in fashion, technology or customs. Official attempts to dictate clothing and pastimes are the most glaring way in which the pop results of 'social prosperity' don't fit the military 'orderliness' that businessmen-turned-politicians still try to enforce. Still, this definition reflects a sincere national pride.

Today, the official culture is propagated to tourists: sanitised village festivals, sound and light extravaganzas, landmarks cleared of their vibrant old neighbourhoods. When the national narrative occupied the mainstream, much genuinely popular culture was pushed to the margins, from herbalism to Thai garments. Discomfiting subcultures – magic tattoos, mediums, blind buskers, ladyboys, phallic charms, naughty massage – face ever-growing disapproval. Yet often what's most fascinating are the things left unregulated and unabashed.

The underground economy is so vast that it operates quite openly, though under increasingly tough scrutiny. Economists aptly call it the 'informal sector'. They mean handcarts towering with furniture, palmists reading fortunes at piers, trash collectors sifting bins, *tuk-tuk* drivers touting gem scams, demimondaines pouting in dayglo, seafood restaurants camped on the sidewalk. These fringe activities reveal an everyman biography – and therein lies their interest.

Since many authentic things aren't now considered *riab roi* (showing tidiness or decorum), to dwell on the humdrum requires delicacy. "To disparage the great is sacrilege and arrogance; to honour the small is either stupidity or sarcasm," writes the pundit Mont Redmond, pinpointing the dilemma facing journalist and historian. "The Thai feeling for such situations is succinctly expressed by *faa suung paen din tam*. 'Sky high, Land Low' constitutes an order of social nature so self-evident that only a *farang* could question it."

left: **Much Thai life is lived on the street, where vendors will hawk almost anything. Around the PC mall Pantip Plaza, that can mean selling used computers on the sidewalk of the information superhighway. The vendor doesn't need a chair when he can balance perfectly in the compact Thai squat.** *PCS*

It often takes an outsider – or at least a detached perspective – to see the patterns. "One must begin somewhere, if only with an unqualified stranger making a trial sampling and giving his reactions," reflects the artist Tom Phillips of his book on Thai postcards. "This may even have its advantages since every country is ordinary and unexotic to itself. Therefore it is often through foreigners that we learn what is remarkable and strange in the places and among the people that we take for granted."

This has been true for centuries. Histories dwelt little on ordinary folk, about whom knowledge relies heavily on Chinese and Western journals. A rare local record of past daily life, the temple mural, dissolves through time and neglect. Over-painting then superimposes that new era's sensibilities, as when murals stopped including playful sexuality in response to missionary censure. Over time, it becomes hard to track changes.

Popular culture has finally become a self-conscious subject of Thai media, since the economic crash of 1997 highlighted the treasures being lost in the boom. With imports suddenly less affordable, Thais had to draw upon indigenous assets. Faced with an encroaching synthetic culture – with its themed, re-packaged past – some Thais revived traditions, as in the North, or sought restoration of old neighbourhoods. Others found joy in the simple stuff that surrounds them. Anusorn Ngernyuang built the Reflections hotel complex to showcase the Thai pop aesthetic through objects like tableware.

Each chapter of *Very Thai* deserves a book of its own and that's what they're slowly getting. Pundits like Paothong Thongchua, Anake Nawigamune and Suthorn

Sukphisit reach broad audiences with their insights on archetypal Thai lifestyle. Films like *Mon Rak Transistor* (The Magic Spell of Radio) and *Faen Chan* (My Girl) made pop culture their affectionate subject. Magazines by and for the *indy* generation often get inspired by indigenous ideas, record the gritty streetlife and dare to offer opinions. The job of 'critic' – reviled for losing people face – became semi-tolerated in the 1990s and raises awareness of things taken for granted. Issues never touched by T-Pop have emerged in Thai rap, and the biting lyrics of rural music find their way to urban ears.

These diverse voices offer fresh takes on what makes something very Thai. In one dizzying spasm, Thailand is experiencing the forces that took a century to transform the West: modernism, beat philosophy, rock 'n' roll, the sexual revolution, hippy peaceniks, punk alienation, rave hedonism, playful post-modernism, religious revival, slacker consumerism, *indy* experimentation, puritan prohibition, and online globalisation. Much of value from the past is being junked in the headlong rush to one of the many ways to be modern. Yet some traditions draw renewed energy from this cultural whirl, which is financed by a booming economy and was sparked in 1992 by the dawn of a workable democracy. In few places in time do so many subcultures exist simultaneously. While Thailand might not lead in all these movements, there's nowhere better to sample the cultural fusion.

Drawing these threads could be done many ways. I've generally focused on themes under-explored elsewhere, so film, dance, design and the more elite arts don't get devoted chapters. Instead, they emerge among many cross-currents that the index is designed to navigate. Many other items must await a future book.

Mostly I've gathered topics based on how they're experienced, which transcends divisions of class, region, age group, town and country, old and new. Of the four sections, 'Street' dwells on public space, and 'Personal' on the private domains of body, home and identity. 'Ritual' explores beliefs and luck. 'Sanuk' (the fun sensibility) covers entertainment and how Thais socialise.

Of course, these overlap. Many activities have public, private and spiritual sides, while *sanuk* infuses all. Cross-cultural business books emphasise how *sanuk* helps the Thais get work done. So I must stress that writing this book, though an all-consuming task, has been incredibly *sanuk*. And I hope it's also *sanuk* to read.

Notes on sources and use of Thai language
I've used Thai words where they help explain the subject. These are defined in the Glossary, which is incorporated into the Index along with dates of reigns and eras. Thai words are italicised and kept singular since there are no Thai plurals, though 'Thais' is a plural of an English word. Hyphens in Thai merely separate syllables that could be mis-read. I've kept transliterations as close to their pronunciation as possible, while preserving the owners' spellings of names. Apologies for any errors in language or fact. My sources are interviews, experience and the bibliography listed at the back.

About the Photographs
by John Goss

Photography for this book began on my first visit to Thailand in 1988, before it became my home. I soon switched from taking tourist snaps to documenting the puzzling sights in street, market and fairground. Most Thais I queried paid little attention to the meanings of the everyday things around them. So lots of these images remained unexplained until this collaboration with Philip to uncover the origins and interconnectedness of things like coins in ears and poodle-shaped bushes.

As with many people, my first encounter with things Thai started with my discovery of Thai food. Perfumed soups, Technicolor gelatinous cubes, drinks tasting like spiced wood in hand-embossed mugs – a sensory overload calmly overseen by portraits of monarchs in every restaurant. While pop in many countries has become appropriated by commerce, in Thailand these mundane marvels of 'found art' remain an unselfconscious part of daily life.

I've tried to record this unsung beauty, free from the posed and styled quality of many books and magazines on Thai culture. These scenes, encountered through serendipity, were not set-up or re-arranged, though a handful of images needed some composing. While Thais love to prepare for portraits, I've sought to record their smiles in a natural, impromptu way. I shoot in natural light wherever possible, avoiding flash, using a range of Sony digital cameras.

Two-fifths of the photographs are by Philip Cornwel-Smith. He, likewise, brought years of images to the book, drawn especially from festivals and performance. As foreigners, we are, inescapably, observers, but we've tried getting to the heart of the action. Philip was stampeded by men in animal trances at the Tattoo Festival, wiped flying perspiration off the lens at the boxing ring, and found himself becoming part of the comedy routine he was photographing.

Some pictures needed to be sourced, mainly related to mass media. We thank those who kindly supplied images in the acknowledgements. Overall, our picture choice covers every taste and every region, because there's more to Thai pop than cosmopolitan Bangkok. These images offer an invitation to experience the mixture of ancient origins and global hybrids, official culture and underground intrigues that envelop anyone on a walk through modern Thai life.

far left top: **The soda fountain of a *nam sa* stall at Talad Ban Mai in Chachoengsao takes the shape of a jet plane, ready to fizz-up syrups, juices or even tea.** *PCS*

above: **A *mai dut* poodle bush clad in blue at Chachoengsao.**

left: **Thailand has a many themed colours. A major one is saffron, seen in these monks' robes at Wat Loka Ya Suttharam, Ayutthaya.**

Street

****

Dinner on a Stick

For the constant urge to snack, streetfood is always close at hand

Thai streets smell of many things. Foremost among them is the pervasive whiff of food. Even where cooking carts have moved on, their traces slick the pavements, their aroma hangs in the air. You can sense clouds of atomised chilli from a hundred paces, not least because it stings the eyes. Indeed, a hundred paces are the most you need travel before encountering something more to eat.

"*Gin khao reu yang*" ("eaten rice yet?") is the original Thai "Hello", not the bland World War II invention, "*sawatdee*". Like Osakans greeting each other with "Earning money yet?", it sets the cultural priority. The implication being, whether you'd dined or not, conversation should continue over food. Tellingly, the term for snacking is *khong kin len* – play eating. Fun food must be available at all times, in all places. And so it is. Bangkok boasts around 11,000 restaurants and fixed stalls in their tens of thousands. Day and night, food vendors gather at markets, hover informally at *pak soi* or ply the backstreets by trolley or by slinging baskets over a shoulder yoke.

Serendipity is guaranteed with roving streetfood, which saves you from doing the walking in the heat. Snacking is the instinct of the hunter-gatherer: grab food when you can. With ever less time available for home cooking, modern Thailand elevates that survival impulse into an art. Snacking accompanies labour, punctuates boredom, makes arduous teamwork *sanuk* (fun) and typifies the Buddhist injunction to live in the moment. And the moment hunger strikes, food is at hand.

Some vendors display pre-prepared dishes, such as vats of stewed pig leg or trays of curry. Others cook on the spot, whether it's boiled, stir fried, deep fried, barbecued, marinated, or pounded with a pestle and mortar.

Thai food's prime format is the morsel. In curry, shrimp-paste dip, *yum* (salad) or most other dishes, the cook pre-cuts each portion so you may shovel and spike with spoon and fork, or nibble it off skewers, often from inside a plastic bag. Displayed in glazed cabinets or arrayed in patterns on trays, racks, grills and griddles,

facing page, left and above:
Sausages and fishballs. A fast snack for a permanently grazing population, meat on a stick is fuel for the Thai smile.

below: **Dessert on a stick for this ice-cream loving kid in Dan Sai, Loei.**

every imaginable *khong khob khio* (thing to bite or chew) sits skewered on bamboo. Myriad parts of pig or chicken get lanced *satay*-style over charcoal: meat, liver, heart, wiggly intestines. Sausages come long, short, round or sliced. Meatballs might be pork, fish or buffalo disguised as beef. Much else gets speared: won ton, cuttlefish, parboiled eggs in their shell and unhatched chick foetus. Even *miang kham* – a do-it-yourself mixture of savoury ingredients you fold into a leaf – has turned into a lazy snack, pre-wrapped and lanced for eating without effort.

Dessert comes morsel-sized too. While friend banana may come on a stick, huge trays atop vendor tricycles tempt passers-by with gelatinous cubes. Speared by a cocktail stick they're concocted from coconut, palm sugar, banana, taro, bean paste and rice in myriad forms.

The archetypal all-day nibble is fruit. Plying his glazed trolley along roads as the sun slowly warms his iced cargo, the fruit vendor performs a well-honed system when hailed. Opening the hinged glass lid, he stabs at, say, an unripe mango with his all-purpose knife, flips it onto a curved metal cutting plate, chopping through to the hard seed repeatedly while rotating the fruit. He levers off slivers of the sour green mango and slides them through the plate's funnel-like end into a plastic bag. This – and other bags of fruit like spiral cut pineapple, bendy lengths of papaya or half-moons of melon – enters yet another plastic bag, this one with handles. Pink sachets of sugar, salt and chilli provide the dip, satisfying the tropical body's need for liquids, salts and sugar to

rehydrate. After a quick swab with a cloth, knife, tray and glass lid get eased into their designated slots.

Another finely honed vendor art is wrapping in banana leaf. Folded around savouries, desserts or an entire meal on rice then secured with a bamboo pin, the waxy waterproof leaf opens as a hand-bowl or lays flat like a plate. Slowly fading from stalls, particularly in Bangkok, banana leaf is increasingly consigned to smart restaurants to convey retro ambiance.

Thais rarely invite acquaintances home in the style of a Western dinner party, so impromptu daily dining on streetfood at holes-in-the-wall, night markets and vendor carts keeps standards high, especially where multiple vendors gather. Favourites naturally emerge, while famed one-dish specialists draw pilgrims for decades. Simple open-fronted eateries are essentially a stall parked in a shophouse, instead of paused under a green umbrella. You pull up the generic plastic stool to the generic steel trestle table under the generic congealed cobwebs.

How differently formal Thai restaurants evolved. "Only with the post-World War II influx of foreigners and Thailand's rapid economic development did Thai cooking begin to be appreciated as worthy of a night out," comments Lonely Planet guru Joe Cummings. Adopting the Western format in the 1960s, wealthy Thai wives in Bangkok's Sukhumvit district converted buildings fronting their compounds into outlets for their cooks. That format persists, joined by shophouse and purpose-built restaurants of increasing sophistication. Yet gourmets often complain the posher the premises, the less authentic the cuisine, with timid spicing, lame fusions, and a Western sequence of courses. In all but the smartest places, Thai dishes arrive like buses. Only when they're ready – and in any order.

Thai cuisine's phenomenal success in the West since the 1980s – coming long after exposure to Indian, Chinese, Indonesian and Indochinese food – was partly prompted by returning backpackers enthusing about what they'd tasted on Thai streets. The government now promotes Thailand as the 'Kitchen of the World'.

Authentic streetfood isn't *riab roi* (politely tidy) or upmarket in the eyes of face-conscious authorities, who constantly seek ways to cleanse and standardise stalls. The Singapore formula of hawker centres located off pavements could well follow. Appearances may deceive, however. Stalls could be more sanitary, but street food tends to get bought, prepared and eaten the same day. Ingredients kept refrigerated for days in restaurants are at least as responsible for any tummy troubles.

Availability and quick preparation means that many Thai dishes count as fast food. Now the urge to nibble extends to sweetened, fatty, additive-laden junk foods. Dubbed *ahaan waang* (empty food), it hails mostly from the West and Japan, as do their main outlets: convenience chain stores. Attracting customers from corner shops and vendors, these clean, brightly-lit franchises glare from every busy street. Designed to promote impulse buys of plastic-sealed preserved snacks, they pull Thais from their past diet through clever marketing, scripted greetings, sheer ease, and a modern, synthetic image.

While obesity now mushrooms among the young, generations of eating at will had kept Thais famously svelte. The health difference lies in the freshness Thai food requires. And since each meal forms an excuse to socialise, the West's nutritious, convivial 'Slow Food' movement's response to processed Fast Food comes naturally to Thais. Their dexterous vendors combine the best of both worlds, supplying Slow Food at fast pace.

Drink in a Bag
Quenching thirst with juices, tea and herbal tinctures

"Waiter, there's salt in my drink!" No mistake, salt often gets added to drinks in Thailand, especially fruit juice. One gulp from freshly squeezed orange or pineapple juice and many a foreigner sputters. Some pucker and return the drink with disgust, others find they like the heady mix of citrus and sodium chloride.

In this sweaty climate, minerals need replenishment, so Thais take all they need (glucose, salt, water, vitamin C) in one go. Or reach for nature's all-in-one rehydration pack: the coconut. The husk gets hacked with a machete into a pentagon shape with a 'lid'. The fruit comes with a spoon so you can scoop out the coconut lining within. Sweet coconut flesh also gets salted, not just in curries but also in many desserts.

Just as in Thai cooking, where condiments balance out the principal flavours – sweet vs sour, salty vs bitter – so with drinks. Salt softens water, and so counteracts tartness from the lime. On its own, tea is bitter; hence teas (excepting green and jasmine infusions) get the sugar treatment. And how.

No drink is deemed too sweet, thanks to lashings of palm water, granules or condensed milk. Instead of by the spoonful or lump, you could measure sugar by its depth: "One centimetre or two?" Then in pours the hot tea, strained, with a flourish, through a sock.

The tea appears brick red, though the gauze sock is stained black with repeated inundations of powdered tea concentrate, brewed earlier in a tin. Most vendor trolleys

above left: **Dark oliang coffee and orange Thai tea join other pre-mixed drinks ready to pour over a bag of ice in Chiang Mai.** *PCS*

above right: **A finely embossed aluminium drinking cup rests on the lid of a ceramic water jar, an hospitable invitation to passers-by to slake their thirst.**

left: **OJ to go. Plastic bags of frosty, fresh-squeezed juice are tied up with a rubber band that doubles as a springy carrying handle. Sip through a straw as you walk.**

pair the tea apparatus with equivalents for coffee. Same drill, whether sweet black Chinese *oliang* or sweet brown *gafae*. Ordered hot, it comes in a cup. Decanted over ice, it can be taken away – in a bag.

Shaved ice gets shoveled into a handled plastic bag, the hot tea or coffee poured on top. It's not handed over until a further slick of sweetened milk gloops from a can. The resulting swirl of white on orange adds an essential touch of beauty. Stick in a straw – plus another for your friend – and you're off. Same goes for juices, shakes, Coke and saccharine soft drinks flavoured red or green. Unlike spill-prone plastic cups, the pendulous bag makes a steady mobile vessel. Just don't try to sit it down… look for a hook!

Since the 1997 economic crash rekindled fashion for things traditional, herbal drinks have joined the plastic bag parade. They're ladled from enormous glass jars, or more authentically from unvarnished, decoratively scored Mon pottery the shape of a lotus bud. Lift the pointed lid and a coconut shell scoop retrieves the diluted, sweetened residue of boiling ambrosially smooth bael fruit, lemon grass stalks, chrysanthemum flowers or rozelle buds, which resemble currant juice in taste and colour. Each harbours medicinal goodness, though the diuretic ones

pose a problem since herbal drinks have become a very common feature at marathon festival shows.

Similar lidded jars and ladles still sit in pairs under shelters in front of some Northern houses. The idea is hospitality, offering water (naturally chilled by the pottery's porous properties) to the thirsty traveller. In bygone days, when these jars were universal up north, water may have been less polluted, but wasn't always pure. Drawn from wells, scooped from streams, or bailed from rain jars of roof run-off, it took on tastes and textures from organic matter, suspended particles and the clammy confines of storage. Hence the appeal of water tinctures. Just as the unwashed douse with perfume, unfiltered water improves when scented.

Evoking a feminine cologne such as rosewater, *nam yaa uthai* emits a pungent floral aroma, even when a water jug contains just a drop. Concentrating blossoms like jasmine, pikul, dafflower and several kinds of lotus, it also contains over 30 kinds of herb, including saffron, Vietnamese cinnamon and two ingredients that make it pink: *jan daeng* and sappanwood. Boiled sappanwood produces *daeng luead nok* (red bird blood), a tonic for enriching human blood. Not all the flowers used impart scent, but each heals the heart, herbalists assure.

When Western medicines threatened the future of Thai treatments, King Rama V registered it among the *tamrub yaa thai sib yang* (Ten Thai Medicinal Recipes). Today, traditional homemakers still serve it, perhaps partly due to reverence for Rama V, whose favorite colour was pink. Its body-cooling qualities were once prized as a disguise for warm, foetid well water, though now either of the two brands – Ya Uthai Mor Mee and the more popular Uthai Thip – conveys a retro panache. A summer cooler, it's the Thai answer to Pimm's No 1. A younger devotee of *nam yaa uthai*, flower designer Sakul Intakul, notes another other property: "Before branded cosmetics, women dabbed it on their faces as a kind of rouge."

Though *nam yaa uthai* steadlily becomes scarcer, and *khao chae* (rice in jasmine-scented chilled water) is only a hot season dish, another tincture remains omnipresent. More appetising than plain water, less piquant than full-strength tea, *nam cha* (dilute jasmine tea) sits in jugs on each table at every simple eating place, from the vendor's metal trestle to the Formica shophouse counter. More often than not, the cup provided is metal. In cooling the contents, metal is prone to condensation. The resultant puddle always seems to dribble onto someone's lap. The reason for the metal is tradition transformed.

"Until two or three decades ago almost every Thai drank from a metal bowl, though I'm the only one in my family who still does," recalls Paothong Thongchua, Dean of Arts at Thammasat University and connoisseur of things authentically Thai. He sips from an engraved steel vessel eight inches across, its rounded base resting on a filigree-rimmed tray that doubles as a lid. "The metal depended on your class: gold silver, bronze, brass, tin and so on. Just as people share food from the same dishes, they drank from the same bowl. Glasses only came in with fashion and concern that germs might transmit."

During meals, it's still possible to see older family members supping from such a bowl. Their descendents may favour modern glass, ceramic or plastic, though the floridly embossed aluminium bowl is still found everywhere, though usually of a smaller size. It often rests upended on the lid of an insulated plastic tub of iced water, which Thais keep handy by the household daybed, in the hut of a security guard, or by the bench of a motorcycle taxi rank.

The electric water cooler has brought the curse of soggy paper cones to gyms and offices, but not to every water dispenser. Metal cups, often with the handle on chain, are still the norm for quenching visitors' thirsts at state offices, museums and temples. The more sanitary public drinking fountain has hardly caught on, despite new ones in downtown Bangkok. People see them being used as standpipes for washing hands and much else. But since Thais prefer their drinks to be shared, they happily sip from the same metal cup or plastic bag.

Sugar
A nation full of sweetness

Thais seem disposed towards sweetness, in language, personality, sentiment, colour schemes and, crucially, food. Thai sugar consumption is about the highest per capita in the world. Perhaps that languid ability to doze in the most uncomfortable positions is down not only to heat, work or digesting sticky rice, but also due to blood-sugar energy mounting until the inevitable collapse.

Thais balance flavours in both food and life. Flatterers are dubbed *pak waan* (sweet mouth) and dainty women *sao waan* (sweet maidens), in contrast to sassy *sao priao* (sour maidens), and people who are stingily *khem* (salty) or sorrowfully *khom kheun* (bitter).

In food, this balance seems a model of moderation until you realise it means that sugar gets added to everything. Even savouries can't be sweet enough. Curries are ladled with coconut milk, brown palm-sugar's used everywhere, and even dried slivers of pork, beef or squid come saturated in syrup. Calorie counters look on aghast as the wok-handler clacks, tings, sizzles and scrapes a healthy stir-fry, then heaves in handfuls of sugar. Once at the table, most lunches get laced with lime, vinegar, chilli and fish sauce plus further granules of glucose.

To keep the sugar rush going, a colour-enhanced rainbow of puddings and candies tempt, though often with a saline tang. Typical Thai desserts are cubed and wobbly, sliced from trays of gelatinous variations on the coconut/palm-sugar/bean theme, often combined with sticky rice. Many old sweets derive from early imports. Aside from introducing the chilli and the tomato, 17th century Portuguese visitors caused the profusion of light, honey-laden breads and eggy puddings. As if equating richness with being rich, heavily yolked desserts often bear flakes of gold leaf. At weddings, bride and groom feed each other syrupy saffron threads and thumbsized golden cupcakes resembling flowers. Vendors also place similar golden filling in tiny crepes cooked on mobile griddles.

Taste for the diminutive, decorative and cute infuses Siamese sweets, from blue-dyed rice and multi-coloured bean strands to fruit carving and miniature marzipan sculptures dyed in exaggerated hues. "The attention to detail within the confections is a sight to behold: the soft curves of the *saneh jant*, the painstakingly-detailed decorative markings on the *tong ake sumpany* and the creation of a crown for the *ja mongkut*," writer Mallika Khuansathaworanit reminisces of sweet nibbles still found at specialist outlets.

The sugar addiction extends beyond traditional treats to newer imported nibbles, from sweetened movie popcorn to chocolate bars made waxy so they don't melt. Kids with a handful of *satang* (pennies) pester shop-keepers to rummage for boiled sweets or durian-flavour biscuits in huge tins with a window to help you guide your hand. Pizza can't be consumed without sweetened ketchup. Teenagers swarm around bread-and-milk bars in malls for toast slicked with margarine, and dusted with granulated sugar or coloured sprinkles. Another variant involves toast spread with a white, red or green gloop: condensed milk, scarlet jam or leafy pandan paste.

The saccharine slick also floods the bakery. Squishy buns emit cloying custards, more condensed milk and a fibrous substance resembling an armpit: hairy pork. Not wild boar with bristles attached (itself a forest delicacy), it is meat teased into strands then sweetened. Cakes veer towards bath-sponge-and-shaving-foam variety. Iced with cute characters and slogans, they can come with pictures lasered onto icing with the texture of cardboard.

The oddest confluence of tastes must be the ice cream sandwich. Scooped into a bun and sprinkled with

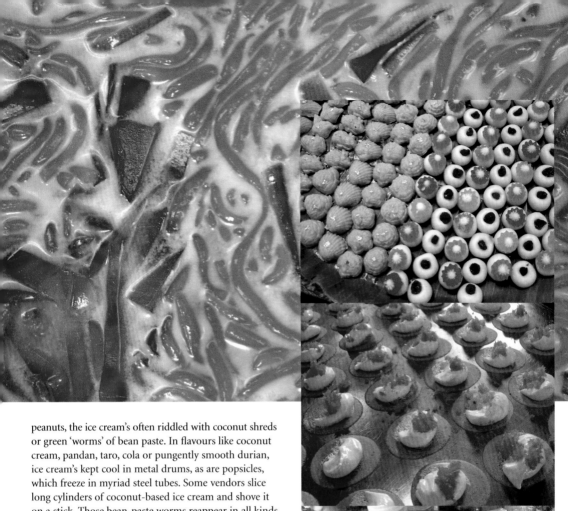

peanuts, the ice cream's often riddled with coconut shreds or green 'worms' of bean paste. In flavours like coconut cream, pandan, taro, cola or pungently smooth durian, ice cream's kept cool in metal drums, as are popsicles, which freeze in myriad steel tubes. Some vendors slice long cylinders of coconut-based ice cream and shove it on a stick. Those bean-paste worms reappear in all kinds of iced desserts, whether swirling in a green slurpable drink or poured over shaved ice in *lord thong ruam mit*, a kind of Thai knickerbocker sundae with sweetcorn, red beans, taro chips and multicolour syrups.

Tea, coffee and fruit shakes, too, receive glugs of evaporated milk, and a final swirl of sweetened condensed milk. Herbal drinks – bael fruit, roselle, lemon grass, chrysanthemum flower, longan – effectively become flavourings for boiled sugar water. While Coke and Pepsi monopolise whatever market they can, in the kaleidoscopic Thai taste, brown Cola doesn't stimulate the eye like bright sugar-pop sodas. Orange Mirinda, Green Spot and red Dang Bireley's are carbonated evocations of the now rare *nam saa* stalls that fizz-up fruit cordials and even oliang coffee through a rocket-shaped fountain.

Thai frames didn't fatten into mass obesity until Western fast food captured the popular imagination and its franchises muscled out indigenous outlets. Now everything's so over-sweetened you can literally inhale it. Just as vaporised chilli oil stings the eyes, atomised sugar with a plasticised aroma hangs in the air of convenience stores, cinema foyers, and mall kiosks flogging flavoured pretzels. You could almost cut this cloying cloud with a knife, and if you could it would make a nice Thai snack.

top: **Worms of bean paste swirl in coconut cream ready to mix with crushed ice, beans, chestnuts and other goodies in the retro dessert *lod thong ruam mit*.**

far left: **Typical Thai desserts.**

left: **Iced popsicles of sugar – and salt! – drawn from moulds spun in a heat-exchanger cart.**

above, upper: **Gold leaf on eggy desserts inspired by Portuguese traders in ancient Ayutthaya.**

above, middle: **Marshmallows on crêpes at a kerbside griddle.**

above, lower: **Water chestnuts diced, floured, boiled and dyed pink, before serving on ice as *tubtim krob* (crunchy rubies).**

Tiny Pink Tissues
Tabletops explained

A perennial mystery to the *farang* visitor is the design of the tiny pink tissue. This wisp seems ill suited to their table manners. Lodged with toothpicks in a sponsored holder of Carlsberg green or Pepsi blue, pink napkins are as much a fixture of street stalls and informal *raan ahaan* (food 'shops') as the condiment holder for sugar, vinegar, dried chilli and fish sauce.

Napkins, *farang* decorum presumes, should be big and substantial. Even if you could place the flimsy single-ply squares across a lap, the fan would blow them away. Waste-conscious *farang* use ever-decreasing areas of one sheet, and sigh when it takes a handful of the paper to mop the puddle from the steel cup of dilute *nam cha* (jasmine tea). Some test it – never twice – with a sneeze.

Westerners use one double-ply serviette to manage several mealtime mishaps. Some even re-fold rumpled cloth napkins and put them back in the drawer. To spotless Thais, such antics are like wearing an unwashed shirt, a crime for which repeat-offending backpackers are often dubbed *farang kii nok* (bird shit Westerners). So why is the Thai tissue so tiny and so pink?

The secret lies not in multiple use of a single sheet, but a different use for each sheet. For Thai needs, the size is ideal. You discard it the moment it's dirtied. Aside from dabbing mouths, blotting spills and coping with chilli's effects on eyes and nose, Thais use tissues for cleaning

the cutlery and crockery. The customer does this. *Before* they eat. Savvy diners don't trust street stalls' murky grey rinsing bowl, hence the Bangkok municipal plan to supply hot water washers to vendors. Thais sometimes retrieve bamboo or Melamine chopsticks from sanitised wrappers, but more usually from communal hinged steel boxes, which also contain flat-bottomed soup spoons made of steel or Melamine.

The pink tissue's essential for wiping the serving spoon handle, which always slides into the food en route to the table. One sheet may come binding the spoon and fork, which are pressed from aluminium of a consistency favored by Uri Geller. Marvel as the spoon suddenly bends! Witness food mysteriously escape the wonky fork! Gasp as its tines splay like a dancer's fingers!

Fingers were the cutlery, in days – mostly now past – when banana leaf wrappings unfolded into a plate. But Thais do find themselves eating many dishes with the hand, though always the right, since the left cleanses where the food exits. With sticky fingers to swab, demand for tissue is high, making cost an issue.

Hence the colour. Ones bleached white may be too pricy (at 22 baht for 500) for poorer vendors to afford. The dye indicates recycled paper costing just 16.50 baht: every half-baht counts. It's pink because extracts of tomato and cinnabar annatto score best at disguising the speckly blemishes from recycling, a dye company explains. And pink proves more appetising with food than, say, blue, brown or green.

Maximising value, some vendors separate lap-size serviettes into single-ply sheets, which they patiently cut into quarters and then fold. Labour is that cheap, money that tight, time that expendable.

Cheapest of all are toilet rolls, which grace many a dining table, though usually hidden in a holder. So ingenious are its disguises that the box for tissue rolls and face tissues has become a Thai craft tradition. Popular finishes include elaborate bead work, dainty lace, carved teak wood, woven reed, knitted frills, interleaved bamboo slats, cutesy doll-like dresses, and Baroque moulded plastic flecked with gold paint. A fixture in taxis, the decorated tissue box has graduated to trendy accessory. Rare is the booth in Bangkok International Gift Fair that doesn't tailor its aesthetic to tissue.

While tissues colonise smarter restaurants using such elegant disguises, at the top end the starched lap cloth now reigns. But imagine Thai distaste at having to keep using a cloth after it's dirtied. At such moments, diners might yearn to reach for the tiny pink tissue.

facing page: **A portable quartet of Thai condiments – ground red chilli, sugar, spicy vinegar and fish sauce – rests in front of a basket of other dining essentials and a complimentary jug of weak Chinese tea.**

left: **Ubiquitous tiny pink tissues perplex many visitors. You need a whole handful of the wisps to tidy up after a pepper crab or roasted chicken.**

below: **At home or in taxis, tissue boxes and toilet rolls don frilly fantasy frocks to distract from their dirt-mopping destiny.** *PCS*

previous spread: **A typical scene found at *pak soi* – the mouth of a side street – in Saphan Khwai, Bangkok.** *PCS*

Insect Treats
A protein hit for farmers becomes a snack for city folk

Fried chicken only comes with two legs per bird, though another deep fried Thai treat boasts up to ten smaller, but scrumptious legs: insects. For centuries a nutritious nibble for impoverished farmers from the Northeast, insects have become a staple snack among urbanites.

Vendor trays glisten with the oil-laced crispy carapaces of up to a dozen different bugs: ants, beetles, grubs and even scorpions. Buckets may hold a mottled slop that closer inspection reveals as ants in varying stages of life: egg, grub, adult. A piquant staple of Isaan and the North, red ant soup finds its way onto Bangkok restaurant menus.

Bugs fall officially into two categories: *malaeng* (six-legs with head, thorax and abdomen) or *maeng* (eight or ten legs, just two sections and no wings). However, most insects are simply called *maeng*, like *maeng da*, a water beetle resembling a large green cockroach.

Though the appearance of insects puts off many foreigners, these alien-looking scavengers are essentially prawns of the land. Pound for pound (and it takes 30,000 termites to make a pound), bugs match the nutrition of freshwater fish and prawns. Bombay locusts are 25.88 percent protein, giant crickets pack 20.72 percent and the greatest energy of any bug: 237.26 Kcal per 100 grammes. Metallic beetles (their iridescent wing casing used in royal jewellery) and dragonfly larvae supply the best dose of minerals, especially phosphorous and calcium. No wonder entomologists and the National Institute of Thai Traditional Medicine champion their health value – and as spin-offs to existing industries.

"In 1987 the Ministry of Health included silkworm pupae on a list of local foods that could be used in supplementary food formulas developed for malnourished infants and preschool children. They are fried and ground into a coarse powder, which is then added to curries and soups," writes Jerry Hopkins, author of *Strange Food*, much of which emanates from Thailand.

So what do insects taste like? *Mot som* seem tangy like their name – sour ants. Their large soft white eggs burst on the tongue like sacs of soft cheese. Other bugs emit a gamey, pungent twang, though frying renders many quite alike to the novice. "Most [beetles] in the adult stage are somewhat nutty in flavour – although I know a Thai woman who insists she can identify the plant the bug had been eating before it was caught and cooked," Hopkins recounts. *Maeng da*, though, zing with a minty-apple taste when pulped into a kind of Isaan paté.

While mashing disguises their shape, frying and steaming preserves them mostly intact – mandibles,

left: **Prawns of the air – deep fried grasshoppers at Pratunam in Bangkok. Just spray with soy sauce and crunch.** *PCS*

top and above: **Select your slither in Chiang Mai's fresh market. Trussed beetles ready for pulping into Isaan pâté, and bee larvae fresh from the honeycomb.**

Farms now breed *maeng da*, scorpions, beetles, and crickets, even *rot duan*, now that its nine-month dormant stage can be sped to under three weeks. Some raise the multi-horned *kwaang* (Hercules Beetle), though Pairath Disthabamrung of the Hercules Beetle Club of Thailand rears them not to eat but as exportable pets and as combatants in a Lanna folk game. "A decade ago, the *kwaang* population had noticeably decreased. What saddened me most was seeing the vendors plucking the beetles' heads off and throwing their bodies into the pan."

Unfortunately, insects may share the fate of the threatened species being poached for wild animal restaurants that illegally thrive near national parks for northeast Asian tourists. The trade in rare edible insects could well come to mirror that in decorative collectors' butterflies or beetles, which can still be bought pinned and mounted off street stalls. Whatever the crackdowns on tiger breeding zoos and animal exchanges at Bangkok's Chatuchak Weekend Market, hunting's a hard habit to break.

Farming insects may be the only way to match the world's appetite for protein. "If you eat insects you don't need pork or other meat," says Rotjana Nusu, a bug vendor in Phitsanuloke. Hence the insects' greatest metamorphosis could be in human eating habits.

antennae and all. Those fearing disease, parasites or pesticides needn't worry; suppliers clean them repeatedly before boiling, while white liquor neutralises the scorpion's toxin. Many remove its tail sting, while the wings of dragonflies and crickets get severed before cooking. Locust legs may also be too horny for some mouths to crunch.

Until the mid-1980s Thai insect consumption was confined to few species and as a dietary supplement rather than a delicacy. "The idea of eating insects became more acceptable about ten years ago when frustrated villagers, plagued by the Bombay locust, began catching and frying them," Uamdao Noikorn writes. "What worries scientists, however, is that the insects are no longer just food for the poor… A shortage of predators could lead to a proliferation of pest insects."

Insects keep many ecosystems in balance. Particularly useful is the *maeng kudjee* – the dung beetle. Though Thailand boasts among the world's greatest variety of this creature residing in a diverse menu of manures, the magnificent giant ones must burrow in the droppings of big mammals such as buffalo, elephant and gaur, which are all in decline.

While some insect taxonomists claim that very few edible insects are endangered, we're newly into their mass marketing and the rarer they get, the higher the price, the greater the incentive to hunt. One of the most popular bugs – brown tipped white bamboo caterpillars, dubbed *rot duan* (express train) for their length and speed – can cost as much as 1,000 baht a kilo. Compounding the biodiversity loss is the waste of bamboo timber.

Vendors
Shops on wheels keep the economy moving

below: **Artificial flowers, ceramic vases, wind chimes, and bamboo stools. Everything needed for blissful contemplation.**

bottom: **A full suite of bamboo furniture being navigated by hand through the back alleys of downtown Bangkok.** PCS

Imagine steering a bicycle through a crowd while pulling half the stock of a shophouse. Picture wending a tricycle through dark alleys, a car-wide dessert tray straddling the handlebars. Try heaving a hot egg barbecue brazier all day on a bamboo shoulder yoke. Contemplate shoving a gas-fired cauldron of soup stock diagonally across an eight-lane intersection. Without lights. Or reflectors. Or a sideways glance.

This isn't a daredevil act in Cirque du Soleil, but reality for the roving Thai vendor. Pedalling, pushing or pulling a *rot khen* (push cart) for a living is the micro-profit career of millions. Huge distances they trudge, motor-powered carts costing more for fuel and maintenance than they save in labour. Though honing shapelier calves than a gym membership, it's increasingly a challenge.

Many hawked items satisfy impulse needs of any time or place; others face a sell-by date. Food carts purvey a staple, often most relished when cooked on the street. Squid – dried, rolled, pegged to a frame, and then warmed over charcoal – sates a particular tastebud in roadside drinkers.

The blasé way that vendors wend through Thailand has barely adapted from the carefree days before rampant industrialisation, when carts not pick-up trucks ruled the dirt roads between villages. Or rather, when supply boats plied the *khlong* (canals) threading through central Thai communities. In today's rare roadless areas, paddle craft still deliver provisions from shop-pier to house-pier. Some prepare dishes in an on-board galley for *khlong* dwellers to relish.

The quaint postcard image of the floating market is fast evaporating, with most survivors reduced to souvenir touting. Yet waterborne commerce is central to the national psyche. Thais embrace modernity perhaps because they discard the past so readily, yet they yearn at the same time for certain emotive icons of Thainess. Upon sighting *kuaytiao reua* (boat noodles), Thais tend to salivate and go dewy-eyed. Hence land-based 'boat noodle' vendors customise their carts or cafés with prow-shaped counters or salvaged boat parts. "People who live along the water in Ayutthaya or Ang Thong will tell you that the old boats are now hot items for sale," remarks Suthorn Sukphisit, a folk culture buff who derides the quality of modern *kuaytiao reua*. "The customers are noodle sellers who display them in their shops purely to give it a certain image."

The confined quarters of a boat honed the ingenious fitting of utensils and containers that compact wheeled carts inherited. From knife, board and condiments to bags, bands and swab cloth, every item has a slot, box, cranny or hook within instant reach. When the Bangkok Metropolitan Authority issued carts with Thai-style roofs during the APEC summit, hardly any vendor wanted to keep one even if they were free (they weren't), because they lacked strength and stowage capacity. "My food cart is more practical and convenient than the BMA's cart though it is worn out," Sawong Srimongkhol told the *Bangkok Post*. Investing in a new cart requires careful consideration for such low earners who may make 300 baht profit a day from selling fruit.

Antique wooden *rot khen* – panels evocatively stained, varnish sensuously charred, grain revealed through wear – now park in homes as décor items, holding pots of

plants not urns of coffee. Their ready-made steel and aluminium successors cost 5,500 baht for a noodle cart, over 25,000 baht if motorised. Though for half that you can self-assemble a cart from brackets, planks and bicycle wheels. Some customise them, like the vendor in Phetchabun who raised the superstructure so he could keep in business during floods.

Centuries of easing smoothly through boat-jams has, fortunately, prepared Thai hawkers for the fact that road traffic, too, obeys the laws of fluid dynamics. Vendors think nothing of setting up folding tables and miniature plastic stools around their cart on the inside of a corner or the neck of a *soi*. Where streams of travellers eddy, customers deposit like sediment at a river bend. Around them, somehow, the bikes, cars and buses effortlessly flow. Millimetres separate diners from moving vehicles. Nothing ever seems to touch. Accidents tend to be minor among parked *soi* carts, though they're a hazard when careering around highways. Tables, chairs, braziers, gas bottles get piled high upon the cart to be wheeled off to some hidden garage before tomorrow morning's dawn trip to the market to buy supplies.

A flexible way to ensure that toil gets fast, tangible results, hawking appeals to the Thai sense of freedom. After staying in the same communal job for generations – rice farming – urban Thais happily hop between jobs, seeking advancement, independence and carefree contact with people. Vendors become part of life's rhythm. You know which cart is coming by its tell tale sound. Ice cream trolleys tinkle with bells, noodle vendors clatter chopsticks on bamboo, brush-sellers squeeze rubber-bulbed horns. Rubbish recyclers induce a sharp whoop from a bicycle-pump clamped to the frame. The black-dye man rattles a stringed bead upon a twirling twin-

faced drum, a remnant of the Chinese ethnicity of the earliest urban vendor class. Now they're likely migrants from Isaan, managed by a Sino-Thai businessman.

For all its quality and charm, vending languishes at the low end of the social scale. Not least because outdoor work browns the skin. In the increasing confrontations with authorities, vendors rarely win, however much they may pelt officials with fermented fish and its verbal equivalent. Encroachers who'd been accommodated for years get evicted in an instant, without compensation and often with no alternative site. When television exposed Bangkok Metropolitan Authority inspectors asking regular bribes from food vendors in 2003, the victims were blamed and shunted away to save face.

While food courts, markets and malls slowly starve the vendor of his customers, the sheer convenience and conviviality of the roving cart will ensure a demand for a long time to come. Street foods are fresh and feature many dishes never found in formal restaurants. "The persistence of the urban informal sector in sustaining an 'urban foodscape' is worth stressing," says academic Marc Askew. "Department store workers gather to socialise around the food stalls of nearby *soi*." Supply is ensured, too, as long as there's a population poor enough to push heavy objects in this heat. However, that may change through the eviction of slum-dwellers to distant suburbs.

An increasing proportion of vendors aren't freelance, but franchisees of both famous brands and less obvious goods on consignment. Those quaint straw hats brush vendors wear don't connote a particular tradition; it's the uniform of those flogging the same company's brooms, mops and dusters. Unsalaried mat franchisee Sawat must travel by bus to central Bangkok, from where he pedals at least 30 kilometres a day around a zone the mat company demarcates. He earns just 5-6,500 baht a month piece rate, spending 150 baht a day to live and 20 baht to garage the cart his supplier owns. "It is good that I don't have to stock anything," he says in a Khon Kaen accent. "My *thaokae* (Chinese shop owner) is responsible for all costs. I will save up some money, then open a shop with my wife."

While vendors have been the ultimate freewheeling entrepreneurs, their livelihood is threatened through increased regulation, consolidation, and upgrading of anything society's arbiters consider 'untidy'. Sanitary standards and zone designation are increasingly enforced, cart design standardised, and road safety measures are bound to follow. With vendor strips more tightly zoned, Singapore's sterile 'hawker centre' concept beckons.

Under the government's poverty-busting asset conversion scheme, carts, stall contracts, vending licences and even supplier endorsements can act as collateral against which the upwardly mobile vendor may borrow. If the risk pays off, expect an increase in those graduating from shoulder yoke to cart to motorcart to truck-based stall to shop. Those that over-reach their potential, however, may face unpayable debts and a fate akin to landless farmers. Vertical integration means the same agribusinesses that

swallow farms also control motorised plastic trolleys of processed ice cream or chicken balls. If the synthesised corporate jingle it broadcasts drives neighbourhoods nuts, consider the driver hearing it all day, every day!

In the West, roving vendors largely disappeared before delivery made a comeback through Internet shopping. While the concept of delivery may well have a future, the Thai vendor must contend with more regimentation and less *sanuk*.

Everyone needs a ladder, clothes rack and furniture, but perhaps not often enough to have a limited range of such huge items speculatively hand-wheeled through congested roads. The next generation may not want the kind of goods that vendors hawk, like gaudy ceramic animals piled amid sheaves of plastic toys shrinkwrapped to cardboard. And there can't be much the future for vendors who boil clothes black in a can attached to their bicycle, given that the result reeks and costs as much as a new market garment. Mega-stores' economies of scale are out-discounting even the low-overhead itinerants' prices. So vending may become a profession out of time.

Trundling the same streets for decades, they seek a chance catch with the same custom-yearning eyes as the *tuk-tuk* driver. As with the *tuk-tuk*, the vendors' variable rates and untraceability fail comparison against predictable, accountable, fixed-priced modernity. The wired *rot khen* of tomorrow might have the responsive on-call character of the centrally-directed radio taxi. But matching any gain in efficiency is a loss: serendipity.

Longtail Boats & Barges
Water instincts guide life on land

Bangkok may be losing its character as the 'Venice of the East' with canals being filled, rivers polluted, floating markets abandoned, but Thai water culture isn't entirely gone. With such a lot of water lacing the land – and often flooding it – boats remain essential for millions of Thais. Ceremony continues aquatically through monks' alms rounds, boat races and various festivals including the royal barge procession.

"Today's rivers, *khlong* and sea lanes are probably more clogged with traffic than ever before," Mark Graham observes. "Boats large and small converge on numerous markets to unload fresh produce. Much of the construction materials must still be transported by barge or tender and tourism has added many new boats. This growth has been echoed around the coast as Thailand's fishing fleet ranks sixth in the world in tonnage." A collage of orange, aqua and kingfisher blue, the trawlers fill their forward tilting turrets with ever more hi-tech gear to locate ever fewer fish as far away as Africa.

River adventurer Steve Van Beek found that more types of boats have been created than have fallen out of use. Some convert boats to new uses; others re-imagine old styles for hotel ferries, floating restaurants, disco rafts. Slowly transport's Wood Age is giving way to the steel and fiberglass pleasure launch, freighter and commuter waterbus. The shallow canoes sculled from stilt house to shop pontoon now come in bright blue plastic.

Boatyards still dot the *khlong*, rivers and estuaries, though scarcity of water-resistant teak and takian wood forces captains into buying a modern replacement rather than repairing planked craft. Even trekkers' bamboo rafts slipping northern rapids now get disassembled, trucked back upstream and relashed.

"Boat building was, and still is today, the best example of Thai carpentry which, in turn, must be one of the most precise crafts in the world," writes architect Sumet Jumsai of this early Thai technology. "The crafts are the product of the tranquil riverine condition and an

above: **A longtail boat moored on the Chao Phraya River.**

left: **Painted eyes help steer this teak barge through the canals of Thonburi.** *PCS*

far left: **Festooned prows at the annual longboat races on the Mekong River at Nong Khai, Isaan.**

expression of an organised society." That tranquility now shatters when an outboard motor saws past. Pootering sampans wobble in their wake, if not totally capsized. Waves that sloping natural banks once absorbed now rebound off vertical concrete anti-flood embankments.

Choppy waters may jeopardise the future of the light paddle boat, just as it made unliveable the rafts that once housed most of Bangkok. Government later banned floating homes as insanitary, though a few survive in Phitsanuloke and floating guesthouses flourish in Kanchanaburi. The Mekong River has become more treacherous for small boats since China instigated the blasting of rapids to make shipping channels. The land-lubber assumptions and rigid materials of China and the West clash with the amphibious Thai approach of flexible materials and accommodation with nature. Yet cultural collisions spawn hybrids. Two iconic Thai craft – the longtail boat and tug-towed barge – mix mentalities and machinery with surprising grace.

Just as hooking a motorbike to a rickshaw created the *tuk-tuk*, so bolting an Isuzu pick-up engine to a boat made the *reua hang yao*. Named 'long-tail' after a trailing drive shaft that can reverse or churn through 270°, the long, sleek craft is tailored to cramped shallow waterways. Made of *takian* wood lacquered with go-faster stripes, the hull tapers like a scimitar to a raised, needle-sharp prow. Its roof displays the telltale arc of all Siamese boat canopies, only made of deckchair-hued plastic rather than bamboo, thatch or galvanised iron. The passengers shelter behind plastic sheeting to avoid spray as the unmuffled engine rips through turbid *khlong* or salty shoreline, scattering swimmers and rattling nerves as the sound reverberates off cliffs and buildings.

"The Isuzu is more powerful and economic than other car engines. Plus it's faster and quieter now we use a turbo," hollers Piya through the din at a Bangkok pier, which all seem to be run with the mafia muscle of a motorcycle taxi rank and are notorious for tourist scams.

island, swapping goods and cash via a bucket on a rope. Like elephants strung trunk to tail, it takes 24 hours to plod from Bangkok's port to Ayutthaya by water, versus two hours by road. Readjusting your body clock to languid Thai time, there's freedom to sense the breeze, witness nature, and hear chanting, laughter and splashing children amplified across the swirling brown eddies.

Since the mid-1990s, the *reua kracheng* has gone from scrap timber value to prized antique. Converted barges moor permanently as guesthouses or restaurants. Others chug sightseers along the waterways or host students on an ecological floating classroom. Some even sit on river-bank lawns to be used as a house extension.

Nostalgia for the ebbing riverine lifestyle shows up in the city, too. Shops serving *kuaytiao reua* (boat noodles) shape their counters like boat parts or harvest wooden sculls from actual use for display only, hastening the demise of the floating market. Even massage parlours come ship-shaped to evoke the floating brothels of decades ago, which persisted on canals until the 1960s.

Thai water culture has always influenced land culture, since rain and flood governed architecture, crops, rites, warfare, travel, everything. Ayutthayan temples, furniture and utensils swoop up at each end like a boat. Plaited fish hang above babies' cots, seated dances evolved partly from boat-bound courting dances, and everywhere images of the *Naga* serpent symbolise his watery abode.

Thais treat all vehicles as boats, painting coachwork as auspiciously as the ornate prow of the *khorlae* fishing skiff. Before any journey or working day, truckers, taxi drivers, motorcyclists and pilots emulate boatmen by blessing the bonnet, steering column or rearview mirror with flower garlands as if it were a bowsprit at the 'head' of the vehicle. This offering to the journey spirit *Mae Yanang* requests luck and protection. Just as well, since Thai driving reveals nautical instincts.

Weaving between lanes, Thai cars slip through gaps as if they were a canoe that would glance not crash. Touting taxis and *tuk-tuk* hover freely rather than stop at reserved ranks. Cars park up to three vehicles deep, rather like tethered boats. Handbrakes off and wheels aligned, 'parked' cars get rolled back and forth to let others in and out with elastic ease, managed by well-tipped attendants. The complex yet easy-going shuffle of cars – seen at shopping streets, car parks and the forecourts of flashy bars and restaurants – resembles activity at any wharf.

Trading and buildings, too, betray amphibious origins. As at floating markets, stalls migrate to and from night markets and vendor strips, piling everything aboard a hand-powered steel box on wheels. The ebb and flow of vendors makes Patpong a 'floating world' in more than the decadent sense. In department stores as on streets, stalls-on-stilts spill out into concourses like the frontages of old water villages. The instinctive overspill of structures onto canals, railways, river and road now gets denounced by politicians as "encroachment". Yet once most Thai construction was temporary and flexible. However much land culture overtakes water culture, the Thai keep a waterworld in their mind and soul.

Serving as bus or taxi, large and small longtails weave deftly between barges, which glide imperceptibly by. The humped carapace of a fully loaded barge resembles a beetle swimming, with eyes painted on the stubby bow, and water lapping at the gunwales. Handsomest among these cargo vessels are the twin-ruddered *reua iamchun* (salt boat) and dumpier *reua kracheng* (rice barge). Formerly inched along by punt, and later by outboard longtail propeller, these *takian*-wood tubs have since been recast larger in iron. Once itinerant river gypsies, barge owners now have their boats shunted like train cars at the whim of a company tug, which strainingly sputters upstream. These brass and wood tugs with frilly awnings resemble the steam packet from 'Around the World in 80 Days'. Only there's no rush.

This passive caravan chain is a very Thai mix of work and play, naps and games, friends and family. "They look like barges with bungalows on the back, but peer into the hull and it's a floating warehouse. I now understand why they often appear to be sinking," says photojournalist Olivier Pin-Fat of a ride he hitched aboard a barge. "In the middle of the river, these boats become a floating town. There's a lot of jumping boats and visiting one another." Vendor paddle boats resupply this moving

facing page, above: **Coconut, gold leaf and garland offerings on a sampan at Damnoen Saduak Floating Market.** *PCS*

facing page, below: **Garlands to honour** *Mae Yanang*, **goddess of journeys.**

left, right: **Auspicious tricolour scarves on the prow of a fishing skiff at Pranburi on the Gulf of Thailand.**

far left: **The conductor's tube stores, scrolls, cuts and validates tickets on Bangkok commuter expressboats, as well as on road-based buses. She announces her rounds with a rattle and clap of the change and metallic lid.** *PCS*

left: **Vendors of** *kuaytiao reua* (boat noodles) **have kept the boat as décor on dry land.**

Truck & Bus Art
Customising vehicles both beautifies and protects

Not often does a lorry lift the spirits, but Thai traffic overcomes grimness through frivolity. Bus, truck, *tuk-tuk* and *songthaew* (pick-up minibus) beguile the eye with grace, colour and art. Their handmade coachwork spans the range of Thai illustration. Some aspires to high art, most show folk stylisation, and others interpret imported graphics. Treat each jam as a gallery.

Looking beautiful may be important, but meaning matters as much. With spirits underwriting any accident,

drivers pay extra premiums for divine protection through décor. Chassis metalwork plays shrine, cabins act as altar, talisman-shaped bolts physically hold the trailer together.

Like temple trimmings, lacquer cabinets and fruit carvings, truck art displays *lai thai*, a visual language of traditional patterns with infinite applications. As ingenious a discovery as Classical Greek proportion or the paisley shapes-within-shapes of fractal imagery, *lai thai* likewise withstands extreme manipulation with ease. Drawn from plants and animals, it scales up to intricate oceans of texture, or scales down to the core motifs. Interleaving the *kanok* (flame) are leaf and shoot, feather and fish scale.

Inspiration for the metal truck bolt is, unbelievably, the flower petal. Joining superstructures of timber and steel struts, the four-pointed *prachamyaam* flower evokes security from the word *yaam* (guard). Augmented by more petals into diamonds and chevrons, it adorns painted door lintels, window frames, wire luggage racks. Today it depicts each terminus on route maps of Bangkok's subway. "The *prachamyaam* symbolises the guardians of the four directions of the universe," Vithi Phanichphant explains. "It's a mandala, protecting everything on board. It even goes onto Thai costume."

As with the truck, so with the handbag. One reason Thai dames favour Louis Vuitton fabric to protect their valuables may lie in the four-pointed flower appearing in its trademark pattern. When the LV monogram emerged in France a century ago, oriental imagery was all the rage, with the *prachamyaam* a possible inspiration.

Placed across the front and sides of trucks, panels in chrome or aluminium act as both sacred and secular offerings. Going way beyond Cadillac-style swoops and flanges, scrolled plates depict lotus blooms or gleaming jeweled rings, while a *naga* water serpent reminds us how buses and trucks are boats reincarnated.

"They're all the same – the spirit of a vehicle is in the upper part of the front," Vithi says. Hence, the driver's cab plays the prow with garlands and coloured scarves placating the journey spirit *Mae Yanang*. Overall, each cabin represents sacred Mount Meru. The Buddha tops this hierarchy of chromium deities. Truckspotters can readily identify characters like the monkey warrior Hanuman, mythical *hongsa* swan, man-bird Garuda, or *thephanom*, the *wai*-ing angel protector.

Engraved into a shield on each side, a horse-drawn chariot carries the sun god *Suriya*, which nothing can outpace – including the aeroplane placard often flanking the rear. Thai folklore thus pre-empts Einstein on the

speed of light. One side may instead depict the chariot of the moon god *Phra Chan*, reflecting the usual pairing of sun (gold) and moon (silver) offerings in altars and regalia. "You see the sun god's chariot everywhere. It was adapted from a sketch by Prince Naris that an Italian painted on the ceiling of a bed chamber in the Grand Palace," reveals scholar Anucha Thirakanont. "Prince Naris would print his sketches to give out, so it became famous and available to everybody." Similarly, Bangkok Metropolitan Authority changed its logo of Indra riding the three-headed elephant Erawan to resemble another Naris sketch. But trucks aren't all traditional art.

Somewhere on any given truck, bus or *songthaew* appears a garish landscape of an idyllic rural hut painted to Western perspective. The Buddha on the cab, instead of being traditionally stylised, gets vividly painted in life-like manner. Why the sudden shift to European style?

"The pastoral scenes came from around World War I, when postcards of scenery came in," says Vithi, noting the same shift appeared in Thai fine art. "The thatched huts derive from Western landscapes, which became big in the 1960s." Having always seen nature as a mythic pattern in temples, Thais now viewed their environment in a revelatory new aesthetic, that of the chocolate box.

clockwise from top left: **Trucks are loaded with symbolic metalwork: a gem for the precious cargo, the sun god's chariot for speed, and a lucky** *Supannahong* **swan barge running the length of the rig** *(PCS).* **Stencils are used as much on trucks as in temples. This engraved aluminium airplane updates the godly chariot** *(PCS).* **A door fastener decorated like an eagle. The bolt washer becomes a protective flower petal** *mandala* **guarding all directions. Mud flaps depict Al Pacino as the buster of corrupt cops in** *Serpico,* **to ward off extortion of truckers.**

Like Constable's Haywain and Monet's Haystacks in the West, the vividly tinted hut by a mountain stream spread into Thai crafts. The day-glo landscape reappears on the *Lanna* umbrella, the lacquer box, and the set of puppet and *likay* theatre. The hut sometimes gets upgraded into a suburban house, as a symbol of modern aspiration.

The latest way to see the world – as a wide-eyed *manga* cartoon – now emblazons trucks and especially buses. Perforated screens for extending advertisements over windows also enable characters and abstract designs to cover the entire surface. Another enduring pop icon glowers from many truck mudflaps: the painted image of Al Pacino from the movie *Serpico*. The character Serpico busted corrupt police – a subtle warning to officers not to extract bribes from the driver in exchange for allowing common violations like overloading or reckless driving.

Truck and bus art thus adapts to changing conditions. Heroes, patterns and talismans continue to keep vehicles safe and beautiful.

Motorcycle Taxi Jackets
Hopping on a bike to beat the traffic

The unsung heroes of Thailand's battle with traffic, motorcycle taxis are a very Thai response to a universal problem. Flitting between jammed cars with knee-endangering speed, the *motercy* is the one sure way to make an appointment. Perhaps with your next life.

Most shuttle customers up and down *soi*, with as many as 100 taxi-bikes gathering at each *soi* mouth in a rank, known as a *win*. A sartorial symbol of streetlife, their *seua win* – zipped sleeveless vests in neon-hued nylon – is a uniform with surprising value. "A glamorous evening gown may be worth less than the weather-beaten rag of a jacket," report Wassayos Ngamkham and Manop Thip-osod. "That's because drivers must pay protection money to the mafia types that run motorcycle taxi queues." Originally of multiple colours and bearing names of businesses or politicians, a jacket costs a joining fee of anywhere from 4,000-100,000 baht. Drivers also pay around 15% of their 400-500 baht daily earnings, enabling *win* mafia to extort 1.2 billion baht a year.

"The *win* owner then pays the police up to 30-40% of his earnings," explains Piak, who drives on a *win* of 16 without an owner. "At the end of the month we each put 100 baht in the kitty and present it to the police station. It's just our way of building good relations."

Prime Minister Thaksin Shinawatra made *win* reform the opening salvo in a 'war on dark influence', a policy to open the black economy to control – and tax. All 114,452 Bangkok *motercy* taxis from 4,324 *win* had to register with the Bangkok Metropolitan Authority by June 2003.

The small annual license fee gets them a numbered orange *seua win* bearing a reflector and the location.

Before the scheme could be applied nationally, non-standard jackets re-appeared and drivers revealed they still had to pay the mafia. The fixed limit of jackets also faces challenges as the city expands and transport patterns change – the SkyTrain and Subway increased demand for bike shuttles. But bikes may face competition from new narrower electric *tuk-tuk* and cheaper tricycle pedal carts with seating under a huge umbrella.

At a *win*, each bike makes about 50-70 trips per shift for a profit of 300-400 baht after fuel, excluding repayments on their bike. Small ranks may work up to 12 hours, though most have a ten-hour day shift and a shorter night shift when fares are slightly higher and *win* fees lower. Fares reflect distance and the wealth of the neighbourhood, with a premium for heavy loads, side trips and foreigners. Only a few drivers have other jobs, but some get more lucrative work as salaried couriers.

above: **Idling bike taxi drivers play Thai chequers with bottle cap counters.** *PCS*

left: **Drivers at a Sathorn bike taxi rank keep fit through** *takraw,* **an acrobatic sport using any body part except the arms to keep aloft a woven rattan ball. This version using a volleyball net,** *sepak takraw,* **is touted to become an Olympic sport. It's a favourite late- afternoon game of labourers nationwide.** *PCS*

left: Do-it-yourself seating. The steering column's transferred to the sidecar so a wheelchair user can ride the motorbike. *PCS*

right, clockwise from top left: An upcountry bike-taxi jacket on Koh Si Chang. Bangkok riders wore divers jackets before they were standardised (*PCS*). Artistic bike jackets, like this one from Thonburi, have become rare. Bangkok's new standard jacket with reflector strip varies in hue by district, some with numbers in Thai.

Companionship, macho joshing and games enliven the wait until their turn to drive is indicated by chalked-up numbers or ignition keys hanging on a series of hooks. Some sew fishing nets, read comics, tend plants or help at nearby stalls. Others doze on narrow benches under ragged plastic shelters, head resting in a colleague's lap. Many play the Thai version of chequers. Everyone squats around an eight-by-eight board scored into old wood or chalked on the pavement, using bottle caps as counters, and doubtless making the occasional bet. To keep going, they swill energy drinks and scoop iced water from a lidded tub using a shared metal cup.

There's more to *win* style than the jacket. Amulets cover the dials, sacred string wraps the steering column and their jacket number may be a 'lucky' one. Stickers, unmuffled exhausts and multi-coloured bolts are secular ways they customise the bike. Usually Japanese, bikes now include the Thai brand Tigar. Leathers, kneepads and boots are unheard of in this humidity, so protective clothing runs to long sleeves and trousers to keep the sun from darkening the skin. Footwear is typically flip-flops, worn with socks, sweater and anorak during 'winter', when the wind chill-factor dips below 20°C.

A few don surgical masks or bandannas in a vain attempt to block fumes. Women passengers often press handkerchief to nose and hold aloft something to shade from the sun, while teetering side-saddle, toes brushing truck tyres. Sitting cupped behind the driver runs the risk of incurring a whiff of 'eau de *seua win*' cologne.

Helmets also offer scope for self-expression. Despite safety laws, however, they're hardly worn in *soi*, almost never upcountry, and often get left unfastened on Bangkok highways. Aside from the expense and cramp on freedom, they're simply too heavy and hot. Instead of wing mirrors inconveniently clipping cars as they zigzag through jams, the mirrors can be folded inwards to create a handy helmet rest while riding. Some perch a helmet above their face, lending them the profile of the monster from *Alien*. If brand names like Safetymet or Ladymet aren't sufficiently hip, riders sport helmets with horn-like spoilers, blue visors or stickers, perhaps to cover cracks. A few don Nazi-style helmets, complete with swastika. To be safe, helmets should fit snugly, but the spare ones for passengers generally have the strength of a plastic salad

bowl. Commuters who bring their own helmet arouse nervous laughter. It's a loss of face for the *win*, and besides, accidents only happen on karma's command.

Each *win* suffers one or two scrapes a week, while bikes account for the large majority of road injuries and especially of fatalities. The government introduced cheap personal accident insurance premiums of just one baht a day as one of its poverty policies. Insurance might reduce the tendency of drivers causing an accident to flee the scene in an act of conflict avoidance. Truckers and car drivers have been known to drive back over injured motorcyclists to prevent them being a witness or a cripple they'd have to compensate.

Registered *win* drivers are eligible for training. Just as well; pathologist Vira Kasantikul found that only 0.1 per cent of motorcyclists involved in accidents had passed a driving course. While car, bus and truck drivers break road rules, too, they get fined far less than bikes, partly because they may have influential connections.

Motercy collect like a swarm of metal hornets at red lights, then zoom off speedway-style. Scary at 50km/h, this primal thrill intensifies at 140km/h in illegal speed duels for cash, pride or girls in cities like Had Yai and Chiang Mai. Late at night, Bangkok's ring-road (dubbed 'Ratchadaphisek Racetrack') draws spectators, gamblers, groupies and competing crews of charity 'body collectors'. Police may chase or impede boy racers, who lie flat on the seat. "When they hit the ground they're already horizontal," quips a letter to the *Bangkok Post*. "Thais call the illegal motorcycle racers *malaeng wun* (flies) because of the way they buzz around – loud, irritating, erratic and dirty," writes Philip Blenkinsop in *The Cars That Ate Bangkok*. "They also happen to die like flies."

In this substantially two-wheeled society, there are few organised motorbike racing outlets, aside from a tycoons' Harley-Davidson club. Circuits, courses and training could create new sport-biking role models, just as licences increase respect for the bike taxi profession. So far, though, *win* reform dwells more on how they impact others – insurance, training, nice jackets – than on *win* welfare. Just as police get comfy traffic booths, *win* need shelter, seating, water, toilets, fair treatment, and safe, affordable helmets. After all, like the hi-tech trains they connect, motorcycle taxis are modern mass transit.

Tuk-tuk

The three-wheeled motor-rickshaw is a national treasure

As with any initiation, people remember their first time in a *tuk-tuk*. No Bangkok trip is complete without a breakneck ride in one of these colourful *samlor* (three-wheeled) motor-rickshaws. Named *tuk-tuk* after the word for 'cheap-cheap' – or after the rasp from its soot-belching motorcycle engine – it simply exhilarates. Careering round bends at a top speed of 37 mph, it feels about to tip over at any moment. You don't need rollercoasters when *tuk-tuk* provide the same thrill for a dollar. That's why people buy *tuk-tuk* T-shirts, toys and key-fobs.

Despite the fun quotient, the *tuk-tuk* is singularly ill-designed for tourism; you can't see where you are, or where you're going. The curving canvas roof blocks all but a ground view of potholes, swerving motorbikes, bus exhausts and trucks threatening to crunch you under their wheels. That first ride leaves passengers winded, dazed and tingling with adrenaline, not to mention smothered in soot upon sweat. In an international AmEx commercial of 2004, a death-defying tour by *tuk-tuk* had Bond actor Pierce Brosnan both shaken and stirred.

Perhaps only eclipsed by the elephant as a national mascot, the *tuk-tuk* symbolises Thailand as the black cab does England or the Jeepney does The Philippines. Some 7,400 *tuk-tuk* ply the capital's markets streets and sights,

over 40,000 more upcountry. Yet national icons don't always receive the respect that seems due, earning more affection once their usefulness has peaked. No longer employed in logging, elephants were reduced to begging on the streets of resorts and cities; spurned by ever more folk, touting tuk-tuk drivers elicit similar desperation.

Bangkok may be pancake flat, but the *tuk-tuk* is speeding downhill. Unfortunately, it combines the disadvantages of both motorcycle and car, with none of the advantages of either. Like a bike, it's open and poorly protected from climate, accidents or pollution, though plastic flaps help shield against rain. On the other hand, it's slow and just too wide to nip through traffic jams. The price of a new model has dropped, while many stand idle as people upgrade to air-conditioned taxi-meter cars. As *tuk-tuk* aren't metered, riders have to bargain. Usually they end up paying more than for a faster, cooler, safer taxi. Worse, *tuk-tuk* have become synonymous with aggressive touting, whether for tours, massages or luring people into gem scams, discrediting the law-abiding drivers.

As it declines domestically, the *tuk-tuk* revels in a new role: cultural ambassador. Enchanted by the vehicle, *farang* started to hold *tuk-tuk* rallies and drive souped-up versions across continents for charity. In 2004, one drove

left: **A whimsical tricycle pedi-cab, the once newfangled son of the rickshaw and now retro-style father of the *tuk-tuk*, waiting outside King Narai's Palace in Lopburi.**

right: **Overstuffed like a circus clown car, the adaptable *tuk-tuk* is a mainstay of Thailand's street market economy.** *PP*

A Japanese invented the man-powered rickshaw in 1833, which reached Siam in 1872. Later, the Japanese added motors and exported them across South and Southeast Asia. In 1959, Thailand imported 31 Daihatsu motor-tricycles followed by 4,000 in 1960. Bulb-nosed early incarnations still carry people in Ayutthaya province. Tohatsu brought in another model in 1963-4, though handlebars replaced the steering wheel, doors were removed and the sides made open-air. Isaan favours a model in which a motorcycle pulls a shiny passenger capsule dubbed *skylab*, after the spacecraft of that era.

Today, seven local companies make all but the Chinese engines here, but the Thainess comes – as in so many other objects – through the application of Thai aesthetics. The early ancestors of the *tuk-tuk* and many of its international variants are somewhat ugly. The modern *tuk-tuk* is rather beautiful. Brilliant colours and flashing starburst lights are only part of the appeal. "The elegant lines of the *tuk-tuk* preserve some of the lines of the Siamese ox cart," observes scholar Vithi Phanichphant of the graceful, dart-like profile. "That line doesn't exist much in the West, even in speedboats, but you see it again in the Thai longtail boat." Coachwork paintings also migrated here from the oxcart via the truck and bus, from where the *tuk-tuk* gained its swirly metalwork.

Less attractive are the fumes and vibration. In 1995, one company launched an electric *tuk-tuk*. Despite being bright pink it never caught on, perhaps because of the square lamps, boxy bodywork and engine noise, which turned from 'tuk-tuk-tuk' into a high-pitched whine. Undeterred, the government made the 2003 APEC summit a showcase for the *tuk-tuk*. George W Bush got to ride a Chai, an all-new electric rickshaw by the Thai motorcycle firm Tigar. But foreign minister Surakiart Sathirathai was quoted as calling the egg-like Chai design "odd" because it "did not quite represent Thainess".

Nevertheless, the government envisions the Chai (and its petrol-driven cousin Thai Chaiyo) as a 'national car' targetting the growing market for neighbourhood

from Thailand to Denmark via the Himalayas and Iraq. A wide-bodied diplomat had a *tuk-tuk* converted to single occupancy. In the 1990s, Thai artist Navin Rawanchaikul made it the mascot of the global art project 'Cities on the Move', which hops between world capitals.

Some *tuk-tuk* were imported into cities like Vienna as a novelty. Since then, modern rickshaws have spread across Europe. Could it be coincidence? In 2002, a British firm patented the MMW Tuk-Tuk motor rickshaw adapted to British road safety standards, around the time an American tried to patent another Thai icon, jasmine rice. Shocked by this double-whammy, politicians woke up to the export potential of indigenous Thai things. Now the Thai *tuk-tuk* might be exported to hot countries such as Brazil, Egypt and Morocco. All of a sudden, the word 'Thailand' was embossed across the back plate, where previously it read words like 'Suzuki' or 'Daihatsu'. These had been appropriate because the *tuk-tuk* concept and much of the design is not actually Thai, but Japanese.

above left: *Tuk-tuk* conversions are a pure expression of the Thai pop sensibility. This mobile bar offers *tuk-tuk* cocktails (a well-shaken mixture of caffeine drink and fumes, perhaps?) along with a smile wherever it parks.

lower left: One of a fleet of hot-rod *tuk-tuk* that carry tourists around the east coast island of Koh Si Chang.

below: An early-model, Japanese-style *tuk-tuk* still offering banana-coloured rides to locals in the historic city of Ayutthaya.

vehicles like golf carts, resort buggies and all-weather alternatives to motorcycle taxis. However, the Chai's still exposed to rain and sun, lacks luggage space and seats only two, instead of the ten schoolchildren, three *farang* or one large diplomat who can pile aboard a *tuk-tuk*. Getting rid of the fold-down rear tray undermines one of the *tuk-tuk*'s few advantages – as a flexible cargo-carrier for purchases strapped on the back with bungee chords.

Long having van and minibus variants, the *tuk-tuk* has growth potential as a mini-truck, but other creative options beckon. Some convert the *tuk-tuk* into vendor stalls or mobile bars with a raised roof. Others take the plastic roof off to make a hot-rod cabriolet. Such uses trade not on utility, but charm. Aside from the cute size, it's the Thai coachwork that makes it loved as a design classic. Just as England's decommissioned red phone boxes get snapped up as garden ornaments, cupboards or shower cubicles, the future of the *tuk-tuk* may not be as a working vehicle, but as a piece of sculpture.

Fairy Lights
Brightening the night with twinkling bulbs and fluorescent tubes

In 2000, Bangkok earned a surprising first: it was named the world's dimmest metropolis. This honour in the fight against light pollution didn't gratify, however, in a land where light isn't just bright, but right. Light confers beauty, wisdom, prestige. So regardless of need, governor Samak Sundaravej ordered streetlamps strengthened.

What Thailand wants in wattage, it makes up for in bulbs, with each fairy light playing a crucial role. Viewed from space, the superpowers sear the eye, while Thailand gently twinkles. On earth as it is in heaven, the coast and highways appear as strings of festival lights, Bangkok's intense tracery resembling, to a satellite, the typical Thai seafood restaurant. Each eatery is a miniature galaxy.

Food, service and music being relatively equal, what makes you select where to eat? Call it the fairy light factor. One string lamely slung from a dust-encrusted tarpaulin? Any port in a storm. Multicolour flashes pulsing in sequence along architectural outlines? Cheap and cheerful. A tree impersonating a chandelier? Classy and relaxing.

It's an understudied fact of human nature that under fairy lights our senses twinge with primaeval memories: fireflies, constellations, moonlight on rippling water. The ambient aura evokes the closeness and companionship when only candles and coconut oil lamps held gloom at bay. To rural folk fairy lights seem modern; to urbanites they flash back to a rural sense of wonder. To all, light has a spiritual quality. Thais donate candles to monks, not just for ritual, but also as a symbolic aid to scripture study. Illumination for both eye and mind's eye.

above: **Diamond necklaces of light hang from the art deco buildings of Ratchadamnoen Avenue for royal birthdays.** *PCS*

right: **Fluorescent tube art announces temple fairs and, here, a wedding in Pranburi.**

facing page: **A floating barge lit up in honor of mysterious glowing lights that** *naga* **serpents are said to send skywards from the Mekong River during the full moon Naga Rocket Festival in Nong Khai, Isaan.**

In dark old Siam, as highly prized as light itself were things that reflect. The shinier the surface, the less light source required, the greater the impact. Silk and bead encrusted costume, mirror tiled temples, lustrous gold – quality and status could be measured by the power to dazzle. And like fairly lights, their fragmented glinting conjured the infinity of Buddhist cosmology. The more reflective the object, the higher the status its owner.

This is clear in Thai performing arts. Compared to the more lightly spangled gear worn by lowly characters, the costumes of heroes and heroines shimmer with a coalescence of beads, crystal, gems and stitched metal thread. Limelit on stage, they looks more powerful, more wise, more charming. In *khon* court dance, lead figures get to wear more glitter. That's magnified in blindingly bright *likay* folk opera, with a further differentiation between Day-Glo hued marketplace *likay* and its gilt-edged, gem encrusted court version.

Light lends prestige, so the more you emit the brighter your prospects, the greater the tribute to those you welcome and worship. Hence the myriad tiny lamps swathing portraits of monarchy, images of Buddha and most spirit houses.

Used liberally for decades, fairy lights have noble predecessors. King Narai's summer palace in Lopburi was a miniature city of concentric walls inset with thousands of Persian arched niches where flames would flicker. Ambassadors visiting this most international of Ayutthayan kings would have witnessed something like Ratchadamnoen Avenue around the birthdays of the present King and Queen. Millions of Thais flock to view this electric firmament, which spreads Kingdomwide. Fountains of incandescence cascade off branches or gather in curtain-like swathes. Flashing wires the height of a skyscraper strobe across displays of royal insignia, their contours studded with tiny bulbs.

Many of the King's Birthday tribute lights stay shining throughout December as illuminations for Christmas and New Year, though shops stock fairy lights all year round. Festivals and cool-season outdoor dining add periodic focus, though there's a more expedient reason.

Because of its classy connotations, fairy lights are a quick fix in cases of *pak chee roi naa* (garnishing the mundane with parsley). Faced with a dreary stall, a tawdry bar, a dingy restaurant, there's no need to call in décor consultants; buy up strings of bulbs from any local store at 30 baht a metre. Coloured or plain; flashing, pulsing or still; outlining architecture or writing out words – all call attention to something otherwise plain. Same deal with the *tuk-tuk*, where brake lights and indicators are joined by starbursts of green, blue and pink. When shops and stalls need passing trade, fairy lights say "buy from me".

Now a cliché, fairy lighting has its detractors, none more rigorous than Thailand's new breed of design hotels that shun quaint Siamoiserie in order to surf the décor wave of minimalist Asian chic. Instead, recessed lighting accents their matt expanses. That restraint rarely lasts. Often a poolside Loy Krathong party sees the first fairy light infestation. Resistance broken, within a week, the entire garden gets festooned like an elfin grotto.

When not twinkling however, Thai lighting places practicality over beauty. Eager to escape darkness, the nation swings to the polar opposite: unyielding bright glare. What else can explain the plague of fluorescent tubes? From temple altars and beach resorts to rooms in home and shophouse, neon beams triumphant.

It may be that the victory of neon is not really about light at all. Incandescent lamps, being a burning filament, feel perceptibly warm and vigorous. Emanating a harsh, greenish blue, fluorescent strips render everything flat and cold. The anaemic result isn't pretty, but feels cool. And whatever feels cool, from talcum powder to menthol inhalants, tropical Thais relish.

Now Thais have done a folk equivalent to the neon installations by Dan Flavin – they've turned strip lights into art. Night markets beckon custom with multiple coloured tubes, arranged in patterns or dangled with

right: **Dazzling like fairy lights, traditional dance costumes, embroidered with sequins and metallic thread, shimmer as the performer moves.**

below: **Trees dripping with fairy lights frame the Grand Palace, and adorn outdoor restaurants across the country.** *PCS*

bottom: **A cocktail vendor lights up a Bangkok night market with a bit of streetside glitz.** *PCS*

random charm. Pointed into arrows, tubes direct you to temple fairs, and once there, decorate the rides with kaleidoscopic flair. Northerners even dangle neon tubes inside the traditional *saa* (mulberry) paper lanterns.

Thais share their love for things luminous with their neighbours. At Chinese festivals, dragon eyes flash, fireworks sparkle and neon signage shouts. Clouds of bulbs garland Hindu deities while oil lamp offerings glisten. Electric haloes deify Philippine Catholic regalia and help customise the Jeepney. Across Asia, myriad tiny lights seem both auspicious in worship and good for business. The Thai applications are no less kitsch, though display the most casual finesse, tapping an instinctive vibe for beauty and frivolity that turns gaudy into gorgeous.

Greco-Roman Architecture
Dressing Thailand in classical chic

Olympian statues hold orb lights aloft – atop a cement shophouse. Cathedral-scale domes cap buildings – 65 stories high. Renaissance balustrades line temple terraces – in iridescent pink ceramic. No building is immune from the Thai enthusiasm for Greco-Roman style. Porticoed lintels, fluted pediments, gilded cherubs and scalloped pedestal fountains adorn not just mansion and country club, but factory, farm and mall.

Their impact is not so much neo-classical as neon-classical. It's easy to dismiss this as pretentious borrowing, devoid of proportion, tacked on without consideration for either Thai or European integrity. In fact, it goes far deeper.

The Thai dub the genre *satai roman* (Roman style), or more commonly *sao roman* (Roman pillar), for pillars play a core role in a culture where houses always sat on stilts. Elaborate rites attend the erecting of pillars for a traditional teak house and the *sao ek* (principal pillar) gets swathed in sacred scarves, holy white thread or leaves of gold after the astrologically timed blessing. Thus it's only natural to prize a fabulously ornate, gilt encrusted Corinthian column especially if the stucco foliation is modified to look like a lotus.

Ultimately, the Thai tap classical imagery for the same reasons Westerners do. Evoking Ancient Greece and Rome summons civilised qualities that people want to project – particularly emergent players seeking to establish credibility. It suggests order, philosophy, history, culture, discipline, ethics, science, taste, logic, beauty, strength… the entire classical idyll, though perhaps not democracy.

Upwardly mobile nations go classical to give them an impression of matching the big powers, which also used it as a stamp of ownership in their colonies. Witness the Victorian façades of Raj-era India and Burma; the Palladian villas of Dutch Batavia (now Jakarta); the arched colonnades of British Singapore; the boulevards of French Hanoi and Phnom Penh. Classicism is the visual language of Empire. Grand, muscular, eternal, it became a must-have for Siam in its 19th century game of camouflage. Decorated in dainty structures intended to convey ephemerality, Siam suddenly had to play look-alike with imperialists so they couldn't claim to 'bring civilisation' as an excuse to invade. Ringed by threatening foreign powers, King Chulalongkorn visited many of the Western countries and colonies, seeing many classical edifices. He soon adopted the traits of Victorian Europe: hats, coats, shoes, trains, moustaches… and Roman columns. What the King commissioned, his subjects emulated. Hence there's a link between classical style and Thai independence. No wonder people are proud to stick pediments on their home – it's patriotic.

Some nationalists rail against this important heritage for not being indigenously Thai, though usually only when someone wants an excuse to demolish a precious landmark like Tha Tien pier market, the National Theatre, or the Thai-Chinese Chamber of Commerce. They recant when it's pointed out they'd be condemning most royal and governmental architecture since King Rama IV, including the palaces of Dusit and Ananta Samakhom Throne Hall, seat of Thailand's first parliament. The greatest classical flowering came in the reign of King Rama VI, with over 20 Italian architects at the court.

Truth be told, the Siamese have been appropriating foreign design throughout history: Chinese, Indian, Mon, Khmer, Persian, Burmese. European classical arrived as early as the 17th century. King Narai's palace in Lopburi was designed by a Frenchman, while the lancet windows found throughout Lopburi show Persian influence and a sense of Gothic. Thais have periodically flirted with Gothic – as at Government House, Wat Ratchabophit and the church at the mostly Baroque Bang Pa-in Palace. Today developers build turreted townhouse terraces with pointed arches, rose windows and concrete spires.

Classical architecture looks harmonious only when in proportion. Here, proportion isn't the point. Unlike in the West, Thai architects have rarely been free artists, but artisans who must realise the owner's requests. If he wants a triumphal arch, that's what he gets – even if it's for a restaurant or a suburban estate. To the Western eye used to restrained Georgian terraces and sober bank edifices, this excess of scrolls and pilasters resembles an over-egged pudding. Classical logic gets lost on smaller scale, too, with bright curvilinear bannisters placed on every new edifice, from shophouse to temple.

Materials also matter. Chiselled stone has an intrinsic quality that painted cement mouldings can't hope to match. If a ferro-concrete frame takes the strain, classical elements also lose structural purpose and end up being worn like costume jewellery. So we get pillars resting on an unsupported balcony, or protruding off a ledge, as if on foundations of air. Some porches soar three storeys high – only to clash with windows shoved horizontally out of alignment. This sends your bewildered eye in diverse directions, not in one glorious upward sweep.

But when an attempt to look classy ends up brassy, the hodge-podge can get by on novelty appeal. The many connoisseurs of kitsch delight in spotting gems of neon-classical; some so bad they're good, others worth a smile or a knowing wink. The West has classical wannabes, too, but because the architects are steeped in that heritage, they can play with the motifs using irony. Warehouses, showrooms and tyre garages attempt the same trick here, but since it's outside Thai tradition it looks clipped on.

Attempts at fusion with Thai architecture often founder since their fundamentals contradict. Thai uprights slope inwards; classical ones diverge to appear straight when foreshortened. Thai pediments form a concave swoop; classical ones form a triangle or convex dome. Thai buildings aim heavenward as if floating; classical edifices weigh heavily upon the ground.

At the higher echelons of contemporary architecture, the buildings by Rangsan Torsuwan achieve a camp panache – they're plain skyscrapers and malls sporting brazenly preposterous drag. So he injects some wit. Take his Chatpetch Tower on Bangkok's Chinatown riverbank. This bulbous cylinder topped by a cupola with two domed gazebos at the base can be seen as a nod to sky-scrapers being dubbed phallic objects. On the tower, Rangsan placed at medieval rose window; not filled with stained glass like his cathedral inspiration, but open as a vent for the car park. A prime post-modernist pastiche, it's now a much photographed landmark.

Downriver, the non-symmetrical State Tower posed a challenge. Rangsan covered its vast bulk with curved balconies, placed porticos on three ledges dozens of stories up, and capped it with a gilded dome. At its foot stands a century-old pawnshop that proves more deftly how an awkward site can be made elegant through simpler classical techniques.

Classicism can unify a streetscape. The palette of lines, shapes and decorative flourishes lends coherence, even if individual buildings greatly vary. And Thailand harbours some sublime classical districts in Bangkok's old town and the southern ports of Phuket, Songkhla and Takua Pa, though all suffer unkind intrusions that spoil the harmony. Bangkok governor Bhichit Rattakul attempted to scale back signage on heritage terraces in a late 1990s UN-sponsored scheme. But civic pride lost out to the desire to maximise profit per square inch.

In fact, classical motifs have adorned Thai shophouses for centuries. The archetypal non-wooden Sino-Thai shophouse seen in the South originated further down the peninsula in Malacca, after the Portuguese displaced its Malay sultanate. The so-called Sino-Portuguese style of tropical classicism acquired its long, narrow format due to a tax on frontage by the next Malacca colonists, the Dutch. The *baba* (Chinese male immigrant) felt at home in these dense, pastel hued terraces, keeping his *nonya* (Malay wife) behind a barrier zone of inlaid rosewood furniture, in rear rooms lit and ventilated by tiny court-yards. And his 'minor wife' next door.

This *baba-nonya* (aka *Peranakan*) style migrated with the Straights Chinese south to Singapore, then north to Penang and finally Phuket. There you can trace Chinese elements like curved window vents and lucky symbolism mingling with pilasters, pediments, balustrades and louvred shutters. The next influence on the style was British. They contributed shady arcades, decorative false balconies, and the Georgian half-circle fanlight above doors and window divided into small square panes. Today, many of these details have resurfaced on ordinary buildings. Hence modern Thai windows with fanlights share an unsuspected link with 10 Downing Street.

above: **Three-storey columns reach the full-height of this gated Phuket shophouse.** *PCS*

left: **Curvilinear balustrades have spread to temples, houses and buildings of every style, often in iridescent ceramic of pink or blue. It's a long-standing fashion. In many places you can spot early ones made of stacked ceramic pots, like these on an old merchant's house on Tha Phae Road, Chiang Mai.**

below left: **Eclectic Thai style – a Corinthian column supports the wooden fretwork porch of a Chiang Mai shophouse clad in plastic signage.** *PCS*

below right: **A cherubic fountain donated to Wat Don Wai, near Nakhon Pathom.**

Gates & Grilles
Marking boundaries beautifully

A recent survey identified a need for Thailand to catch up with regional rivals in academic prowess. Except in one respect. Thailand boasts Southeast Asia's best – and most expensive – school gates.

The proportion of funding poured into plaques, pillars and ironwork seems to outpace that spent on teaching. Travel the country's roads and it's apparent this status symbol isn't exclusive to schools, but conspicuous evidence of pride in progress, from civic compounds and factory gates to gaudy mansion railings and golf club archways, complete with clocktower.

Architectural one-upmanship is nothing new. Temples (*wat*) have long had their porches adorned to soar gloriously above plain timber housing. Historically,

temples had far grander construction materials, such as glazed roof tiles in the distinctive pattern of green and orange rectangles derived from cloth covers on the tented roof of a royal barge. With wealth generally increasing, the human impulse to upgrade has seen commoners cover everything in shiny ceramics: roof, railings, walls and, yes, gleaming, wipe-clean gateposts. Now condominiums look like 40-storey bathrooms, accessed via towering screens of gilded wrought iron, twice the height of the security guard heaving them ajar.

Despite Thailand's class system, upward mobility is not just possible, it can take mere dressing to achieve. Look like a winner and you surely must be a winner. To keep ahead of the neighbours, wealthier *wat* leave antique architecture to moulder while erecting gold-painted portals inlaid with kaleidoscopic glass mosaic. Golden gates indicate good karma.

Gates, of course, are a building's face. And face must be built up, burnished and bowed to. Each social class has its own way of shouting about how impressive they've become, with the nouveau riche shouting the loudest. Hence the neo-classical embellishments found in suburbs, where developers erect vast gated housing estates, industrial parks and country clubs with towering arched sentry posts and engraved marble name placards.

Amid all the glamour and exuberance lurks the prime reason for gates in the first place: security. Communal trust still keeps open the gardens of ordinary villagers, perhaps edged simply with planks or planted thickets. But those with status want walls and railings, gates and guards. Ironwork solved the resulting dilemma: how to shield what you've got while also showing it off.

Hence the forbidding private enclosures that scar beautiful landscapes, and turn residential *sois* into cement corridors. A neo-classical mansion on Phuket's sea gypsy island Koh Siray even resembles a medieval *wiang* (fortified town), with railing-fringed walls upon embankments ringed by a moat-sized ditch. Outside gated compounds, where there isn't a security guard, bourgeois Thais bask behind fences of fierce iron spikes, and walls embedded in the top with shards of broken glass. Quite different to the open front lawns and flowerbeds of Western suburbia.

Underlying this impulse to wall off one's private domain is the Siamese sense of *riab roi* (decorum). Gates are not just a superficial frontage, they order, control and beautify. Ornate doesn't equal ostentatious when extravagant decor is the prevailing social standard for what's considered proper. Restrained design is less likely to gain

acceptance into the ranks of the exclusive and may cause puzzlement like 'dressing-down' does in clothing.

Security in many countries leads to the grimmest of environments, but in Thailand even defences are cheerful and succumb to carefree fashion. Patterns in the sliding gates and window grilles preserve an archive of design since the 1960s. Echoed in cement block tracery, modern Thai metalwork would make *Wallpaper** magazine swoon. Diamonds and honeycombs tessellate, ovals and circles overlap, while long stepped rectangles replicate the format of traditional teak paneling. Baroque gilt fencing expresses the 1990s-boom taste for Frenchified Louis Napoleon décor, and walls often contain blocks with air-gaps that show the Mercedes tri-star logo. Minimalist style now favours chrome tubing and plain slats of stucco or wood, more integrated into modern architecture.

Over time, railings became integrated with sunshades until balconies were fully enclosed, with roof gardens typically capped by oppressive metal cages. What keeps people out, though, also keeps people in. As Thai firemen impotently lament, residents burnt behind their bars forgot what's most precious to protect.

Wat aren't immune to such conspicuous protection of possessions. Historically open to community use, they were also liable to antiquities theft. So since the mid-20th century, when raids on artifacts became an industry, *wat* have kept their treasures safe behind metal bars. And in doing so they invented an art form.

Vihaan shutters open onto strip-metal outlines of angels. *Thephanom* (guardian angel) *wai* in windows, often echoing their image similarly outlined on shutters of lacquer or mother-of-pearl. Typically painted in vivid hues, temple gate ironwork may depict chakras, chariots and the lotus at various stages of blooming.

Traditional *lai thai* patterns and the 2-D mural drawing style lend themselves to silhouette, thus religious railings update the fine-lined aesthetic found in Thai lacquer-work and shadow puppets.

Metal grilles thus have the power to preach anything their owners wish: materialist grandeur in the suburbs or heavenly splendour at the *wat*. Surface in Thailand can be much of the substance. And so gates can be a gateway to the culture.

above left: **Geometry in temple fair colours shows individual flair at this suburban home.**

above, right: **Gilt ironwork and Corinthian columns turn shop-house into showpiece.**

left: **Balcony security grilles act as a gallery of early modern motifs – and trap city residents behind bars in case of fire.**

Security Guards
A salute to the whistle-happy man in uniform

Walking through any upmarket Thai district, it's not unusual to get a salute. Behind the clicked-heel, hand-to-brow reflex of the *yaam* (security guard), a beaming grin emerges. The uniformed man at attention really enjoys the salute. He was raised with a sense of deference to strangers, but his pleasure in politeness may lie simply in face-to-face contact. To someone confined to this spot day-long, day-in, day-out, a resident strolling past his apartment block is light relief from saluting tinted-windowed cars.

Every few metres in urban Thailand, you'll find a *yaam*. Doffing his cap, helping cement trucks reverse, wielding a red flashing baton so a big car can push in to traffic. All manoeuvres are conducted with bursts on his whistle.

Yaam love their whistles. If there's a meaning to the shrill rasps they emit – as there is to the warbles, shrieks and quavers of boatmen's whistle – it's not a language known to drivers. But noise is good, positive, colourful: the sound of doing something. He looks the part, too.

In the West, uniforms have degenerated into pseudo-leisure wear: bulletproof anorak chic. Still enchanted by Ruritanian finery, *yaam* get dandified with embossed buttons, clip-on ties and, most crucially, a loop of rope brocade around the left shoulder. The uniforms aren't uniform, however. Security firms admit they adapt these styles from military dress, hence it appears like every compound has a private army. Indeed, the profession is rather like a privatised army, given the entrepreneurial sidelines of certain officers. They tap into an industry of 2,000 firms and 200,000 personnel worth 36 billion baht a year – that's a billion dollars. Not to mention the boon to the brocade and whistle industries.

Some security outfits are, notoriously, ventures by influential army officers with surplus time, manpower and protection to offer. The blurred line between state and private guards, allows them to impose authority on their own turf, with minimal accountability and murky allegiance. The 2003 surprise late-night demolition of a block of bars and shops at Sukhumvit Soi 10, Bangkok, was the work of "uniformed men". Applying to half the male population, it's a euphemism that in all such strong-arm cases is kept conveniently vague by accuser and accused, witness and reporter alike. At such times, the Bangkok novelists' hype about the capital's "seething underbelly" feels uncomfortably close to reality.

Security for some is a must. Gold shop guards wield shotguns, and factory watchmen preempt arson, though few legit businesses warrant scare tactics. But the real driving factor may be display – the impression of having

much to protect gains as much face as actual possession. Whatever the local crime rate, no self-respecting office, condo or housing estate could contemplate not hiring *yaam* to match the marble name plaque and wrought iron railings. Hence the sentry boxes on driveways, the arming of doormen and porters, the primping of parking attendants to bodyguard proportions. Judging by staff apparel, the plainest concrete block must be a palace. And with 'Palace' (or 'Mansion' or 'Chateau') tacked onto its noble name, who's to argue?

For all the pomp, the main *yaam* activity is waving gloved hands and filling names in registers. They're less likely to wield their truncheon or pistol than be found snoozing, snacking or chuckling with colleagues, maids and deliverymen. If they're lucky enough to have any company, that is. For Thais wired for group *sanuk*, sitting solo in an aluminium booth for 12 hours is dullness verging on torture. All that keeps the *yaam* going are obligation, wages and heroic patience. Plus pride in that lovely uniform. Although one must not carry the uniform too far. Municipal beach patrols in Hua Hin feared arrest for lese majesté because the gold and scarlet garb they were given resembled royal barge crew-wear, complete with turban-style head-dress.

Curiously, the most satisfying of all security jobs – imperiously selective nightclub bouncer – barely exists. The young rich expect (and get) red carpet entitlement, while riff-raff wouldn't dare enter the same venue. An internalised sense of hierarchy pre-sorts wheat from chaff, though high-class hookers invariably breach the few door policies attempted. With Thai crowds so well behaved, the only rowdies worth ejecting can't be touched: belligerent sons of politicians.

"The *nakleng* (hooligan) is aware that he can always emerge victorious by not abiding by the rules of the game," states William Klausner of the sense of impunity that afflicts not just nightlife, but business, communities, politics, everything. "One evades, one avoids, one does not challenge. There is fear that such power, if disturbed, challenged, confronted, will become even more arbitrary and will express itself in a vengeful, dangerous and violent manner." When influential people have been arrested for nightclub violence, the police themselves get publicly threatened, cases founder, reporting dwindles.

Refusing a social senior's face is fraught at the best of times, so imagine the fallout from a *yaam* barring the scion of an influential family. (At the very least, none of their clique will return. Ever.) Hence anyone looking

suitably haughty can usually sail inside. No need for any elaborate infiltration scams, just act with a sense of entitlement and say you're with someone the *yaam* wouldn't dare interrupt to ask. To ensure you're on the guest list next time, place your namecard in the prize draw bowl. Or claim you're a "journalist." It's amazing the buffet-grazing opportunists who gatecrash parties where royalty, ministers or celebrities preside.

Post-9/11 paranoia may finally push up standards – plus wages and training – for the under-motivated *yaam*. Hosting the APEC summit grew the industry 10 per cent in 2003. Plus they got new toys to deploy, from under-car mirrors to machine guns. Perhaps the thing security guards keep most secure is their jobs.

above left: **Hard at work in a car parking booth wearing faux-army khaki.**

above centre: **Pollution masks compromise the whistle reflex of the security guard.**

above right: **Saluting in a helmet strangely reminiscent of traffic police.** *PCS*

right and far right (*PCS*): **Guard firms revel in names like 'Guts Investigation', 'Stateman' and 'Doing Well Security', with badges, brocade and coats of arms completing the uniform.**

Blind Bands
Bringing joy to the street

below: **Streetside bands can swell to ten members, requiring aptly named 'roadies' to assemble the instruments on stools.** *PCS*

Bumper-to-bumper vehicles aren't the only kind of Thai street jam. In an impromptu musical jam, trios play sidewalks, ten-piece bands gig by the roadside, lone a cappella minstrels serenade stalls. Pavement players may be a common sight across the world, but in Thailand there's a difference: most of the *wanipok* (buskers) cannot see.

Blind musicians cover every age, region and genre, from folk to rock to ballad. Some sightless soloists rove, waving a cane or gripping a sighted assistant. Head swaying like Stevie Wonder, the singer phases poignantly in and out of microphone range. The busker or assistant sling an amplifier around their neck, or support it on a pole, while one of their hands holds out a cup.

Static groups make the best music, gleaning donations into a large steel box. Guitars, chime bells, pipes and drums turn the sidewalk into a stage, typically under a footbridge. Wired to amps and large speakers, the Electone synthesiser perches on plastic stools. Usually women star on vocals, while a male keyboardist plays

extrovert lead, grinning like an Asian Ray Charles. At the simpler end, you might find faint melodies emanating from an elderly couple folded onto a tiny patch of paving. Granny warbles over granddad's plaintive scrapings on the *pin*, a kind of three-stringed mandolin. They're from the north. Migrants from the northeast more likely wheeze elegaically through the region's trademark bamboo harmonica, the *khaen*, to lyrics in Lao of rural toil.

It's debatable whether *wanipok* mask, or merely add to, the ear-damaging noise pollution that Thais endure. Traffic sounds reverberate off concrete, shop and bar speakers out-blast each other, PA systems shatter nerves frayed by ads that squawk a sales pitch as you pass. Even exercisers in Bangkok's Lumphini Park face karaoke being amplified at 7am. Busker quality varies wildly, though to ears unattuned to the musical qualities of the Thai language, many renditions flirt perilously with discord. Connoisseurs bear with excruciating moments for serendipity's sake. Round the corner might lie a gem.

right: **blind troubadours wander the sidewalks solo with a cane, amp slung round neck, or guided by a sighted relative.**

below: **Many a sightless chanteuse sings like a dove, though their plaintive voices get poor acoustics from Bangkok's towering SkyTrain stations.**

Their blindness adds piquancy to the fact that most popular music deals with pain or loss. "They can play many styles, from *luuk thung* (folk) to *luuk krung* (urban ballads)," says Jirapat Jetnipit of the Thailand Association of the Blind. "But they're most likely to play hits, so they know the public would give some money." For it is their livelihood. "Each clink in the box means food, education and a future for my sons and everybody in the family," says Amorn Samakkarn, who plays the *pin* near the Grand Palace. "I can't afford to get sick or die."

Founded in 1988, the ten-piece band Thep Prathan Pohn (Angels Grant Wishes) gets 700-2,000 baht per day. "It's not reliable, but on average I earn 100-150 baht a day," shrugs Bang-orn, 57, of a smaller act that plies a mall forecourt in Bangkok's Silom financial district. "My boss divides the money for us. It's better than doing nothing. I don't know what to do if I stay at home. I can't do much there; everyone else goes out for work. If I come here to sing, at least I'll get some money."

With so much social respect bound up in being able to provide for one's family, the priority is on integration and self-help skills. Lose one sense and other senses make up the deficit. Hence organisations guide the sightless into jobs that optimise hearing (music), touch (massage), or even the sixth sense: luck (selling lottery tickets). In similar fashion, the deaf find a role using touch (making toys and gifts at the Silent World Craft Centre) or sight (as souvenir vendors). Along Bangkok's Sukhumvit and Silom roads, teams of all-deaf stallholders barter prices visually using fingers and calculators, while 'chatting' in one of the world's most sophisticated sign languages.

Other professions are now opening up. The Fine Arts Department teaches the disabled cultural skills from weaving and wood carving to dance and music. Others tackle electronics, athletics, herbal healing and computer programming instead of the clichéd options. "I used to think selling the lottery was the best job for the blind, but I realised this is the worst, because it's too dangerous," cautions Jerawat Laowang, who now grows *lamyai* fruit in Chiang Mai. "Many of my disabled friends have been robbed or hurt in car accidents. Farm work is one of the most desirable jobs for the blind." Still, for blind city folk, music and massage can provide a life-long income.

Over five percent of the public is handicapped, but 87% of them languish as rural recluses. Belief in bad karma makes imperfect bodies something shameful to hide. The disabled are banned from inheriting land redistributed by the state to the poor and don't get any farming subsidies. Government agencies lag in hiring the handicapped. In 2004, a new Health Ministry regulation threatened to ban the disabled from healing professions, including massage. *Wanipok*, too, must constantly run the gauntlet of officialdom. City authorities often hassle them, evict them and confiscate their equipment. "When they get caught, we contact the Bangkok Metropolitan Authority to return the instruments," Jirapat sighs. "We're tired of this kind of thing. It's a real problem."

Cluttering the street can't be the reason, since vendors occupy more space and get away with far greater mess. The rare occasions they get a space, it's in low-trafficked spots, complains Jirapat: "Crowded spots are reserved for vendors. It's because the BMA gets money from vendors. Musicians can't pay, so they don't get space to play." That would require a licence. Licences for anything are a kind of currency. Issued usually by police, they determine who can do what and each has a rate of return. With music venues milked like dairy cows, no way could mendicant minstrels be allowed to bust the monopoly, even if most pose little competition to professional players.

There is another reason, again to do with face. Busking is begging set to music, and begging has a bad name in Thailand. There's always the suspicion that mafia are behind them. "I think there aren't any gangsters exploiting them. It's not profitable," Jirapat counters. "Blind people set up bands on their own. There might be some sighted assistants carrying instruments, driving or buying food, but most are relatives."

Finally solutions to the cat-and-mouse game are appearing. Already well organised, *wanipok* could pursue the model of London's underground which now licenses the best ones to play at numbered pitches, sponsored by a beer company. In 2003, the BMA's Department of Social Welfare inched in that direction with a 100 million baht scheme offering a platform for blind bands of ten or more players at parks and malls and payment of 10,000 baht a time, in exchange for quality standards. Audiences forgive bum notes less than passing pedestrians do.

Few appreciate the cultural contribution *wanipok* make. Veera Somboon provided an insight in 2003 with *Tamnan Salok Haeng Kitayarn*, a novel about a blind busker that spotlit unsung truths. One is that the *phu noi* (little folk) of the street often have a revelatory story that *phu yai* (bigwigs) are too blind to notice. Another is that musical traditions (and antique instruments) survive largely thanks to the dedication of independents, rather than to official preservation orders. Most poignantly, Veera celebrates music as an effective means to understand human existence and to grasp compassion in a way mere words can't manage. Veera notes that music affects people most profoundly at transitional times of day: on waking or nightfall, starting or stopping, changing attire or activity. Hence the street buskers' synergy with rush hour, of which Bangkok has 24 a day.

Encountering a blind band is a life lesson. A triumph of beauty over pain, of spirit over body, of talent over intolerance, they perform a true social service. Blind buskers more than play the blues; they really live it.

top: **In Chiang Mai's 'Walking Street' fair, a busker sings through his loudspeaker while tapping his cane to the beat.** *PCS*

above: **A migrant busker in Silom banking district, plays an electric mandolin and chings tiny brass cymbals between his toes.** *PCS*

Soi Animals

The urban zoo – cats, dogs, birds, snakes, elephants

Among the most arresting sights in cities are animals. Stray dogs snooze in street and temple. Cats raise oddly bent tails. Elephants beg at tourist spots. Pythons nest in gardens. Night air hums with frogs and cicadas.

Hasty modernisation has regimented life, though not the casual way Thais relate to nature. Animals were so integral to rural life, wildlife so seemingly inexhaustible, and animal products so valuable, that nature got taken for granted. Now many Thais abhor that animals must endure constant avoidable tragedies under the law of the concrete jungle. Elephants suffer injuries from urban hazards. Squirrels get electrocuted scurrying along old power wires. Vipers are killed with the quickest weapon to hand, though constrictors may get taken to refuges.

Problems arise from a fracture between Buddhist compassion and harsh street realities. A million dog bites a year – over half on small children – spur calls for canine registration, sterilisation, extermination. Yet most Buddhist Thais oppose culls, and baulk at the cost and discipline of managing the street menagerie. Hence the gesture of putting out food. The dogs' lazy, lolloping ways aren't just down to heat, but a malnourishing diet of rice scraps causing disease and a constant presence of mangy mutts. Starving them is worse; they go feral and attack.

As with many other social problems, temporary purges save face. Ahead of the 2003 APEC summit, the Bangkok Metropolitan Authority controversially trucked some of Bangkok's 100-150,000 strays to a makeshift pound near the Cambodian border, where care, shade and food proved inadequate. Daunting challenges face a planned network of pounds, pet ID cards, health checks and tagging of neutered strays. Past pounds have lacked resources and space. Plus people continue to abandon pets in schools or temples, risking a 5,000 baht fine. Pedigree dogs confer status – fostering canine boutiques, delis and spas – but demand much of their handlers. Thus Alsatians, Spaniels and Rottweilers also end up traumatised victims of the street-mongrel hierarchy.

Championing the adoption of indigenous dogs like the Ridgeback in his 2002 Birthday address, King Bhumibol launched a book and a clothing brand named after the stray he trained, Thongdaeng (Copper). The police also tried to turn strays into sniffer dogs, though few proved obedient. The Thai Ridgeback is among the world's oldest breeds. Lauded as a hunting hound in old manuscripts, it occurs in cave paintings and Baan Chiang graves up to 5,500 years old. Though popular in the US, Ridgebacks lack the global fame of the Siamese cat.

Several feline breeds originated here, from the Siamese and Khorat to part-Thai cats like the Oriental, Snowshoe or Himalayan. The smoky 'points' on nose, ear, paws and slim tail of a Siamese pop up among Thailand's diverse moggies, many of which have twisted tails. Aghast visitors wonder if they've been injured or even mutilated by man or beast, although the deformity is genetic.

Throughout Southeast Asia, Charles Darwin noted, "the cats have truncated tails about half the proper length, often with a sort of knot at the end." He might not have believed the origin myths. One says that cat tails held Buddha images so protectively they rigidified. In another, a bathing princess kept her rings on a cat tail. Because they slipped off, next time she or the cat – tales differ – knotted the tail. Just as Thai optimism holds that bird droppings 'bless' those splattered, a crippled tail augurs luck. Ancient treatises describe 17 domestic cats of which two with kinked long or short tails bring wealth and power. Though Bangkok's 25,000 stray cats can fend for themselves, people put out food, partly as they catch vermin, but also because killing a cat equates to killing a novice monk. So vets hate putting cats down.

Out of cats' reach, cages of songbirds hang from the eaves of many homes, especially Muslim ones. The cages of bent cane or bone have an ornate hook and a cloth shade. The pricy birds, some endangered, twitter for their owners' pleasure and may compete in cooing contests.

At Baan Ta Klang village in Surin, the family pet is rather bigger: an elephant. When Southern Isaan was second only to Africa's savanna in 'big game', Surin's Kui tribe rounded up elephants for war or labour, keeping several under their extra-high stilt houses. After local forests were felled, fodder became scarce and expensive, so the village herd declined to just a few dozen.

With Bangkok's vacant lots offering better natural foraging, Surin elephants become itinerants, plying streets so people can pay to feed them sugar cane – or to duck under the belly for luck. Since hot roads damage elephant feet, they trudge through lighter night-time traffic wearing reflectors and lights, still risking harm from sharp objects, potholes, drains, wires, cars. Many Thais fret that the national animal, which once appeared on the flag, should beg, but outrage exceeds answers.

Cities keep banning them, but grand plans fizzle out despite private initiatives. The mahouts lack plausible options, so some elephants work in illegal logging under doses of amphetamines. A government idea to purchase elephants for forest work undervalues the mahouts, whose skills and companionship are essential for elephants to survive safely. Yet most interest in the mahout school at Lampang's National Elephant Institute comes from tourists. Including a hospital, sperm bank and pachyderm art and music (both taken seriously by Western critics), this northern enclosure offers non-exploitative solutions, but languishes in a funding crisis.

Of the 2,000 domesticated elephants left in Thailand, many northern ones unemployed by the 1988 logging ban now offer rides and tourist shows. About 2,500 survive in the wild, though threatened by ivory poaching, live export, violence by encroaching farmers and the killing of mothers to grab babies for tourism, which entails allegedly cruel training. Authorities bask in the prestige and Thainess of elephants, but can't seem to manage their care and survival. Some experts predict extinction in a decade or two, since captive elephants hardly breed. That so many creatures remain visible in towns highlights the Thai bond with animals, yet their grim coexistence shows it's become a dog-eat-dog world.

right: **Truncated cats' tails aren't malformed or mutilated but genetic.**

far right: **Stray *soi* dogs nap with a neigbourhood boy at Sathorn Pier in Bangkok.** *PCS*

Blue Pipes & Hanging Wires
The whimsical art of visual pollution

Uniting Thai architecture, roads and vistas, two things snag the eye: hanging wires and the blue PVC pipe. You can't miss these contributions to probably the world's most cluttered streetscape. Wires old, new and redundant tangle our surroundings in brutal, slashing lines or whimsical knots, severed ends swinging like electric eels at head-height. Defying logic and memory as to what connects what, cables tangle into garlands several dozen thick. Blue pipes meander over teak house, temple and waterfall. The eye may bypass them to dwell on beautiful details behind, but the camera doesn't lie. Taking a wire-free photograph defies all but the deftest lensman. The most photographed sight in Thailand is the hanging wire.

To its natural and historical wonders, Thailand adds an abundance of avoidable eyesores. Even heritage sites succumb. Cables asphyxiate landmarks, lamp posts upstage Sukhothai's spires, colonnades disappear under commercial signage. Vast billboards blight landscapes.

Many are the devices met on the sidewalk obstacle course. Walking requires a slalom round pots, poles, lumps of cement, sawn off metal rods and imploded paving – assuming there *is* a pavement. Bigger intrusions force people into the road: phone boxes, footbridges and police booths. Other impediments wander: parked cars, vendors, food tables, clothing racks, beggars, buskers, restaurant signs on wheels, trash bags, construction materials, election boards, store displays, people sleeping, motorcycles parked and speeding. Walking in Thailand is quite a trip, in every sense of the word.

Street chaos enmeshes Asia, though its extent in Thailand astonishes. Local factors make authorities less keen than planners in the West to hide away utilities that are proudly displayed as symbols of independence and modernity. Just as plumbing implies hygiene, wires mean communication and the electricity that powers progress. "In 1893, Bangkok became the first Asian city to have electrified trams (Japan would not switch until 1903)," Steve Van Beek writes. "The city was also a pioneer in the use of telephones." Piped water served Bangkok by 1914, though its first sewage main was only recently dug.

But what was novel then is a given now. The planners' mentality owes much to the mid-20th century 'development mindset', when countries put pipelines, dams and power stations on their stamps and banknotes as icons of a new culture. Ironically, this fetish for conspicuous industrial carbuncles now brands a country as less, rather than more sophisticated. As Asia pundit Alex Kerr explains, similar thinking scars every vista in Japan, a huge influence on Thai taste and aspirations. Soiling the nest spoils a country's prospects for the post-industrial future, where being truly modern demands something else – like burying pipes and wires.

While concrete, cars and billboards show material advance, old buildings, mature trees and walkable street-scapes struggle to be valued in the 'development culture'. Aside from a few monuments, no laws or listings stop heritage buildings from being demolished or ineptly modified. Prioritising wires over everything caused the

right: **A tangle of do-it-yourself cabling bridges the information superhighway to back-alley shophouses.**

facing page, left: **The Pompidou Centre in Paris wears its bright plumbing on the outside; so does the northern village of Mae Salong.**

facing page, right: **Roadside trees get sacrificed for webs of wiring like this masterpiece of abstract art in Bangkok.**

brutal amputation of most roadside trees, which then provide less shade. A severed branch may take decades to grow back, but it must make way for this flexible wire right now. This can damage development. Widening of the road to Hua Hin could have incorporated the rain-trees that lined it for miles. Instead, their replacement by pylons robbed the resort of a prime asset.

Yet Thai culture offers solutions. Trimming trees is a Thai art, seen in the patient pruning of *mai dut* topiary. But utility workers aren't professional tree surgeons. They hack branches without concern for its shape, shade or survival. The jagged stumps of lopsided 'amputrees' invite rot and disease, while the resultant thicket of sprouts require far more 'tending' than before. Behind this butchery lies a latent fear of forest. The urban jungle doesn't tolerate encroachment by the natural jungle. Foliage grows so fast here that progress is equated with cutting the forest away. Now it has little chance to grow.

To help slow this Thailand Chainsaw Massacre, some monks bless trees with coloured sashes. It took embassies to save the trees on Bangkok's aptly named Wireless Road. Recent Bangkok governor Bhichit Rattakul failed in trying to scale back signage, but got half a million trees planted, though officials often cut mature trees to plant overpriced saplings for show rather than shade. The same happens at new parks, where there's more cement than greenery. Officialdom views parks as show-pieces – spaces more for respect than relaxation. Even temple foliage gets denuded to show off the buildings.

Neglect of the streetscape has social origins too. The wealthy avoid walking. It's not just the heat; rank infers they shouldn't be seen expending effort. Their car is a bubble between private domains that limits their engage-ment with the masses. So Thailand doesn't go for pedes-trianisation for its own sake, unless it's for events, which always fill up with markets. Culturally, public space has been regarded as an amoral domain ruled by spirits and beyond personal ownership or control – except when VIPs visit. For international set-pieces like the Asian Games or the ASEM and APEC summits, the clean-up is total and devastating. Multi-billion baht budgets fund monumental sculptures, mass tree slashings combined with plantings that wilt a week later, and vast signs to hide historic neighbourhoods branded as slums.

That monument mindset focuses on major buildings while treating the overall streetscape either as a free-for-all or a rigidly ordered set. The Rattanakosin Island Plan aims to demolish several old neighbourhoods to 'restore' Bangkok's core into a depopulated hub of landmarks with Paris-style open vistas that never actually existed. Critics lament the loss of living culture, both to Thais and to tourists for whom the plan is tailored. Herbal apothecaries would go, while convenience chain stores could stay as they 'cater to tourists'. It's all or nothing.

Balanced plans have been drafted, but only partially implemented. Schemes founder when state agencies compete for turf, while boondoggles often favour vested interests over civic responsibility. The compromise to

align pavement obstacles and leave 1.5m passing space had piecemeal results. Since a pledge to bury wires in 1999, Bangkok has barely buried a mile, while Shanghai interred thousands of miles of cable, vowing to cut any wires illegally slung. Fresh impetus came in 2004 with a dynamic new governor, Apirak Kosayothin, pledging to beautify the city as well as respecting communities.

While inertia reigns, people get used to the visual chaos, hence the shock and initial denial when Phuket and Chiang Mai fell into the 'getting ugly' category of *National Geographic*'s 2004 tourism survey. As Kerr says: "People who are born and live in such an environment know of no alternative. The result is that the public, as well as planners and architects, think this kind of look is an inherent part of modernisation."

Faced with wire poles and pipes, the Thai make use of them. Some poles get festooned with foliage, while the blueness of the water pipe pleases in its own right. While less obtrusive pipes – yellow for electrics, grey for sewerage – do get hidden, the blue PVC must be liked better, since that's the one people use to make clothing racks, furniture, frames for stalls or carts, all of which are prominently displayed for effect. Perhaps instead of burying wires, they should just make them blue.

top left: **A pottery handicraft urinal. With or without blue drain pipe. Up to you.** *PCS*

lower left: **A home-made water sprinkler keeps the grounds green at Wat Chaiwattanaram, Ayutthaya.**

top right: **Don't park here, but admire the barrier, created from blue water pipes.**

lower right: **An ingenious lamp turns water pipes into electrical ducts at Bangkok's Central World Plaza.** *PCS*

Trash Recyclers

Freelance gleaners make the most of rubbish

Under cover of night they come. Residents wake in the early hours to the sound of rubbish sifters rummaging through their bins to take what they can sell. By the time official dustmen arrive, half the bins' content has gone.

A comment on the country's widening wealth gap, this enterprise highlights public and official ambivalence about separating and recycling trash – and a lifestyle that willingly throws away resources. Into the resulting mess, the freelance forager thrusts a willing hand. "There are two types: *khon geb khaya* collect or steal stuff, whereas *saleng* only buy unwanted items," says Natthaphon, 23, a *saleng* who joins his mother and two elder brothers in buying-up a chunk of Phitsanuloke's scrap. A rung higher up the hardscrabble hierarchy, *saleng* – a term indicating the Chinese ethnicity of Thailand's earliest 'rag-and-bone-men' – make a decent living in a socially useful role that's part of daily streetlife.

"I quit working in a BMW car factory to do my father's business when he retired," recounts Natthaphon from his red, three-wheeled trolley. "My mother uses a pick-up truck, not a tricycle. She could earn 1,000 baht a day. I earn about 500 baht." Assembling BMWs clearly hasn't influenced the design of the bare assemblage of steel, rubber and grease that constitutes his tricycle. He rides the largest size sold by his *saleng* depot, costing 23,000 baht. It's pedal powered, though Bangkok's traffic has lead to an upsurge in motorised versions. On luxury models, a collapsible umbrella shades and shelters the driver and his scales, though not the assistants dozing in the load tray's lumpy mattress of jumble.

"I buy almost everything: glass, paper, plastic, metal, wood, newspaper, books, magazines, electronics, usable tyres and sometimes clothes," Natthaphon says. He makes 4-5 baht profit per kilo on the 3-5 baht a kilo he pays for things the processing centre can ship in bulk to recyclers. He may pay a premium for other useful items, prizing things that won't need repairing before resale.

Squealing their trademark bicycle-pump 'horn', *saleng* trundle urban streets from 9am to 3pm on weekdays and all day weekends. They complete for only a small fraction of the trash, however, while the wider problem eludes solution, as mountains of hazardous, mercury-seeping waste pollutes groundwater. Recently, *khon geb khaya* in suburban Bangkok swiped tubs of apparent trash from a prominent company's doorstep, only to lose fingers, sight or life to the radioactive contents.

Thailand produces 14.2 million tonnes of industrial and consumer waste a year according to World Bank figures in 2003. Thailand only reprocesses 11 percent of

a possible 4.5 million tones, compared to rates of 30-50 percent in Korea, Singapore and Japan. Excluding *saleng*, the state recycles just 3 percent. Schemes involving colour-coded street bins have foundered through lack of enforcement and the changing of bin colours. Bin men have been spotted dumping divided trash into the same truck. The solution rests in education, discipline and civic pride. A new generation Bangkok governor, Apirak Kosayothin, promises to foster the separation of waste in households and workplaces. Its collection would build on the profit-driven *saleng* system that Thais are used to.

NGOs have long treated *saleng* as a socially positive means to educate about waste and to get the poverty-stricken organised and more appreciated by society. A successful pilot scheme in Isaan's Khon Kaen province now runs municipal trash collection. Yet officialdom feels queasy about such a dirty profession that spotlights a source of shame. A few truly desperate gleaners pick through what ends up at the suppurating, volcanic land-fills on which those scavengers actually live.

Thailand is actually a well-swept country, only the sweepings end up soiling forest and field, canal and coral reef. Though a proverb decries 'hiding an elephant corpse beneath a lotus leaf', bureaucracies tend to do just that.

Thoughtless pollution has been a cultural blindspot across Asia, with minds fixed on development, not its costs. Attitudes like *riab roi*, cleanliness and unblemished beauty also mutate so that old items of superior craft or materials often get discarded in favour of shiny new replacements. And as in many societies, one measure of wealth is what you can afford to throw away.

In the Arcadian past – when wrappings were bio-degradable reed baskets, wooden boxes or banana leaf pinned with bamboo slivers – whatever got tossed, the climate soon decomposed. Not so those symbols of modern life: the plastic bag and water bottle. Flagging trails through 'protected' jungle, the spent plastic bottle becomes a marker buoy on picturesque beaches or indicates waterfalls suitable for swimming.

Elaborate over-packaging is part of the Thai shopping experience, which retail writer Anon Nakornthab sums up as "buy ten buns, get eleven bags". Convenience stores are a major culprit, distributing needless plastic as a policy. But that's what consumers want. "If we give fewer bags or don't give double bags for some products, they'll complain," explains Suwandee Chaiwarut of Big C super-stores. But with consumer trash expected to grow 25% by 2010, the cabinet wants to reduce the use of plastic bags. Bangladesh and Taiwan recently banned them, but research shows Thai shoppers won't carry re-usable cloth bags. Thailand's 7-Eleven boss thinks it'll take years for Thais to accept Body Shop-style questions like "do you want a bag?", let alone "do you *need* a bag?"

far left: **Even dustpans are former junk, in this case halved metal tins, shown with an array of Thai brooms.** *PCS*

left: **Water bottles converted into trade talisman goldfish by scissors and spray paint.**

Anti-litter campaigns appeal to public pride, but to confront Thai offenders is taboo, and clean-ups can cause loss of face. Slammed for moving vegetation on Phi Phi island, producers of the film *The Beach* made no friends by removing tonnes of locally-generated trash and pointing out how anchors and fishing tackle wrecked the reef. Also, to clean up is a low-status job, which is why drains are dredged by prison chain-gangs. To retrieve the wrapper you've just dropped is to ape that stooping servant.

Nevertheless, as the English say: "where there's muck there's brass." Someone will see a way to reap the 16 billion baht of resources that goes unrecycled every year. Thai entrepreneurs have now shown how eco-friendly containers made of hemp or cassava could become a viable industry. While some see a biodegradable future for trash, others have turned rubbish into art.

Those plastic bottles can become fish amulets or be cut and painted into toys and mascot animals that so appeal to the cute tastes of teens and young adults. Drink cans get sliced into wind mobiles or cut into patterns, hole-punched and laced into handbags and handicrafts. The same method can turn a Coke tin into a cap and a cardboard whisky box into a broad-brimmed hat. Several artists turn engine parts into sculpture and many firms recycle rubber tyres and buffalo carts into furniture.

Improvising with odds and ends has long been a trait of Thai folk crafts, as well as makeshift vendor carts. Appropriately, Thailand boasts a diversity of beautiful organic brooms with which to brush: bamboo poles bound with bristles from the *ton mai kwaad* (broom plant). Dustpans are even a model of recycling, being diagonally halved tin boxes on poles.

Attitudes can change. The 1997 economic crash punctured the middle class aversion to anything second-hand and there remains a residual 'retro' market for used goods among some who can buy new. When the likely environmental reckoning comes there'll simply be no option but to scrimp, retrieve and reuse. The whole country will have to play *saleng*.

above: **A Si Satchanalai lady dons a hat stitched from whisky bottle boxes for keeping out of the sun at a festival.** *PCS*

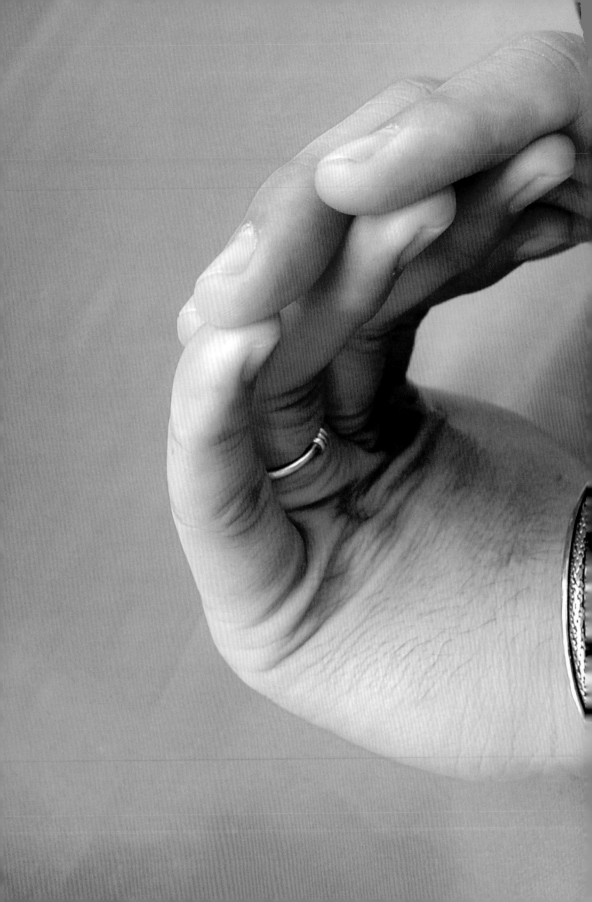

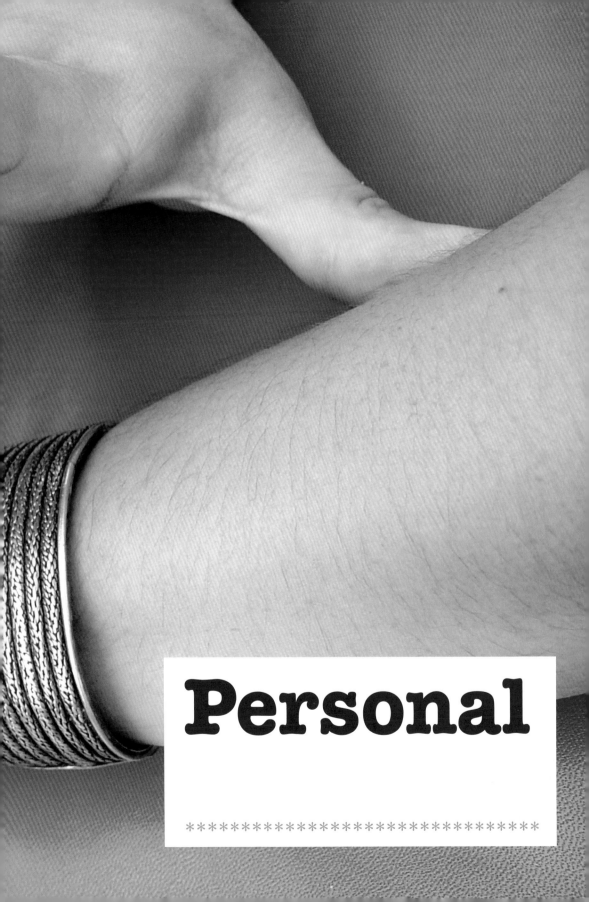

Personal

****

Uniforms
The delight in dressing alike

previous spread: **Most Thais can make complex double-jointed dance gestures. They train to bend back their fingers and elbows through dance lessons in school. Mothers may also put kids' hands in warm water then flex the fingers back.**

The Thai love their uniforms. Dressing alike sets the tone from farmer and guard to silk-clad *khunying* (titled lady) and police in brown polyester so tight it looks sprayed on. A society attuned to hierarchy needs clothing that helps people deduce each other's relative rank and thus which vocabulary to use.

While fashions define contemporary social 'tribes', traditional uniforms are genuinely tribal and thus regional. Many hill tribes still don trademark dress, not just when hawking their regalia as souvenirs. Still widely worn, the archetypal farmer's outfit – the unisex *moh hom* suit of indigo pantaloons and jacket shirt – began as Thai Yai tribal wear. Yet the *moh hom* was an ancient import: Asian trousers originated in either Persia or China, which also inspired the jacket's cloth buttons.

Ancestors in this humid land wore little, but what they wore branded them. Influenced by India, indigenous Southeast Asian clothing is essentially the untailored rectangular sheet. It's worn panels sewn together in a tunic or dancer's cape, or worn wrapped, as a monk's robe, *pha khao ma* loincloth, or longer, looser *jongkraben*. Now mainly seen in pageantry or on hotel doormen, the *jongkraben* features yards of cloth wound around each leg then passed between and tucked in at the small of the back. The simpler *pha sin* tube skirt has a hem pattern to identify each village, though that's rarely the case now as the practice declines upcountry and the urban rich buy *pha sin* for formal dress or as table runners.

Official uniforms have long imitated foreign fads. Nobles under King Rama III wore things Imperial Chinese; Rama IV adopted sartorial accents from Napoleon III of France, while Rama V donned military dress like European kings. King Rama V modelled the structure and uniforms of the new branches of the armed forces and bureaucracy on Western colonial forces, employing Europeans to help set them up. He also created the *rajapataen* (royal pattern) national costume, combining a silk *jongkraben* with long white knee-socks,

shoes and a white jacket with a low 'Nehru-style' vertical collar. This jacket still dazzles at official functions and on election posters, pinned with medals. "At that time, naval power was the big thing, so white was in," says scholar Vithi Phanichphant. "The stocking socks and shoes were Western." Some say the jacket is Prussian; others say it came from British colonial style, as did the army khaki.

The new Thai police force, under direction of a Dane, adopted a darker khaki. Styled after British Malaya and Hong Kong, police khakis had "the sharkskin look like Charlie Chaplin, with loose trousers, tight jacket, small shoulders, no padding," Vithi records. "Padding came in during the 1940s, but by the early 1960s, everything had to be slim and cut like the Mod look. That's why today's uniform is kept close, showing off the muscles." A zip behind false buttons makes the jacket snug, even for older officers with a belly. One modern result is sexual harassment: 400 calls a month to the 191 emergency line are lewd propositions to policemen, 60% by men, reports the *Nation*, which adds: "Websites show pictures of handsome police in their tight uniforms, and feature advice on how to win their hearts."

A hangover of dictatorial times, the macho uniform culture resurfaced twice recently when police arrested army officers while the suspects wore military khakis. The army insisted that uniforms must first be removed and then only by army officers. "To lose face isn't merely to lose one's own face," Eric Allyn explains. "One loses the face of one's family, group or even all Thailand."

Military-style codes also applied to civilian dress through draconian 'cultural mandates' by dictator Plaek Phibunsongkhram around World War II. He denied entry to anyone in Thai clothing at government offices. The rules later relaxed, but the habit stuck. Bureaucrats had to swelter under suit and tie without air-conditioning until a 1960s military ruler, Thanom Kittikachorn, had them wear the safari suit. Ideal for the climate, it survives in the multi-pocket jacket shirt still keeping drivers, officials and provincial godfathers in dapper comfort.

top left: School uniforms on parade at the King Rama V statue in Bangkok in styles of a century past: girls in sailor suits, boys in Scout-style shorts. *PCS*

left: Phrae folk celebrate Thai new year in the unisex indigo *moh hom* farmers' outfit for which Phrae is famous. *PCS*

top right: SSSS-size uniforms get ever tighter and shorter among university students. *PCS*

above: A hotel doorman dons the *rajapataen* (royal pattern) uniform of white jacket with Nehru collar, sash, silk *jongkraben* sarong, white knee socks and dress shoes.

right: **A traffic cop in his body-hugging khaki uniform on duty in Loei, Isaan.** *PCS*

far right: **Workers' clothing is so standard nationwide it becomes a** *de facto* **uniform. Despite the heat, a sweeper in Kamphaeng Phet wraps head-to-toe, with face visor, to remain as clean and untanned as possible.** *PCS*

left: **Knitted balaclavas keep dust and especially sun off outdoor labourers and construction workers. This oarsman glides through Khao Sam Roi Yot nature reserve near Hua Hin, checking his fish traps.**

With women playing fashion catch-up with the West, Thai clothing came to look old-fashioned and needed updating. For the royal couple's long foreign tour of the early 1960s, Queen Sirikit modernised classical Siamese garments using Thai silk, a fabric that Jim Thompson was popularising abroad. A total of seven national dress outfits catered for day or evening functions. Dressmakers still tailor these templates for society ladies.

So male national dress could be just as glorious in fabric, colour and Thainess, King Bhumibol instituted the *phra ratchathan* in the early 1980s. A buttoned jacket shirt with a low Nehru collar in hand-loomed silk or cotton patterns, it comes in a long-sleeved variant with sash for evening wear. The then prime minister General Prem Tinsulanonda remains its most celebrated model. The subsequent rise of businessmen to power, however, again caused the Western suit to dominate, though now a jacket's more comfortable in the arctic air-conditioning.

Education instills the idea of uniforms as part of being modern. Yet school outfits haven't changed much in over a century, since it was modern to dress boys like Edwardian Scouts and girls in Victorian sailor suits. Boys in state schools continue with English-style tan shorts, while private schoolboys graduate from red to blue shorts. College and university students can wear long trousers, but students of all ages and both sexes wear white shirts embroidered with the name, number, in blue for state schools, red for private schools. Girls' uniform dates from when Madame Cole founded the Presbyterian Wanglang School for girls in 1874, which became today's elite Watthana Vithayalai School. Above pleated knee-length blue skirts, billowing white smocks have puffed sleeves and droopy blue bows at the round collar, which often extends into a naval flap at the back.

Regulation schoolgirl hair is the 1920s flapper bob. Introduced by style leaders like King Bhumibol's aunt Princess Valai-alongkorn, it was worn by the late Princess Mother into the 1990s. In 2004, a teacher accidentally lopped off a girl's earlobe when brusquely snipping her locks to the regulation length.

The schoolboys' quiffed haircut is a military crew cut adopted nationally from the influential Vachiravudh School, which was founded by King Rama VI on the rod-backed Western and Japanese cadet template. A military government rule enforced school boy and girl hair styles nationwide from 1973 until 2003, when each school was allowed to decide. Few schools relaxed the rules, in case preening took precedence over study.

Schools are just as regimented about clothing. "When we stood in line at 8am for the National Anthem, my school teacher would inspect the hem of the shorts," Paothong Thongchua recalls of a 1950s discipline still in place. "If it didn't look right, he'd measure it. It mustn't be less than 5cm above the knee, with 10cm of spare cloth around the thigh." Even so, teens try to make the baggy uniforms fit tighter, while shortening shorts and hems. Female university students (who also must wear uniforms and insignia brooches) can now choose a SSSSS-sized blouse. "Over 80 percent buy tight-fitting shirts," says a vendor near Chulalongkorn University. "The girls want them short so their navels can be seen."

Found throughout the region from Sri Lanka to Indonesia, state school uniforms were also influenced by the missionary-run schools to which the elite sent – and still send – their heirs. Wags quip that the only conversions Christians made in Thailand have been in clothing, and only then because missionaries brought modernisations that rulers enforced as the standard.

top: **Graduation gowns at a stall by Ramkhamhaeng University. The translucent one mimics court Brahmin gowns, the others adopt Western styles.**

left: **A Phitsanuloke election poster shows the respect always accorded to official uniforms and the trend towards suits.** *PCS*

"To do things the *farang*'s way was then considered part of culture," wrote the late prime minister and cultural authority Kukrit Pramoj in 1970. "The remnants of that 'compulsory culture' are still perceptible today. Nobody would revert to traditional Thai dress, since in this case, compulsion has ultimately engendered a habit." Later social commentator Sulak Sivaraksa lamented that "anything Siamese was old fashioned, decadent and to be looked down upon. I'm afraid this concept still prevails in most fashionable circles in all Siamese cities."

With global fashions now dominant, Thai dress has become a way to stand out from the uniformed crowd. As well as foreigners who cherish romantic notions of Siam, it appeals to independent minds and those devoted to preserving authenticity, like the choreographer Peeramon Chomdhavat. He stitches the most elaborate dance costumes of modern times, and also wears jackets of Rama IV era cut to functions. Other designers turn northern jackets and fishermen's pants – baggy cut-off trousers wrapped like a sarong – into trendy items some affluent Bangkokians treat as leisure wear.

These exceptions belie the impulse for groups of Thais to dress alike, ingrained over eons when dress delineated class and both sexes wore shaven-sided haircuts with the top shaped like *dok krathum* petals. Labouring workwear is so consistent it's a de facto uniform. Fishermen's pants are still worn in boat and field. Knitted balaclavas protect labourers against sun and dust. Gardeners and cleaners do the same using straw hats slung with a cloth visor that shrouds neck face, leaving a slit through which to peek. Some urbanites follow ex-Bangkok governor Chamlong Srimuang in wearing the *moh hom* in solidarity with the many farmers who wear it daily. Whether for work, study or prestige, uniforms tell Thai people who they are.

Hi-So
Inside high society: famous families and new money

Announced with a fanfare of flash bulbs, diamonds and Dior bags, Thailand's leading debutante of 2003 wasn't the season's most eligible daughter, but a website: *www.HiSoParty.com*. Launched by the eminently well qualified brother and sister Inthira and Patpong Thanavisuth, the e-magazine signals changes in the privileged echelons known to all as *hi-so*. This slang for 'high society' extends well beyond the old-school criteria of birth and breeding. Understated Old Money taste has been joined by nouveau riche, their trend-literate heirs and waves of wannabes, maybes and willneverbes.

To be *hi-so* requires more than a good family, wealth, connections, qualifications and official honours. In this multi-media age the true *hi-so* must present themselves prominently in public, in the press, and as the website name implies, at parties. 'Breakfast at Tiffany's' is a mere bagatelle; the committed *hi-so* fills their Mont Blanc diary with 'lunch at Emporium', a 'launch at Gaysorn', 'hair at Chalachol', 'tea at The Oriental', 'cocktails at the Dusit Thani ballroom', 'dinner at The Face', and 'drinks at the Met Bar'. Not so different that any world city, some may say, only there's a degree of spectacle in Bangkok that puts St Tropez in the shade. And an openness that's uniquely accessible.

This lifestyle of fabulous engagements fills the front of all Thai glossy magazines, from women's monthlies and lifestyle bibles to the Thai version of Britain's *Tatler*. Much the same faces pop up in the same hierarchical positions in the layout every month. Features often dwell on at-home interviews with *hi-so*, or society girls may demurely model pashminas or tiaras. With websites, now partygoers (and the working women readership) can coo over snaps from last night's party online – or on their phone. "We publish pictures the next day without waiting for a month. Members can even download images onto their handset and forward them to friends," says *HiSoParty.com* editor Preeyamon Thanavisuth, who's proud of getting older dames Internet savvy. They also

above: **Starring at the launch of** *Lips* **magazine, Lee Puengboonpra (far right) later became publisher of** *Hi!* **Magazine.** *M-SB*

left: **The** *HiSoParty.com* **launch. Runcha Boribalburibhand gives a bouquet to the webzine's editor Preyamon Thanavisuth (left) and publisher Inthira Thanavisuth (middle), along with fellow socialite (second right) Romanee Thienprasiddhi.** *HSP*

'arrive'. Dolled up in look-at-me outfits or gimmicks like mane hair, hats or glasses, most newcomers still play the part through looks and charm. Those with less to offer try to befriend or stand next to a 'somebody'. The pretender may even rent her gown and gems from a shop. "Photographers, seeing this diamond-studded woman, assume she must be a VIP," says *Thai Rath* newspaper's Apiradee Pinthong. "Eventually her photo appears in several magazines and bingo, she's a *hi-so*."

Not just charity galas, couture catwalks and anniversaries attract such red carpet coverage. Every launch of a beauty cream, gadget or accessory jostles with junior *hi-so* in training. Number-one-sons and haughty PR girls mingle with beautiful young things of indeterminate origin: swaggering offspring of officers, try-too-hard bankers, *luuk khreung* (half-Thais) with international school accents. Many aspire to enter *Society*, *Thailand Tatler* magazine's annual directory of the 500 foremost faces. Many even don't mind making *Tatler*'s 'Fashion Crimes' edition, because nothing succeeds like excess.

"Too many people are being called *hi-so*, which I don't think is right. They're more high-sociality," muses Inthira, who recalls how a decade ago functions would require a ticket, a table booking, or at least an invitation. "Now sponsorship comes in a lot and it's become an insult to sell tickets." Today anyone can walk in – and frequently does. Thus bar openings, 'thank you parties' and even embassy receptions throng with low-rent hangers-on subsisting on a diet of buffet grazing, freebies and watered-down whisky soda.

"Door policies will never happen in Thailand, believe me," Inthira insists. "Thai people cannot lose face. If you're not invited, they'll let you in anyway, but maybe talk behind your back." Gossip dominates cocktail chat, but only the nicest pleasantries get published unless someone errs beyond the pale. Insiders claim the secrets revealed on a different, less discreet online gossip column don't ring true, but all *hi-so* have a vested interest. Credibility relies on keeping face. After videos of a politician's daughter having sex leaked out in 2003, her reputation was tarnished, however unfairly.

There remain many levels of *hi-so*, reaching up to royal circles where protocol reigns. Any self-respecting functions needs the presence of a *khunying*. The recent re-gearing of parties to a younger, trendier crowd hasn't alienated such grand ladies. "Now the older tend to dress younger. We see 60-year-old women wearing short skirts," Preeyamon says. This is part of a general social shift from unquestioning deference to elders to a growing cult of youth and commerce. "We want to let people see more that *hi-so* is about successful people, to encourage the younger generation to learn from these people. And there's no secret; it's just working hard."

High society also draws respect through good works, though some cynics see charity being used as a tool. "A disheartening trend has emerged: the disappearance of *noblesse oblige* among the younger generation of the women elite," columnist Sanitsuda Ekachai writes. "For them, the road to fame and recognition is no longer their

get thousands of log-ins from expatriate Thai and *hi-so* on holiday, studying abroad or literally flying out to the shops. Thai Airways can fill regular planes to Milan.

A brace of Sino-Thai corporate wives have enlivened the scene, achieving acceptance though the same savvy that built their businesses. No one makes a more spectacular entrance than paint mogul Lee Puengboonpra, her remarkable outfits framing a remarkable emerald. Amid her entourage, she's invariably escorted by her sons, one of whom, Pattarapon, edits a Thai answer to *Hello!* called *Hi!* A jaunty abbreviation for *hi-so*, the gold-embossed glossy exists to record these precious moments and ensures an orbit around this champagne supernova.

Some resent less informed media pronouncing that certain celebrities are suddenly *hi-so*, since the merely famous may lack the funds or skills to glide though that world. The press can also fall for self-publicity. Though manners can't be simulated, there's no limit on imported labels or trips to the 'nail spa' for ladies determined to mother's route of charities. Flaunting their wealth is the name of the game. And no one bothers to ask where the money came from."

Hi-so also symbolises Bangkok's dominance, since the scene ignores the provincial elite. And not all see such glamour as a role model. Thailand's biggest rock band dubbed themselves Lo-So in counterpoint. Their hit 'Mai Bpai Pantip' equates to Elvis Costello's British anti-Sloane anthem 'I don't want to go to Chelsea'. Increasing ranks of aspiring Bangokians, however, must 'go to Chelsea' to progress, while some socialites feel that expectations of attendance at the ballooning number of functions – often more than one a night – are a burden.

"At management level you now have to participate in social events, so you're seen more, know more people," explains Preeyamon. "So many contracts and projects get signed through friends." No longer just for ladies who lunch, but also for men and women who do billion baht deals, *hi-so* is the new golf.

above: Hi-so events are designer showcases; here Dior adorns Marissa Mahavongtrakul. *TT*

left: One of Thailand's best-loved high society figures, Darunee Kritboonyalai – chanteuse, actress, businesswoman – has a stunning new outfit for every event – and shoes to match. *TT*

Nicknames & Namecards
What Thais call each other is a serious business, whether lucky, rhyming, or cute

"What's your name?" asks a Bangkok English teacher. "Yes," the Thai student replies. "No, what are you called?" rephrases the American teacher. "Yes. My name is Yes, Khun Yes," repeats the student, wondering why his English name wasn't understood. Thai nicknames are often as startling as they are playful. He could just as puzzlingly have replied "Oh", "Eh", "X", "Boy", "Not", "Joke" or, wait for it… "God."

In all but form-filling and formal situations, the Thai use *cheu len* – play names. You can know someone for ages before learning their real first name and maybe never hear their family name. Even rank bends to this cute, intimate habit, with generals often referred to as Big, hence newspapers call ex-prime minister General Chavalit Yongchaiyudh 'Big Jiew' (big little). While some *cheu len* sound fun – Eew, Oui, Oei, Nooi, Dtik – most mean something. Many are unisex (Nong is younger sibling), but several define gender (Chai is male or victory, Noom is lad, Ying is female) or stereotypes. Boy's names may mean brave, strong or noble. Girls usually get very delicate, pretty or charming names, often Thai words for flowers, gems, scents, or wistful things: sky, star, moon.

Nicknames may describe the baby's size: Lek (little), Noi (small), Yai (big), Uan (fat), Goi (little finger); or skin tone: Daeng (red), Dum (black), Som (orange). Non-human names apparently fools evil spirits from claiming kids. Hence people answer to Moo (pig), Gob (frog), Poo (crab), Mod (ant), or Gai (chicken), and even to farmyard sounds: Oud (oink), Guk (cluck), Jiab (chirp), Juum (splash). But what's charming in children – Jim (pussy) or Juu (willy) – may embarrass adults.

Once expressive of rural culture, nicknames now reflect modernity and globalisation. Old *cheu len* may re-appear in English: Fern, Ant, Rose, Ink, Oak, Bird, Baby.

Others use foreign words, often shortened from the end, like Bo (from Jumbo), Taem (from Je t'aime), Sin (from Cinderella) and Lo (from Marlboro). Most of the English alphabet can be nicknames, some spelled with just one letter: A, B, F, J, K, M, O, Q, X.

Among imports, few pick proper names like the singer James or model Cindy. Most indicate trends or interests. Wealth: Gift, Bank, Mink, Oil, Pound. Brands: Benz, Ford, Sony, Nokia. Hi-tech: Neon, Beam, Intel, Com (from computer). Food: Cake, Mint, Candy. Drink: Pepsi, Milk, Fanta, Beer, Ice. Adventure: Map, Earth, Nato, Bomb. Leisure: Art, Balloon, Film, Guitar, Pencil. Sport: Golf, Game, Bad (from Badminton), Coat (from Coach), Man-U (from Manchester United). Some mark events, like the Olympic medalist's baby Athens.

Nicknames like New and Win have a lucky cachet, something essential in real first names. Since surnames were introduced only in 1926 to aid bureaucracy and communications – and to emulate Western tradition – first names remain the formal way to address anyone, whether doctor, parent, boss or minister. This applies to foreigners too, thus Tony Blair becomes Mr Tony.

Parents choose from *naam mongkhon* (auspicious names) suggested by a monk for lucky or astrological qualities. For example, each birth day of the week is apportioned a chunk of the alphabet, from which the first letter could be chosen. The nicer sounding the name the better. To make it euphonious, some select one that alliterates with the family name, like Choopol Choompol or Kasem Kasemsan. Others use the poetic device *khlong jong* to create rhyming chains of serial names, whether of city gates or siblings. An example from a names column in *Ploy Kaem Phet* magazine cites these brothers in order of age: Sariphong Worawit, Goradit Woragarn, Boriharn Woragit, Bandit Waragoon, Paitoon Ratsami.

Surnames must have a meaning, and get ever-longer, because they combine a finite supply of auspicious words. While ethnic Thai names have one or two sylla-bles, Sino-Thai monikers stretch to three, four, even seven syllables, like Ngoenprakairat (shining silver like a jewel). Sino-Thai surnames may also incorporate the ancestral Chinese clan name like Lee or Lim, though its meaning might be translated into Pali or Sanskrit to look more Thai. Thus in the Silpa-archa political dynasty, *archa* (horse) derived from the Beh (horse) clan.

Protocol demands the exclusivity of the many royally bestowed surnames and their English transliterations, which may differ from how they're said. Thus Dr Sumet Jumsai campaigned to get the celebrity Areeya Sirisopha

left: **Multi-cultural nickname –
some Thai, some imports, some
hybrids. Riled by 56% of primary
school students having English
nicknames, the Culture Ministry
collated a booklet and website of
Thai nicknames as part of
proclaiming 2007 the 'Year of
Promoting Correct Thai Usage'.**

below: **A polite way to give and
receive a namecard. Pinch the top
corners so the card faces the
receiver, who proffers the right
hand supported by the left.** *PCS*

far left: **Not what you think.** *Porn*
**is an auspicious word used in
many Thai personal and business
names, meaning 'blessings'.** *PCS*

to drop the surname Jumsai, which her family had
adopted. This was academic since everyone calls her Pop.

In fact, Thais often – and easily – change their name.
Some fall foul of chance: Prateung (enhance) became
slang for ladyboy after a song lyric, a rapist blighted the
nickname Dtuii, and the film *Bangrajan* starred a buffalo
called Boonlert (great merit). Giving animals human
names is taboo. Others want a monk to suggest something luckier. After Aphichet Kitikorncharoen of the
boyband D2B fell into a coma, he was renamed Panrawat
– Mr Remain Alive. Fans still call him Big.

Names remain quite fluid. Since 2004, Thai women
need no longer take on their husband's surname. And
double-barrelled ones may be imminent. "It'll be great
to have a kid with the last name Benedetti-Khemklad,"
says actor Somchai Khemklad, who married singer 'Nat'
Myria Benedetti. "Wouldn't that be cool?"

Since surnames never caught on except among major
families, it's often only encountered on receiving a namecard. This device is universal, not elite, with countless
print shops offering elaborate designs and finishes.
Unlike the casual tossing of nicknames, namecards
embody the giver's face, so their exchange involves care,
especially among Sino-Thai. Bowing slightly, you pass it
with the right hand, or pinching the top corners so it
faces the receiver, who handles it carefully. Imagine the
slur of writing on the front or the back, putting it away
without a glance, especially into a back pocket. With so
much face at stake, no wonder Thais stick to nicknames.

Female Grooming

Women's dress is so important
it's a matter of national security

"We have to ban spaghetti-strapped tops and very short shorts. It's a shame to wear clothes like those," decreed then Culture Minister Uraiwan Thienthong ahead of the 2003 Songkran new year. Instead, she advised women playing in the ancient water-throwing celebrations to wear sarongs to help the government's One Tambon One Product village crafts promotion. Few fashion conscious females obeyed. After all, flirting had traditionally been condoned in such festivals as a way to manage emotions pent-up the rest of the time. Now it's the reverse; festivals are being made a genteel respite from what many elders reproach as a new decadence in female fashion.

Whether in formal fabric or spaghetti straps, Thai women remain among the best groomed people on earth. Visitors marvel at how prettily they frame their natural blessings of smooth skin, fine features, petite figure and lustrous hair. On special occasions, use of gold, silk and flowers lends traditional costuming a divine mystique. Designers today find fresh uses for local textiles like tie-dyed *mudmee* silk, especially in skirt-suits worn by grand *khunying*. In everyday wear, too, female Thais display awesome pride in appearance. Uniforms abound, waitresses glide with prim politeness, office ladies totter off to lunch in elegant outfits. Even the poorest look spotless. All maintain immaculate hair, from matronly bun or practical bob to long, shampoo-commercial locks.

In this social hierarchy, style starts at the top. And the top part of top people is the hair helmet. Few Thai things mesmerise the foreigner more than *khunying* hair. Experts dispute its origins, though as star hairdresser Somsak Chalachol declares: "We're among Asia's best in *phom klao* (gathered-up hair). We're very meticulous. We've benefited from a relatively solid hair-dressing culture." Solid hair-dos indeed appear in temple murals with the long tresses of male and female royalty plumed up through narrow coronets.

"Then suddenly in 1700, Siam cut their hair really short, even shaving the sides, leaving a little on top and long sideburns for the ladies, wrapped into a curl and decorated with flowers," says scholar Vithi Phanichphant. This unisex style was called *dok krathum* because the top was sculpted into a *krathum* flower shape using wax and oil from blackened pans. In the late 19th century, women grew this a bit longer, combing the hair strands high and back so they stuck up some two inches. The resulting squarish dome is still worn by many old women.

Other pundits see Chinese and Japanese influence in *phom klao*, beginning with Princess Dara Ratsami, who refused to cut her long northern hair on marrying King

Rama V. As academic Anucha Thirakanont relates, "she saw Japanese style hair in the local adaptation of *Madame Butterfly*, and it became a fashion among her quarters in the Bangkok court." The look continued through northern royalty to the late Princess Kokaew Prakaykavil na Chiang Mai, whose blue-rinsed coiffure became a landmark on the *hi-so* circuit.

Bangkok dames then adopted the bob and other international styles until all currents met in the Beehive, a style in vogue when today's women-of-a-certain-age were young. While some still sport a towering Beehive, most *phom klao* recall court styles, especially of Queen Sirikit.

left: **Hair doesn't get much higher than this. A woman in traditional dress, lacquered to withstand the hot, windy weather at a festival in Sakhon Nakhon.** *PCS*

above: **Since the late 1990s, Thai fashion has taken off into realms of couture. A gown by Nagara for Jim Thompson at Elle Bangkok Fashion Week.** *JT*

"They don't want to cut their hair short, but they still want an older style, so they pull it back," Anucha adds. Underlying *phom klao* is the sacredness of the head. Raising its height implies superior qualities. Thus long-haired women often sculpt a lacquered frontal 'swan flick'.

As important as hairspray is white make-up. Paleness raises status. Keeping out of the sun is vital, and people spend 1.7 billion baht spent annually on skin whitening creams. These can at best only restore the skin's natural shade, and some can be poisonous. To look truly pale requires powder. Lots of it. Thus women of all ranks may smear their faces with talc or with *nam ob*, perfumed lotions (like Mong Leya or Quina brands) containing *dinsor phong*, a white clay from Lopburi now used in Thai spa therapies. It both heals and cools.

"Originally, we preferred yellow skin to white skin," Anucha reveals. "We didn't use powder, we used the yellow turmeric root. But during the Ayutthaya period we had a lot of Chinese and European influence, and they are

above: **One of seven national costumes originally designed by HM Queen Sirikit in 1960. These updates of traditional clothes continue to influence formal and evening wear today.** *TT*

right: **Many Thai women do indeed seem to have an advanced whitening complex. A display of pale-skin cosmetics by the Thai beauty chain store Oriental Princess.** *PCS*

always pale, so we put white powder on the face and body." Unfortunately, group photographs can resemble mime troupes, since camera flash highlights unpowdered neck, ears, arms and edges. Meanwhile, Thailand has become a world centre for cosmetic surgery, and not just for anti-ageing. Countless clinics meet demand for a narrower farang-length nose with a bridge, or eyelids with a fold.

In clothing, conventions went further, since the state played stylist. Around World War II, the Phibunsongkram regime tried to replace Thai *jongkraben* (sarong leg-wrap) and uncovered shoulders with skirt-suits, hats and shoes resembling the Andrews Sisters. The habit stuck and traditional costume looked dated and doomed until creative re-interpretations of Thai costume became de rigueur. Queen Sirikit created seven national costume designs in the 1960s that remain stunning templates for day and evening wear today. This encouraged the revival of historic textiles and antique belts of gold or silver filigree. Competition for the classiest lidded box-handbag also revived crafts such as nielloware, *yan lipao* vine weaving and iridescent beetle wing-case appliqué.

Simplified for everyday wear, and with a higher hem to save cost, this glamorous costume has morphed into a suit of silk armour for businesswomen since the shoulder-padded 1980s. "Nowadays it looks very sharp and hard, not draping, because they put in a Japanese lining and pressing by heat makes the silk thicker and harder," explains Paothong. While middle class women pick ever trendier prêt-à-porter, many prefer bold patterns and frills in temple-fair colours. Regardless of age or income barriers, cute mascots gambol over watch, brooch, hairgrip, handbag.

Many who were raised under Phibun's draconian 'cultural mandates' still adhere to his equation of Thainess with 'civilised' Western grooming and national security. Senior ladies should be *sa ngaa ngam* (gracious, elegant) and young women are expected to be *rak suay rak ngam* (love to be pretty). Controversy comes when women choose to be sexy.

As in the West during pop's early decades, blaming the clothes becomes a way of blaming the youth. While the media promotes imported labels without questioning how *hi-so* women pay such prices, youngsters get con-demned for prostituting themselves to afford the same brands. Skimpy clothing like spaghetti straps gets blamed for the teen trend called *gig* (casual sex flings, ie 'minor boyfriends'), while men keeping *mia noi* (minor wives) retain respect. Signs warning against sex on buses caused a furore by reprimanding only the women. Other rows ignited over SSSSS-size university uniform blouses, and teens wearing no bra or just nipple stickers.

A defining event in the battle over women's dress was *Thai Rath* newspaper publishing a shot of supermodel Methinee Kingphayome's nipple popping out of her dress on the catwalk in *Elle* Bangkok Fashion Week 2003. "Culturally speaking it's not right," said the male Culture Minister, Anurak Jureemas. "We will make sure bare breasts are illegal and that both the models and the media are held accountable." Soon afterwards, the official

below: **The wreath-style coiffure named** *faraa* **(after Farrah Fawcett) frames a typically white powdered face at a provincial festival.** *PJ*

Bangkok Fashion City showpiece attempted to manage local fashion and in the process set a dress code.

Contradictions abound. Young women are encouraged to be modern, but scolded when they're up to the minute. The government wants Bangkok to rival Milan as a fashion city, but cracks down on the very fashion features – like bare shoulders and cleavage – that are integral to the international catwalk elite that Thailand seeks to join.

"Our youth are forced to stay a step behind the *farang*," wrote cultural authority MR Kukrit Pramoj in 1970 with pertinence for today's social order clamp-downs. "Now some people are thinking of forbidding young women to wear mini-skirts – not realising that Thai women began to clad themselves in Western dress not by consent but by submission… I know it leads to feelings of despair and confusion. Compulsion in matters of culture only creates pressure to such an extent that they will dispense with all forms of traditional culture altogether; but at the same time, they are not yet able to accept more sophisticated forms of Western culture."

The official tone implies a return to past standards of Thainess. Perhaps it more closely resembles bourgeois primness, which the West initiated when it went through the industrial and social changes that Thailand's now experiencing. "What is being labeled 'un-Thai' here has nothing to do with history and tradition, but is totally modern, rather urban and very Western-influenced," writes *Nation* columnist Chang Noi. "Historical dramas play a part. The costuming is splendid, but to render the females authentic would mean cropping their hair short, blackening their teeth, and leaving their breasts exposed." The Songkran ban on exposed shoulders included the authentic Siamese breast wrap. As Thai textile historian Paothong Thongchua explains: "in the old days our costume was open on both shoulders or covered only one shoulder, while the villagers went topless."

Among the masses' everyday wear, differentiation between male and female attire was negligible until just over a century ago. Today, the well-off dress mostly according to international fashion trends. Yet among the masses of vendors, farmers and labouring folk, people share a unisex casual uniform of T-shirt, loose trousers and flip-flops. The hair of rural and labouring women is also often cropped short. But one crucial accessory remains common to every sartorial class: a permanent, dazzling smile.

Male Grooming
Looks matter to a man

Lip-gloss glistening, eyelashes subtly kohled, foundation coating a moisturised complexion, the blow-dried young man flashes one trimmed armpit as he grabs a pole on the SkyTrain. His girlfriend wears less make up than he does. With a new breed of *jao sam-ang* (young dandies) treating the SkyTrain as a promenade, the *Bangkok Post* proclaimed in 2003: "the City of Angels appears to be well on the way to becoming a Mecca for metrosexuals."

Coined in the West for a new breed of sensitive, well-groomed men, this buzzword seems confined here to label-clad straights who use cosmetics, but tell surveys they're "manly metrosexuals" who must look good for work. "My wife's friends were worried enough to ask her if I was gay because I'm so high-maintenance," admits Vasu, a 31-year-old architect into lotions and spa serums.

In fact, Thai men have long prized graceful appearance and manners, as temple murals amply testify. Thais adopt trends so eagerly that pundits miss moments when the Kingdom's ahead of the curve. The *Post* claimed "men with long hair use plastic hairbands thanks to David Beckham", yet since the 1980s Thai men had used head-bands to hitch back the centre-parted bob, wire clips to restrain their bangs and arched combs to gather hair at the back, geisha-style. Beckham hadn't worn the band before his football tours to Thailand.

Several cultural traits make men keen to groom. The model of Thai manhood isn't sweaty, musclebound Rambo, but refined, soft-spoken Rama. Chetana Nagavarjara notes a "disregard for male robustness, and a bent for 'effeminacy' on the construction of the hero figure" in classical literature. Make-up in *likay* folk opera must emphasise the prettiness of the *phra ek* (leading man), which the largely female fans demand. Similarly, youths are happy to primp like Japanese boy bands in order to please their girlfriend.

Underlying the Thai proverb 'a chicken's beauty is due to its feathers, a person's because of dressing well', as Mont Redmond points out, "it is assumed that all humans desire to be beautiful, and that being well dressed is as natural to man as being fully feathered is to a chicken." Despising uncouth macho laddishness, today's real men still largely aspire to courtesy, conformity and plumage befitting rank. Older men thus exude status if *taeng tua dii* (good dressers). Political faction leaders outshine each other with Versace shirts.

"The social ideal for a man isn't brawn but brains," writes Eric Allyn. "Moderation is perhaps the cornerstone of Thai masculinity, [which] isn't fraught with the kind of anxiety that American standards induce, where it requires continual proof." That's changing. Faced with Calvin Klein ads, some Thais consider their compact, well-proportioned frames scrawny. Hence the gym craze.

Preening also has practical origins. Heat and dust necessitate frequent showers and skin protection. While male cosmetics may be new, Thais have long used powder. Talc holds both sweat and sun at bay, keeping skin pale, dry and cool. Some men now use anti-UV moisturiser topped by powder or foundation. When Bangkok's first smart, non-hotel spa opened in 2001, half its customers were men. Again, the leap is little, given eons of pamper-ing muscles through massage, purging pores with *plai*-infused steam, and toning the skin with turmeric and herbs. Ultimately, though, looking handsome is not about brand-name conditioner, but social conditioning.

Males of all ages check their appearance in every mir-ror they encounter. Anything amiss and the world has to stop while shirts are straightened, stray hairs flattened, collars and cuffs arranged just-so. Some apply powder to blemishes or mop oils from their face with blotting papers. It's not vanity; if anything they're modest and conform to group style. Nor is it really about hair, clothes, nails, or skin; it's about face. Looking slovenly loses face, which is why Thais dub the often dishevelled backpackers as *farang kii-nok* (bird-shit foreigners).

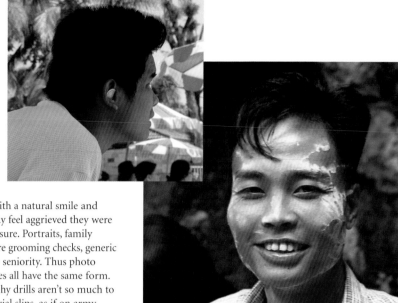

right: **Wearing a coin in the ear is a kind of working class male jewellery – but grew out of a way to carry change.**

far right: **Powder is integral to Thai grooming. After bathing, the masses randomly apply baby powder or mentholated prickly heat powder to keep face and body cool, and to guard against tanning, like this Lampang lad. Many young urban men now put on moisturiser, then powder or subtler foundation, while a few metrosexuals use lip gloss.** *PCS*

Photographed off guard with a natural smile and relaxed demeanour, Thais may feel aggrieved they were denied the chance for composure. Portraits, family snaps, group poses – all require grooming checks, generic postures and arrangement by seniority. Thus photo albums and media social pages all have the same form.

The mirror and photography drills aren't so much to beautify, but to prevent sartorial slips, as if on army parade. "The spit-and-polish of military discipline has been fused with common Thai notions of tidiness, propriety and orderliness (*khwam riab roi*)," says Craig Reynolds of past dictatorships' impact of on grooming. "Military order and bourgeois orderliness are amiable companions."

Schools and conscription still induce life-long martial obedience through dress codes, morning salutes to flag and anthem, and the quiffed crew cut many Thai sport beyond graduation. However, few children now sport top-knots on their shaved scalp, which are believed to protect the child's *khwan* (life force). Fewer than 50 now attend an annual Brahmin shaving ceremony and the rare top-knotted pre-teen acts shy due to curiosity, teasing and peer pressure. Beliefs also lead to mockery of baldness. The patterns of how hair recedes supposedly indicate a man's personality, often negatively.

For centuries, Thais dressed according to rank. Many times, authorities have tried to impose Western clothing so as to look 'modern', but often with out-dated results. "Those in power would prescribe to the youth to act in such and such a way, but when the vogue in the West does change, they, being unable to keep up with the innovation, would either resist or sometimes forbid any novelty," wrote the late prime minister Kukrit Pramoj in 1970. "When Western-style trousers began to get tapered off, people were forbidden to wear narrow trousers, the officials being threatened with penalties reserved for hooligans." This mindset continues among businessmen-turned-ministers, buttoned up in suit and tie.

Men who don't submit to uniforms or fashion adopt a practical neighbourhood look: XL T-shirt, baggy pants, flip-flops. No wonder football strips and outsized hip-hop gear appeal; they update the loose, climate-friendly cut of traditional garb. Upcountry, many still wear the indigo *moh hom* jacket shirt and fishermen's trousers –

cut-off pantaloons that wrap like a sarong. Families in residential *soi* may appear outdoors of an evening in pyjamas, popping into 7-Eleven or chatting with neighbours. After showering they naturally wouldn't get back into today's grubby clothes or soil tomorrow's clean set.

The most resilient traditional clothing remains the *pha khao ma*, an all-purpose chequered cloth used as bath wrap, towel, sash, turban, bag or bedsheet. Where once they varied from small loincloth to large blanket, *pha khao ma* today come medium sized after standardisation for military conscripts. Historically, a loincloth was all most men wore. Today, the heat still prompts men to remove shirts in farm or side-street, while loitering urban workers yearn to do the same by hitching their shirt up above their midriff.

That would leave bourgeois Thais aghast and so would other grooming traits that were once respectable but now have fallen from grace, such as long nails. "Among working people it's a way of saying you're more refined," says scholar Vithi Phanichphant, of this ancient Chinese and Javanese symbol of the leisured elite. "It's also useful for scratching." You can't grow nails in farming or in construction, but you can in jobs a rung higher, like driving, retail or factory work.

Most common is to extend the little finger nail beyond the adjacent knuckle. Fortune tellers claim it helps balance life, just as they recommend rings if palm lines exit between fingers. "We think it's very lucky in Isaan," explains Pete, who boasts two pointed half-inch pinkie nails. These can help grooming tasks widely considered acceptable in public, like picking your nose or popping zits. Similarly, tuk-tuk drivers use the 'two-baht razor', pincering two one-baht coins to pluck unsightly whiskers or to straighten lucky mole hairs.

coins for the bus or the shop. It's now more for fashion than convenience." Ears have since had to cope with inflation pushing coin size from 50 stang to 1 baht, 5 baht, even 10 baht.

While wealthier Thais see such fads as a low-class way to show off – branding the wearer as a *jik koh* or *nakleng*, a hoodlum or tough guy – some deliberately offend mainstream taste. Their favoured weapon: hair. Whiskers enjoyed only brief respectability when Rama V promoted waxed moustaches to match the centre-parted haircut he'd adopted from Europeans. Otherwise, facial hair implies non-conformity. In the hippie era, Art For Life activists protested against dictatorship by growing long, straggly manes and wispy beards. They still do, and a few cultivate dreadlocks. More recently, 'indy' youth showed its individualism by sprouting bohemian goatees or hip-hop/nu-metal chin tufts.

"Dressing down is sporadically tolerated as an eccentricity of the well-to-do, but weighs on one's status if indulged for too long," Mont Redmond writes. "Overdressing is a more dangerous error, a sign of gate-crashing ambition, and is ostracised accordingly." Hence whether metrosexual or martial, fashion-conscious or casual, Thai guys dress to impress.

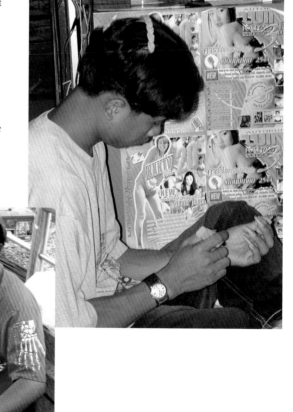

Private grooming is another matter. Some men insert one or more moveable *mook* (pearls, though usually a glass or plastic bead) under the skin of the penis. Intended for female pleasure, *mook* proliferate among prisoners and those into body modifications like tattoos. Western-style piercings have a small urban following, though unlike the Burmese and some northern groups, Central Thai men historically left ears unpierced.

Instead, some workers place a coin in the ear. "People love something shiny around their ears. They used to have flowers there," notes Vithi. Paothong Thongchua dates the trend: "We never had it before we had buses, around 50 years ago. The ear was a handy place to keep

above: **Once standard, now rare, top-knots have historically been worn throughout childhood until ceremonially severed by a Brahmin priest.** *PCS*

right and far right: **Thai men wore hair bands long before David Beckham did. The garland seller in Bangna wears an 'Alice Band' to pull back his bangs; the lad in Pantip Plaza PC mall uses a geisha-style comb to gather his locks, and also grows the long nails brandished by many Thai workers as a sign of prestige.** *PCS*

Kathoey & Tom-Dee
Beyond male and female to 'angels in disguise'

Few features of Thailand beguile and perplex more than *kathoey* – ladyboys with a visibility and grace way beyond global norms. The country probably has no more homosexuals than any other, rather that the Thai physique, smooth skin, love of beauty, refined culture and tolerance enables more of them to flower.

Sirens of popular culture since ancient times, *kathoey* now face increasing prejudice as Thailand undergoes a sexual revolution. Western gender concepts have been adopted not just by conservatives, but also by liberals: independent women, lesbians and men who are homosexual, transsexual or straight 'metrosexuals'.

Kathoey maintain a high media profile, though it's increasingly unflattering. They act in soap operas, become celebrities, jest in comedy routines, and have spawned a genre of movies. The huge box office success of *Iron Ladies* – the true tale of a *kathoey* team from Lampang facing prejudice on becoming National Volleyball Champions – embodies their ambiguous status. In a

culture enamoured of appearance, *kathoey* receive compliments on their features, costumes and make-up, being fêted in festivals and beauty pageants. Beauty becomes business for some, forging careers in make-up, costuming, fashion, modelling, photography, advertising, media. Others work in restaurants, retail and family firms. However, non-acceptance by many employers leads many *kathoey* to profit though entertainment and their 'unique selling point': female impersonation.

Evidence suggests a historical geisha-style role in the pleasure industry as dancers, 'companions' and bawdy performers in *likay* folk burlesque. In modern cabaret – a Bangkok fixture since 1920s Chinatown – *kathoey* became regular showstoppers by World War II, when hostess cabarets entertained not just Thai boys' nights out but Japanese, then Allied troops. Today's glamorous all-*kathoey* cabaret spread from the GIs' R'n'R resort of Pattaya in the late 1960s to become one of Thailand's most famous tourist sights and cultural exports. While traditional dance struggles for a stage or a home audience and rarely tours abroad, *kathoey* floorshows pack huge theatres nightly. Especially popular with north Asians, ladyboy shows also wow international platforms like the Edinburgh Festival and London's West End theatreland. Authorities often wince at the kudos, since they tend to associate *kathoey* with libertine behaviour, promiscuity and prostitution.

Thais make a distinction between gender – a public identity to be kept *riab roi* (proper) – and sexuality,

above and right: **Divas and clowns at the Phuket Gay Festival. Home-made mardi gras outfits and ugly drag make-up are staples of both parades and ladyboy cabaret shows.**

far right: **Thais call such visions 'Angels in Disguise'.**

which remains undiscussed, unrestrained. Thai society tends to regard sexual urges – at least for males – as natural and requiring plentiful, but private outlets. Hence polygamy, once banned, resurfaced through minor wives and the fancifully themed playgrounds of the sex industry. With women's virginity still a commodity to be guarded, *kathoey* have offered a non-disruptive outlet for single males. Openly beyond the pale, *kathoey* trade societal respect for an outlaw freedom that excites many a libido. With bought sex often now viewed as preferable to mistresses, demand hasn't dampened for *sao praphet song* – the second type of woman.

"In Thailand, the notion of a homosexual act resulting in labelling or identity is thought preposterous," writes

Eric Allyn. "It is also a sex-positive society… the Thai view the sex drive as another 'mood'." That rainbow of moods contrasts to the West's black-and-white opposites of Adam and Eve. Surveys find diverse, changeable opinions about what constitutes "sex" and what is merely *len pheuan* – playing with friend – a euphemism for female-female dalliance that can be used for men, too, or the rarer term *len sawaad* – playing at love. The term *seua bai* (bisexual tiger) and advice column replies seem to regard broad tastes positively. Society still regards outwardly masculine homosexuals as 'real men'.

Kathoey, derived from the Khmer word for 'different', originally embraced all sexual minorities, including transvestites, hermaphrodites and lesbians. Since the 1970s, that definition has progressively narrowed to mean extreme effeminacy. Among the reasons are sex change surgery, international publicity forging a *kathoey* cliché, and the growing identification of middle class homosexuals as gay – straight-acting men who want a masculine partner. In building self-esteem, gays regard this imported Western concept as modern. Partly unwilling to forego male privileges, some feel little affinity with *kathoey* as a dated embarrassment like other village culture. The muscular physiques of the growing gym craze depart further from the lithe, tall ladyboy profile.

While sex isn't taken too seriously, making sexuality public forces repercussions. Thai families never ostracise a child over sexuality, though some Sino-Thai might. But all avoid discussing it, even if a couple lives together. Being a good, discreet person is what matters. 'Coming out' confronts that "don't ask, don't tell" equilibrium. *Kathoey*, of course, have always been unambiguously 'out' and played specific roles in village life and festivals. Since the late 1990s, the gay pride parades held annually

above: **A *tom* (butch woman) in military drag at the Phuket Gay Festival, to gain attention from a *dee* (feminine lesbian, slang from the word lady).**

right: **The 'Second Kind of Woman' has a special place in a culture where the 'Third Sex' is an established part of society and belief. This is a moment from the Bangkok Pride Parade.** *PCS*

in Bangkok, Phuket and Pattaya have seen many gays come out. However, to 'out' someone else disgraces the exposer and earns the victim sympathy. Thus gay gossip about celebrities and politicians arouses only cryptic allusions in the media, never scandals.

Occasional homophobia arises from imported moral standards, expressed by officials in terms like *biang tahng phet* (twisted gender). Buddhism's more compassionate, seeing *kathoey* suffering as pre-ordained by certain sins committed in the last life. The third sex appears in both Buddhist scripture and animist Thai creation myths. Many animist societies involve *kathoey* in rites, especially as mediums. Terms for *kathoey* like *nang faa chamlaeng* (an angel in disguise) allude to that sense of specialness.

Their acceptance contrasts with misapprehensions about lesbians, who call themselves *tom-dee*, derived from *tom*-boy and la-*dy*. Tom-dee couples display their roles very visibly, a *tom* in macho outfits and short hair protectively handles her demure *dee*, often indulging in drinking, gambling, ribald speech and other 'male freedoms' to prove her tom-ness. Since *tom-dee* adopted a more public persona in the 1980s, headlines have speculated that a supposed increase in lesbianism was due to girls' schools and a declining quality of men.

top: **Thai Male homosexuals increasingly identify with the Western concept 'gay'. At the Bangkok Pride parade, muscle boys transform into traditional gods from Hindu mythology.**

above: **Subject of the biopic** *Beautiful Boxer*, **transsexual** *muay thai* **star Parinya 'Nong Toom' Charoenphon pictured in a 'boxing bra' before her full sex change.** *M-KBJ*

Sapphic sensibility occurs fleetingly in temple murals and historic court documents, though the public tends still to regard it as a phase or never guess its presence, since people of the same sex being, living or even sleeping together raises no eyebrows. A *tom* may refuse to be seen naked by her partner. This maintains illusion and hides a body they fear can't compete with men, to whom they're perhaps convinced the *dee* will likely later defect. That's largely not true, yet *tom* often succumb to the broken-hearted fatalism also found among *kathoey*.

Quite different to gays, *kathoey* frequent straight bars to find 'real men' who might like their combination of an accentuated feminine body without a female mind. Transsexuals report the *M Butterfly* syndrome of unawares Western men getting a surprise bonus in bed.

Since 1972, up to 1,000 people a year have changed sex here. Promotions of medical tourism curiously ignore gender reassignment, so foreigners seek out skilled Thai surgeons informally though networking centres like the Bangkok bar Casanova, where the clientele compare workmanship. When one gets an innovative implant or surgical tweak, friends follow. Hence the uniformity of high cheeks, flat foreheads and pointed chins. Things can go wrong. Some may need repairs. Fake 'doctors' have caused problems like nipples rotting off by inserting not silicone but saline-filled condoms. Sunny UFO, a boy-band idol who changed sex, went public about his sub-standard face implants having slipped, then fused with muscle tissue to the point that it's hard to scrape out.

The contrasting low visibility of old *kathoey*, hints at consequences to body and mind of radical surgery and high-dose hormones. In their prime, however, most look simply stunning. Would-be *kathoey* typically seek out an 'elder sister' to mentor them through make up, posture and survival skills. Schools often have *kathoey* cliques from a startlingly young age. Accusations of "recruit-ment" and "leading youth astray" pepper sensational news reports involving hysterical, homicidal or suicidal

kathoey. Rumours of thievery particularly hurt *kathoey* feelings. Because sex can't legally change here, they also endure constant bureaucratic humiliation and cannot legally be raped, since the rape law doesn't cover men.

Some *kathoey* partly welcome periodic attempts by ministries to ban or limit the outrageous stereotypes of screaming queens on television. "We've been exploited as a commodity, as seen in the recent spate of gay movies," rebuts Prempreeda Pramoj na Ayutthaya "Most people think we're publicising ourselves. In fact the producers are rarely homosexuals." The actors are also typically straights in a mocking drag act.

Slowly, realistic gay characters are emerging on-screen, helped by positive gay role models and respected *kathoey* personalities. Boxer Nong Toom won over a skeptical public through dignity and discipline. Language teacher Khru Lily became a Thai Oprah Winfrey, filling theatres by making literacy fun. The 'out' business pundit Dr Seri Wongmontha recently starred in the bigot-busting movie *Saving Private Tootsie*. His transsexual co-star – make-up artist and model Ornapa Krissadee – circulates in high society. By contrast, many *tom* have risen more smoothly to the top echelons of business and society, perhaps because maleness earns higher status than femininity.

Gay tourists flock to Thailand for its mythic status as a gay paradise, not necessarily for sex but for the unique sensibility and tolerance. Yet instead of embracing the lucrative 'pink dollar' like rival tourist destinations, Thai officialdom suddenly adopted a stern, moralistic tone from the West, dating from before today's globalised pluralism. They've also attempted to ban *kathoey* from teacher training colleges, harassed gay magazines and companies, and raided world famous gay saunas and clubs in an effort to ape Singapore's puritanism. Meanwhile, after learning that creative industries require a liberal climate, Singapore loosened its social corset in an attempt to seize Bangkok's crown as Asia's gay capital.

After millennia of integration, *kathoey* suddenly face a rights issue. But they do have a vote. In 2004, three of the candidates for Bangkok governor sought support from homosexuals angered by unprecedented discrimination. Gay campaigner Natee Teerarojjanaphongs announced he'd stand for the Senate, and Thanyaporn Anyasiri, 2002's Miss Tiffany and Miss Queen of the Universe, proclaimed: "I want to be the world's first transsexual prime minister so I can legislate laws that promote homosexual people's equality."

Full equality might be a prudent idea. "Absolutely everyone without exception has been a *kathoey* because we have gone through innumerable cycles of birth and death," cautions Bunmi Methangkun of the Buddhist Aphidhamma Foundation. "And we don't know how many more times we will be *kathoey* in the future."

left: As far from the cliché of a flawlessly feminine beauty queen ladyboy as you can get. Ugly drag brings smiles to all, and is a staple of Thai comedy on stage and TV.

Massage
Ancient techniques for healing and relaxing the body

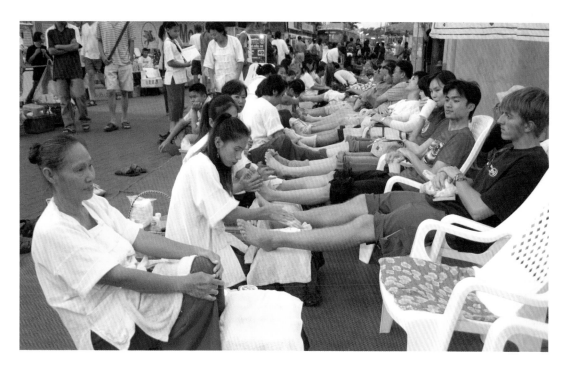

Thailand has two massage cultures: clothed and unclothed. Don't confuse the two. Enter a parlour signed *nuad* (massage) expecting *nuad paen boran* (literally 'ancient massage') and you get, ahem, 'young' massage. This might involve ancient techniques, but more likely oil, a towel, soap and something extra. To outsiders, mention of 'Thai massage' triggers nudge-nudge wisecracks about a notorious nightlife scene that's bubbled for half a century. That cliché has been lucrative, yet limiting for the international potential for traditional Thai massage, a therapy that really heals.

Dubbed 'dancing meditation' and 'yoga massage', *nuad paen boran* is like having yoga done *to* you rather than *by* you. Along with postures that stretch muscles, loosen joints and detoxify internal organs, it involves sometimes painful acupressure along 10 invisible *sen* (energy lines) to release blocked energy. This Vedic Indian science over 2,500 years old was imported by Buddhist monks around 18 centuries ago and, like herbal healing, historically centred on the *wat*. Wat Pho in Bangkok remains the leading school and exponents preserve the *wai khru* worship of not just teachers, but the art's purported inventor, Buddha's physician Shivaka Kumar Baccha. Behind each contortion lies a philosophical concept.

A masseur "is practicing the physical application of *metta*, or loving kindness advocated in Theravada Buddhism," Chamsai Jotisalikorn writes. "A truly good Thai masseur performs his art in a meditative mood, starting with a prayer to centre himself." The therapy is reciprocal. The masseur needn't be strong since they rock their body weight gently through precisely leveraged postures using knee, feet and elbow as well as hands. So the masseurs receive a workout as they massage. It can be painful when suppressed tension releases, particularly when masseurs crack fingers, loosen knots or tread on the patient's back. As some procedures carry mechanical risk, cognoscenti request an older *mor nuad* ('massage doctor') when seeking treatment for an ailment.

Some *mor nuad* are blind. Massage is a major profession for the unsighted, as it is in several Asian countries. "They can concentrate on massaging more than sighted masseurs can. They have purer intention," says Petcharat Techawatchara, president of the Foundation for Employment of the Blind, whose trainees are 60 per cent males. Most sighted masseuses are women. "Women can massage customers of any age and gender, but sighted male masseurs of women could be inadvertently seduced by their visual perception."

A full session takes two hours, but casual massage moments permeate daily life. Mothers massage babies, teenagers knead grandparents, vendors and motorcycle taxi drivers squeeze the shoulders of colleagues. Roving masseurs pamper vacationers on the beach, while fairs feature open-air stalls of massage and foot reflexology. Before Japanese massage chairs colonised transit lounges, Bangkok Airport had a *nuad paen boran* parlour. Now Thai Airways offers in-flight massages, and petrol stations provide reviving rubs for drowsy drivers. At nightclub urinals nationwide, customers suddenly feel a hot towel on their neck as an attendant massages their shoulders. This well-meaning act can put people off. Whatever the embarrassment, you tip, for massage of all kinds is piece-work with meagre salary, if any.

Saved from oblivion after Ayutthaya's devastation, and later institutionalised by King Rama VI's founding of a massage association, *nuad paen boran* had a renaissance through tourism and Western interest in Eastern healing. Thousands of foreigners now come here to learn it, particularly the softer northern style in Chiang Mai. Thai classical massage is becoming a global brand. Now that therapeutic massage can rival naughty *nuad* as a money-making industry, the government ranks parlour licenses in rising categories: from hanky-panky to therapy to spa.

Though top-end spas uphold stringent etiquette, in less classy parlours the entrepreneurial urge may sometimes cross the professional line. As can happen world-wide, propositions get whispered in either direction, or hands may slip... Two American women complained to a Bangkok magazine of being felt up by health club masseurs, unaware that the four-star hotel is a discreet haunt of upper-class Thai seeking a tickle. Even the rare blind masseur angling for a bigger tip has been known to press the wrong point accidentally-on-purpose. Though if rebuffed, their credible excuse smothers any offence.

While Western spas push notions of the silent retreat, Thai massage tends to be social. Traditional masseuses often chatter between curtained cubicles, where groups of salarymen expect to banter with giggly maidens. The sexy parlours are equally social. A drinking-buddy night often ends at a sauna-cum-massage emporium. Losing male virginity from a professional is a long-standing rite-of-passage, only slipping recently with the spread of pre-marital sex. Barn-like 'steameries' fringe many towns, themed according to varied peccadilloes and nationalities. The originals – with Vegas-style names in English, Thai and Chinese in neon – still line Ratchadaphisek and

New Phetburi Roads in Bangkok where they first oiled GIs during the Vietnam War. "The Thai have taken the Japanese conception of a massage parlour – just as they took the Japanese conception of an American style bar – and taken it to logical extremes," wrote author Andrew Harris. "There is a peephole in the door, but the law is flexible and says nothing about installing a small curtain to cover the peephole." Some spas repeat that today. More notoriously, short-time motels get dubbed *man rood* – pull curtain – after the drape hiding the car.

In the 1960s, Chinatown's seedy opium dens went legal by converting smoking divan rooms to *nuad*, while purpose-built parlours evolved their kitschy style and elaborate procedure. A patron often dines or drinks while being advised by a mamasan about the skills of each masseuse (or masseurs, in the many gay equivalents), who sit semi-dressed, often behind a two-way mirror. He then selects one (sometimes two) by quoting the number on a badge on their underwear. A similar drill applies in go-go bars, which originated in 1920s Chinatown cabarets rather than Patpong as many presume. Though seemingly de-humanising, the numbers derive from the taboo against pointing, hence actually preserving a modicum of respect in a career with fundamentally so little.

While go-go bar flesh-pots and their touting demi-mondaines decline with changes in taste, government raids and increased options for amusement, naughty *nuad* parlours show staying power. Drawing on a long history, discreet, orderly pleasure outlets for men's urges still enjoy wide acceptance, at least in preference to men taking minor wives. They also appeal to Asian visitors, and Thai trade and tourism increasingly focus on the region. When zoning nightlife closing times, politicians spoke prudish words yet favoured strips of *nuad* and go-go bars over more sophisticated bar and club districts frequented by the jet-set and globalised clubbers. Wags wondered which world they understood best.

Co-existence of the two massage cultures depends on authorities turning the other cheek. But thanks to the spa boom, traditional healing now boasts the greater momentum. Pushing a more wholesome fantasy of 'tropical paradise' through images of models in a petal-strewn bath, the Thai spa involves a variety of treatments to heal, pamper and stimulate. In a prim twist on the ribald *nuad* 'double massage', some spas enable a couple to get massaged together – on separate beds in the same room. In this era of politically correct surveillance, ancient massage has a modern future.

Inhalers
Aromatherapy becomes a daily habit

Forget Fendi bags, mobile phones and coloured tooth braces, the commonest Thai accessory is *yaa dom* – the nasal inhaler. The little white nozzle plugs into both the nose and the national psyche. Should the temperature drop beneath 30°C and the nation plunge into sniffles, a dab of menthol or *yaa mong* (a fragrant fatty ointment, like Tiger Balm) rubbed under the nose should suffice. But even when not suffering a cold, half the population habitually pops open a plastic tube of *yaa dom* and sniffs.

Fashion, tradition and hypochondria may play a part, but a breathing problem exists. The way the Thai now live traumatises the nasal passages, causes constant chills and dulls the immune system. Constant ducking in and out of ice-cold air-conditioning isn't the sole culprit; millions wake up wind-dried from sleeping through the gusts of a fan. Then throughout the day, stress-induced over-breathing gets the chairbound urbanite panting through his mouth. Respiratory illness is gagging Thailand. The capital's fumes and cement dust permeate the Central Plains, while smoke from burning forest and fields choke Northern valleys throughout the hot season.

Though seemingly a relief, one blast of a sinus dilator overrides the body's defences and lets the toxins in. The light tides of air that Thais practise in meditation would

ease irritation. Medicated puffers don't end the problem; they prolong it. And so treatment turns into habit.

Yet traditions support the vapour fetish. Today's inhalers continue an indigenous healing culture of aromatherapy and a delight in things perfumed. Masked by menthol salt and camphor oil, a potpourri of herbs and bark both cure and calm. As well as in *yaa dom* and *yaa mong*, pungent ingredients combine in another old balsamic curative, *yaa hom* (fragrant medicinal pellets).

"All Thais keep a bottle of traditional *yaa hom* in their medicine cabinet, to be inhaled as a quick-fix remedy for everyday ailments," finds spa writer Chamsai Jotisalikorn. Held in a canister of embossed metal, the pellets may also be dissolved and drunk, while many of the components find their way into herbal temple saunas and the steamed herbal compress often used in Thai massage. "Traditional *yaa hom* is a mix of herbs and flowers, whose key ingredients include refreshing menthol, sensuous ylang-ylang, sweet jasmine and *chapak* blossoms. It's believed that a whiff of this can treat faintness, cure dizziness, soothe headaches, banish nausea and relieve gas."

Aside from morphing into today's lipstick-shaped plastic inhalers, how did *yaa dom* stay hip? Toted like any other cosmetic, it serves as a socially accepted prop.

far left: **Some of the aromatic** *yaa mong* **herbal balms that Thais rub on various ailments.** *PCS*

left: **Millions of Thais sniff** *yaa dom* **inhalers to clear congestion from pollution, mask odours and make their nose feel cool. Some walk along with one or even two kept in their nostrils. "I once saw a rich man driving his Merc with an inhaler stuck up his nose," recalls writer Dominic Faulder.**

below: **New and old versions of the inhaler. Menthol masks other herbs in the modern plastic** *yaa dom* **tube, while the pellets inside the aluminium** *yaa hom* **canister smell altogether spicier.** *PCS*

bottom: **Siang Pure Oil is a Chinese-derived aromatic ointment cure-all adopted by Thais.**

Yaa dom plays nose-crutch in the manner of that mouth-crutch, the cigarette. Freud would have a field day.

Noses must be keep clear, since the Thai subconscious is moved more than most by scent. Perfume powers the culture, from tangy shrimp paste and aromatic jasmine rice to the floral water tincture *nam yaa uthai*. Scent's ability to transport the mind has religious uses, as with incense, garlands and *nam ob*, a pungent, powdery liquid used in rites as well as grooming. Constant bathing and clothes washing ensures one's personal bouquet makes the 'sniff kiss' a mutual pleasure. "If you do smell, you have the chance of having it pointed out to you," Kat's column in the *Nation* points out. But there is a popular remedy: "Mentholated powders leave your body feeling like one gigantic breath mint for hours."

Olfactory sensitivity has a downside, however, just as wearers of digital hearing aids complain of background noise. With many streets and waterways so malodorous, *yaa dom* is often sniffed to mask or purge any stink. "I like *yaa dom* because it keeps a nice smell in my nose," Thammasat University student Bay muses. Ultimately, the appeal of inhalants may have less to do with how they smell than how you feel. Most important of all, says Bay, the sharp minty zing of *yaa dom* feels cool. That's something essential in this oppressively hottest of climes.

Sniff Kiss
Romantic, respectful or simply cute, the hom kaem lifts the heart

Eskimos rub noses. Westerners join lips. Starlets air-kiss everyone. The French involve first both cheeks, and then the tongue. So how do Thais express amour? They sniff. A light, quick inhalation, somewhere around the cheek, is the acme of endearment. The *hom kaem* (sniff kiss) confirms both unconditional love to one's child and understated passion between lovers. Parents bestow a reassuringly benevolent *hom kaem* upon their offspring's cheek or forehead, a private communion whoever might be watching. It also continues into adulthood, as when an adult touchingly receives a *hom kaem* from his mother on, say, collecting her from hospital.

Aside from the exalted, innocent *hom kaem*, what motivates lovers to sniff kiss is another matter. The kissee's spine tingles, hairs raise, knees weaken. Acquiescence may well result. It's the Thai way to reach first base. For the inhaler, any sharp in-breath wobbles the senses, but when infused with ardour, it giddies.

Sniffing comes as naturally to Thais as breathing, though it may puzzle partners from other cultures. "Is this a comment on my hygiene," they wonder. Partly, yes. In the Thai social code, cleanliness is next to cuddliness, a prerequisite for bodily contact, for social acceptability. What possibly started from a parental check on bathtime diligence evolved into a general sign they care. No wonder hygiene ranks high when seeking to mate.

Internationally, many relish pungent pheromones – some to the point of fetish. Yet before bed, the Thai demonstratively shower. And expect a partner likewise to bathe. Thais prefer to avoid anyone who's remotely *men* (malodorous), but they may luxuriate in their beloved's pure and gentle aroma. As an adjective, *hom* means 'nice smelling' (as in *khao hom mali*, fragrant jasmine rice). Smelling nice is a Thai cultural obsession, and one that pays dividends.

Science is proving that love, like memory, is a slave of scent, our strongest sense. And in the pursuit of sweet pheromones, Thais leave all in their trail. In a mid-1990s US-run survey, around 10,000 respondents from multiple countries each ranked the scent of diverse nationalities on a scale of *men* to *hom*. With no whiff of favouritism, the Thais won by more than a nose. Officially the world's best smelling people, Thais can put their *hom*-ness down not just to their thrice-daily soap and powder regimen, but apparently to a diet light in dairy, meat and the ranker spices, but rich in pore-purging coriander, chilli and lemongrass.

A nod to animal instinct, the *hom kaem* also implies human sophistication. It turns that base urge into a quality control technique – and a tantalising erotic game. Clarity and refinement in breathing is a sacred principle of ancient Asia. It heightens awareness, concentration and performance in disciplines like meditation, martial arts and – as Tantra and Taoism assure – sexual prowess. Energy that courses through the body's chakras and meridian lines has the character of a 'wind', a concept found in breathing exercises like Indian *pranayama*, Chinese *qi* and Thai *lom phran*. If the breath pulses smoothly, then so do the muscles, the nerves, the organs.

By the same token, the Asian body is sacred. Even in the tightest of confines – market, train, even disco – the Thai dread to violate personal space. Seat of the soul, the head is most taboo to touch – an occupational hazard for lovers. And hairdressers. Barbers and masseurs still sometimes request permission to handle the head, and between nervous couples on a date, that remains a loaded question to breach.

In public, touching is taboo between the sexes, yet encouraged in bonding with friends of like gender. That's largely changed among urban youth since the mid-1990s, though hand holding between rural boys and girls remains rare. Kissing in public is almost never seen, even in libertarian Bangkok, even on racy TV soaps, even between wedding couples. Faced with such decorum, Thai would-be lovebirds may demurely exchange a sniff. In private it could later lead to more, or maybe not. One never knows. Hence the exquisite pleasure of the *hom kaem*: respectful, tantalising, indirect, Thai.

Village Home Décor
Pillows, jigsaws and waterfall posters comfort rural Thailand

Each visit to a village home is a unique experience, yet patterns emerge. The consistent architecture and décor results from climate, customs, beliefs, materials, needs, neighbours' involvement, and social conformity. You can tell which region you're in by the standard shapes of the wooden stilt houses. Meanwhile, the cement houses that inexorably replace them look as if picked from the same catalogue. In place of carvings, boards and finials come balustrades, tiles and plastic chests.

Tastes and taboos change far more than climate and land, so many rural houses remain elevated. "Exposure to heavy flooding and strong winds meant that the stilts had to be high and braced, hence the triangulated structure," explains décor writer Chamsai Jotisalikorn of the Central Plains style. Though now less common, that tilt recurs in doors, windows and cabinets, even in modern designs. Across arid Isaan, house walls are vertical, and in the hillier North sides often angle outwards. The South adapts the central style with wider eaves against blustery storms. Concrete houses, likewise, keep out sun and showers with cement overhangs from balconies.

Historically, farmers migrated and populations often had to shift on an overlord's whim. So when the Siamese moved house, they moved the house. On arrival they re-pegged the teak boards and rewove panels of rattan or bamboo. Thai houses became as modular as a flatpacked kitchen from Ikea. In some ways, this fits the modernist dictums of both LH Sullivan ("form follows function") and Le Corbusier ("the house as machine for living"). As Chamsai says of Le Corbusier: "his breakthrough recipe for the International Style included, buildings raised on stilts to encourage airflow, a free-flowing floor plan, and a roof garden for social activities – the defining characteristics of the traditional Thai house."

Many cement houses take a reverse tack, while staying uniform. Terraces of Chinese-style shophouses block breezes and leave no room for greenery. And as floods of housing estates prove, building at ground level on a floodplain unlearns centuries of wisdom. It then requires embankments to constrain rivers that yearn to burst.

Architecture pundit Stuart Brand advocates that successful buildings "learn". Wooden Thai houses did this, adapting organically to agricultural lifestyles. Modular components enabled multiple formats that can grow, shrink or morph according to function, family size or fortune teller's divination. While concrete shophouses are put to many uses, their standard size, narrow shape and fixed pillars often prevent appropriate layouts. With no room to expand, shophouses often get dishevelled with kitchen shacks, blocked-in balconies, extra sleeping berths and workshops spilling into public space.

Until flat roofs came, the shape and materials of the roof defined both regional style and rank. Many rural

far left: **Cute has colonised a side-table made from a tree-stump in a teak house in Mae Chaem, near Chiang Mai. Villagers love landscape pictures; this one appears on a tablecloth instead of a poster.** *PCS*

left: **Framed jigsaws and football imagery are village favourites. This one in Sakhon Nakhon, Isaan, shows Thailand's first footballer to play in the English league, nicknamed Zico.** *PCS*

right: **Every home has its glass display cabinet of collectibles. This one, unusually, includes books among the sweet animal souvenirs.**

Thais still thatch with coconut frond, *nipa* palm or teak leaf. Wealthier homes use tile or, up North, teak shingles. Corrugated tin began as a status symbol and along with fluted fibreboard came to dominate rural rooftops. These blended into the landscape, though today's bright blue roofs atop whitewashed walls scream their conspicuous consumption across valley, coastline and village.

Stilts create a multi-purpose, ground-floor 'basement' for eating, dozing, working, weaving, playing. It also stores animals, tools and vehicles, whether cart, pick-up truck or boat. There's often a broad bamboo platform for activities by day, and shooting the breeze by night.

Lined with potted plants, the verandah serves a similar purpose, though only part of it is sheltered. It connects multiple houses with the kitchen, the rooms often being of different heights according to hierarchy. Concrete houses instead have a sheltered area tiled in cool, glazed ceramic. Shoes, being of even lower status than feet, aren't allowed on platforms, nor inside any house.

The broad floorboards gleam from burnishing by decades of bare soles, and by the ebb and flow of minimal furniture according to immediate need. For the floor is also the seat, the bed, the table. Debris gets swept up instantly, however much cobwebbing jungles the rafters. If this resembles Japanese tatami rooms, that's because Japanese house formats originated in Southeast Asia.

Twice daily, bedding migrates between floor and glass fronted cabinet, as in many urban homes. Swollen stubborn in the rains, prone to looseness in the dry, the doors screech and rattle open on pulling the ribbed white porcelain knobs – a noise as integral to the village soundtrack as the pok-pok of pestles and the crack upon tin from a storm's first plump drops. This cabinet may be so large it forms a partition to allow privacy for the elders. Each cabinet pane frames a kaleidoscope of fabric. Kapok fibre mattresses depict *manga* characters. Lime nylon fringes velveteen blankets in red plaid. Special-occasion silk shimmers with silver threads. Embroidered pillows reveal their construction from stitched oblong tubes, whether boxy or the triangular *mawn kwan* (axe pillow).

In the past, furniture had to be portable and light enough for prefabricated homes, whether floating on or raised on poles. So Northerners, for example, ate off light lacquered *khantoke* (raised trays), and often still do. While Thais have traditionally snuggled into soft furnishings, Sino-Thai shophouse décor reflects the Chinese penchant for ground-based masonry. Having maintained ancestral homes in the same village for millennia, the Chinese developed heavy furniture you never need to move: think boxy rosewood with marble inlay.

Wealthier Thais in sturdier homes, however, adapted Chinese furniture to local use, from cabinets to the low *tang* table-cum-bed. Each leg forms a lion's paw, with status shown by the carved claws of seven, five or three talons to the stylised stubs oft-seen today. Furniture still reflects rank. Richer villagers typically have a set of huge chairs, often in a sheltered, tiled area visible from the front. When modernising, the masses keep furniture light

and mobile: tiered wire baskets, aluminium cupboards, plastic stacks of drawers on casters. Just as popular among the middle class, these are the real mainstream of Thai furniture, not the exported contemporary designs.

The consumer boom causes limited storage spaces to spill over with trinkets and brand name flotsam: Hello Kitty notepads, Ultraman dolls, football kits, gold plastic clocks resembling a wristwatch. An overloaded power reel feeds wires to appliances: ghetto blaster, mobile phone, rice cooker, and the TV that invites villagers to buy and borrow in pursuit of the Thai Dream.

Décor has shifted from rough, dark timber, to smooth, whitewashed cement, with light filtered in through glass louvres upon bright synthetics. Floorboards hide beneath a patchwork of linoleum, partly to protect irreplaceable timbers. But clammy, insulating lino impedes convection and becomes an incentive to install air-conditioning. Most villagers make do with plastic floor fans or the retro ceiling fans with brass blades whirring above a cluster of

white flower-like lamp shades for that instant 'old Siam' ambiance. Otherwise, light is fresh-feeling fluorescent.

Covering half a wall – like a portal to a cooler world – is a vivid, often iridescent poster of a chilly landscape: jungle waterfalls, snowy Switzerland, springtime China. Villagers also pin-up posters of Premier League footballers, soft drink ads with toothsome youths and a more treasured possession: the framed jigsaw. Instead of being re-pieced over again, the full image gets mounted like a trophy – especially if it depicts a waterfall.

Time seems measured in the mildew that each rainy season blurs the photographs of past generations, group holidays and graduations. Graduation is a prized passport to prosperity and the picture also shows a member of royalty, handing out the diploma. Above this preside portraits of the king, often from a calendar. Ancestors reside on a high shelf in Northern houses, while in all regions an altar houses Buddha images, offerings and urns of late relatives' ashes. The residents sleep with feet pointing away from these sacred sites. Bigger homes may have a Buddha room, though rarely in apartments.

Modern homes do boast indoor kitchens, though many people prefer keeping the oily fumes in a lean-to shelter out back, or in a separate building. Village *hong nam* ('water rooms') are also moving inside, complete with tiling and shaggy mats in cute shapes. But many still have privies in a cinderblock outhouse near the water standpipe. Under a bare bulb is a non-flush squat toilet and nails for hanging a sarong or towel. Soap, toothpaste and toothbrushes rest atop the walls under a bare bulb.

Hong nam are well named, for water soaks everything. Bathers ladle water with a plastic dipper from a built-in tank or ceramic *mangkorn* (dragon) jar. Showers are less common, and never curtained. Bathroom doors may be plastic, since wooden ones swell from the splashing and need heaving shut so the bolt can slide through the bent-nail restrainer. Since poor plumbing is a prime reason for tearing down old houses, the architectural baby's being literally thrown out with the bathwater.

Since modern living demarcates activities to separate rooms, aficionados seeking to preserve wooden houses reassemble several, so each house can act as a dining room, a lounge, a bedroom. Jim Thompson's House in Bangkok is the template of how to interconnect old houses. The original look requires linking them via an open-air verandah. "Our forefathers did not live in such divided territories. They would eat and sleep and enter-tain under that very same roof, so they did not have to walk about with umbrellas," quipped ex-prime minister MR Kukrit Pramoj about moving between rooms in rain at his assemblage of old houses in Bangkok. Those build-ing new teak houses tend to use Thai pavilions as a hat upon a concrete modern house. Others merely decorate homes, hotels and restaurants with village décor motifs. Such fancies are a luxury for most villagers, though some do wall-in the stilt area to create ground-floor rooms.

With Thailand modernising so fast, little thought has been given to how the countryside and canalscapes might

best be re-used in the coming post-agricultural, post-industrial era. Western cities turned villages into commuter dormitories and weekend retreats, or even relocations for non-polluting companies seeking quality-of-life cachet. That bonanza awaits only villages that preserve their charms while they are upgrading their amenities. Just as cottages became expensive real estate in the West, the old houses that Thais now associate with poverty have the potential to become desirable homes for the moneyed. The Bangkok elite already seeks weekend homes in the North and on the coast. When urban bustle starts to pall, decentralisation policies finally happen, and transportation makes mass commuting possible, village and canalside living will be chic.

above: **Portraits of King Rama IX and fading family photographs in an old village shophouse on Phuket.** *PCS*

left: **A portrait of the king on a calendar, and new year tinsel flank a poster of a cool waterfall – a common sight in hot rural Thailand. Viewed from inside a stilt house in Sakhon Nakhon, the pictures adorn a wall that runs between the pillars to enclose the kitchen and bathroom.** *PCS*

Furniture for Fun
Reinventing the chair – and Thai ways of sitting

What to make of a restaurant diner sitting on a chair cross-legged? Or of a middle class family gathering on the rug in front of their nice new sofa? Not all Thais seem comfortable in Western seats. Given no chair tradition aside from pulpits and thrones, Thai seats often surprise. The sides of many *sala* (pavilions) form a graceful seating ledge from slats of wood, creating the undulating lyre shape found throughout Thai crafts. Similar flowing lines reappear in recycled furniture that utilises rubber tyres, tree roots or parts of a buffalo cart. In a more street mode of improvisation, the poor construct benches from off-cuts of wood, foam and vinyl.

Other furniture simply makes ground-style seating more comfy. Wooden benches and sofas often come deep and broad enough to fit fully on top with legs tucked back beside the thighs, Thai-style. Stools with six-inch legs act as a clean resting perch while squatting – another favoured seating posture, since Thais can balance for ages while folded into the most compact space imaginable. Originally of wood, tiny stools now come in multi-coloured plastic; some are even sawn-off stacking chairs.

Until recent decades, most Siamese had barely any furniture. "In Southeast and East Asia, the Chinese are the only people who sit on chairs; the rest traditionally sit, eat and sleep on the floor," writes architect Sumet Jumsai. "For the Thai, the floor therefore represents the most sensitively finished part of the house (so) people remove their shoes when entering it." Hence the sublime teak boards polished by a constant shuffle of pillows and mats, feet and bottoms. Platforms enabled multi-level floor seating to suit the multi-level hierarchy. As Mont Redmond remarks, "the traditional Thai house itself was already like one big chair, hoisted aloft on its stilts over flood and dust."

Thai handymen continue to recreate the floor context as a broad platform, often of split bamboo, for putting outdoors or under shelters, whether for work, play or festive activities. Inside houses, the Chinese-influenced *tang* (low table or bench) also provides a broad surface. With no arms or back, it comes in various sizes for different needs: stool, daybed, table, dressing table, canopy bed. The daybed's so ubiquitous that Thailand's answer to *Wallpaper** décor magazine is called *daybeds*.

top left: **Tiny stools bring Thais as close as possible to ground seating. Perfect for low tables at a Chiang Mai market.** *PCS*

left: **Vendors hawk woven plastic mats – and uncut sheets from foil snack packaging – for picnickers at waterfalls, festivals, concerts, and here for kite-fliers at Sanam Luang park in Bangkok.** *PCS*

top right: **With wood running out, people cast logs out of concrete and paint them like Technicolor timber.**

The daybed might be the most-used seat in the house, but give it a vertical back, and the resultant hard Chinese-style sofabed gets sat on far less and may end up used more as shelving for unsorted stuff. Needing space to spread, many families prefer to sprawl on floor mats, doing homework, preparing food, making things, dozing. When sofas came into vogue, it was as a Western or Chinese status symbol intended for show. Mansions and smarter shophouses shield the private space with uncomfortable rosewood inlay armchairs and sofa. You can imagine deals being negotiated while perched on these severe constructions, but not relaxation. Their modern equivalent is the sets of gargantuan elephant-shaped chairs carved from a solid tree trunk.

Westernised lifestyles, however, increase acceptance of seats. "People who have chairs tend to sit in a chair," declares Thinakorn Rujinarong, chair historian and president of the Thai Interior Design Association. While that's undoubtedly true, chairs often go unused, partly due to differences in status. Seats elevate some above others, and thus confer rank to, say, owners of florid, gilded armchairs that make Versailles look shy – a style that Thais dub *Louis*. When seniors sit down, juniors position themselves lower. Among familiars and equals, if people outnumber seats, all gravitate groundwards.

Groups act closer and more convivial at floor-level, especially to work, eat or party. The comfiest cushions are square embroidered pads stuffed with kapok fibres, often stitched together into a foldable mattress with a *mawn kwan* (triangular axe pillow), itself a Thai icon. Modernising the rolled reed groundsheet, folded mats of woven plastic in fanciful patterns can be tied up to look like a briefcase. Vendors sell them at festivals and con-certs, along with the most minimalist seating imaginable: sheets of metallic plastic wrapping from snack factories.

However, Thailand developed a huge export furniture industry, thanks to its lumber resources. The local market was enhanced in the 1970s and 80s by still-continuing annual sales of low-cost, high quality furniture made by prisoners from confiscated illegal logs. When timber ran low and taste got more sophisticated by the late-1980s, the prison director invited Thinakorn Rujinarong, his son, to recruit designers to enliven the dowdy range of Chinese cabinets and rattan colonial planter's chairs. No planks, no problem. The buzzword was re-cycling: used tyres, junk metal, old wood, polished tree roots, hollowed out sugar palm stumps.

With the rise of pick-up trucks and tractors, emerged a source of beautifully sculpted carpentry: buffalo carts. In December 1989, the artist Saiyaat Sema-ngoen first displayed the cart's conversion into benches and tables, complete with clacking wooden cow bells. The seat and flatbed form natural benches, the curving yokes make sensual armrests, the axles make lanterns or table legs, the balustrades make supports and grilles. Most emblematic is the cartwheel. Cut into half-moons across the back, placed in walls as windows, or set in concrete as floor décor. "Imitators all over the country started copying my work – even the Department of Corrections," Saiyaat reflects. "Oxcart wheels, farming implements, old boats… they all started turning up in furniture."

Though the quality often lacked Saiyaa's joinery, cart style tapped the Zeitgeist. Country music was in vogue, prompted by Thai graduates returning from American universities. Some like beef magnate Chokchai Bulakul even established restaurants and ranches with wagonwheels integral to the cowboy chic. The aesthetic also suited the earthy, progressive championing of farm values by the Songs for Life movement. Their venues brim with heavy cart furniture, forest vines and that emblem of lost rural innocence: the buffalo skull. Ironically, demand for components so gutted Thai cart heritage (or possibly saved that heritage from being burnt or trashed) that wood yards harvest them from Burma, Laos and Cambodia. Workshops even carve new 'used parts', ageing the wood by soaking or burial, just as is done with reproduction carvings passed off as antiques.

While wood decays, the Chinese-derived stone bench resists the climate and thus is found kingdomwide in gardens, parks, streets and beaches. Cut from cool-feeling terrazzo, benches often come in sets of four curved ones surrounding a circular table inlaid with a chess board. Producers often tile them in cute patterns or dye the concrete. Nostalgia for when everything Thai was wood led to the next best thing: wood-effect cement. Moulded to resemble knobbly tree trunks, the bark and grain stand out in green or red paintwork to create a 'natural look' for national park picnic spots.

Another symbol of that recycling wave is the truck tyre bin. Also found in neighbouring countries, it inverts the tyre and uses off-cuts to make lid, legs and handle. Sprayed in primary colours, it graces roadside, village and suburb. Tyre workshops dotting the countryside also craft Bridgestone baby chairs, Goodyear sun-loungers and Pirelli lotus ponds. Thus Thais turn environmental hazards into art.

The latest gimmick is weaving chairs from weeds, turning Amazonian water hyacinth from a canal-choking menace into a light, soft furnishing fibre. Sculptor Nirandr Boonnetr even grows furniture, training trees using grafts, glass and stones into topiary you can sit on. Taking seven years to grow, his first armchair came complete with drink holder. London-based designer Ou Baholyodhin exemplifies the more minimalist trend of distilling classic lines into sleek furniture for Jim Thompson Thai Silk. Several contemporary Thai interior designers were architects made redundant by the 1997 crash who've created new furniture concepts by mining indigenous forms and materials with wit. Planet 2000, has earned international acclaim for amoeba-shaped stools of tangled rattan. Whether recycling materials or imagining new forms of seating, the way that Thais come to love furniture is to make it fun.

Alphabet Tables
G is for Chicken, K is for Egg

Students of the Western alphabet quickly set aside spelling prompts like 'A for Apple', 'B for Boat'. Learners of Thai instead maintain a lifelong relationship with the 44 words that contain the 44 consonants. As the Thai A to Z runs G to H, people nickname it *gor gai tueng hor nok huuk*: 'G Chicken to H Owl'.

More than a learning tool, it resembles the international radio operator's "T for Tango, V for Victor" as a way to clarify spelling. This need arises from the 44 consonants duplicating just 21 sounds – 9 when ending a word. Listed in an order based on how they're shaped by lips and tongue, there are 6 kinds of T, 5 Ks, 4 Ss, 3 Chs and so on, each spoken with a trailing 'Or' vowel. For example, the three Ps are labelled *phor phaan* (pedestal),

above: **When the Siam Ruay shop at Chatuchak Weekend Market put retro illustrations of Thai letters on T-shirts, others copied the graphic idea. This one shows the consonant chart, from G for Chicken to H for Owl.**

right: **Children's tables showing the pictorial consonant chart end up being used by adults, too, for anything from eating to tarot card dealing. Each letter has word to differentiate it, which these tables cutely illustrate.**

phor samphao (sailing junk) and *phor pheung* (bee).

Transliteration minefields come from Romanised spelling adopting these overlaps, redundant letters and pronunciation of Ls as Ns, Rs as Ls, Js as Ts. Thus a sign for Patpong reads Phat Phongs, Surawong reads Suriwongse, Chonburi reads Cholburi. Attempts to clarify can confuse, like Ph and Th marking softer Ps and Ts. Phuket gets called Fucket, when it should be Pooget.

Illustrations of the words grace letter charts adorning posters and table tops used for anything from lunch and lottery selling to fortune telling. "There are various styles of letter chart, with many linguists in the Rattanakosin period creating their own," says Associate Professor Ingorn Supanwanich. One of the earliest and easiest, *gor gai tueng hor nok huuk* became the standard.

Its imagery exudes Thai culture. From the temple: *sor sala* (pavilion), *khor rakhang* (bell), *nor naen* (novice monk). From the jungle: *chor chang* (elephant), *ngor ngu* (snake), *sor seua* (tiger). From the farm: *khor khai* (egg), *khor khwai* (buffalo), *bpor bpla* (fish). From mythology: *sor ruesii* (hermit), *yor yak* (giant). From nationalism: *thor thahan* (soldier), *thor thong* (flag).

The chart also standardised letter shape, which evolved from a South Indian script. The loops simplify earlier complex strokes. Before the US missionary Dan Beach Bradley initiated Thai printing in 1839, writing had been limited and local. "It's funny that a foreigner set the standard for writing Thai," chuckles typography expert Pracha Suveeranont. "There was no private reading culture. Thai society was oral. They wrote far less. There was no standard, but it was not a problem. Monks read out for others to listen."

Originating in palace and *wat*, letters were sacred, used for prayers, rules and oaths. Khmer-derived *khom* script, thought to be magical, still commands awe on tattoos, amulets and blessings. Hence the late emergence of leisure reading. 'Pocket books' for youngsters have recently boomed, though few older folk curl up with a novel. Like all solo pursuits, reading seems anti-social, un-*sanuk*. Despite 95% literacy, surveys find Thais read an average of eight lines per day, much of it in comics.

Still, most Thais today could decipher the 16th century *Jindamanee*, the first Thai language book. It already featured sample words for multiple letters, since ancient Ayutthaya adopted not only words from Khmer, Pali and Sanskrit, but duplicate Khmer letters to spell them. These elaborate letters appear in long, difficult words. They then get distorted or truncated, because spoken Thai originated as a monosyllabic tongue akin to Chinese.

Later borrowings from English, Chinese, Portuguese, Malay and French add to the convolution.

No language calibrates hierarchy as finely as Thai, with multiple ways to say 'I' and 'you'. Indo-Khmer spellings dominate official wording and the vocabularies for kings, monks and nobles. Thus they're defended by the Royal Institute, which in 1950 codified more than a century of early dictionaries. The Royal Institute continues to apply classical spellings to modern things. Just as 'television' pairs Greek and Latin words, so its translation, *toratut*, fuses Pali and Sanskrit terms.

Language reforms reflect power. "Elites might implement a writing system to create a national identity," Pracha explains. "Like Americans tried to show their independence by simplifying English." On uniting the first Thai nation seven centuries ago, King Ramkhamhaeng incorporated tones into Thai script, and put vowels in line with consonants. However, vowels soon drifted back above, below, after or before the consonant they follow. There are 32 vowels. These can blend to make 48 sounds, with up to three vowels surrounding a letter, or may be pronounced without being written at all.

King Rama IV tried to modernise Thai and under Rama V in 1888, Prince Damrong wrote a language book. Another attempt to put vowels in line failed in 1917, and the introduction of surnames in the 1920s only increased the everyday use of Sanskrit-Pali spellings.

More radically, the 1940s dictator Phibunsongkhram culled some redundant letters and respelled words phonetically, as had been done in Laos. Disliking the loss of traditional meanings, Thais reverted from Phibun's impositions, but kept his invented greeting "*sawasdee*". Officialdom still makes a laboured point of explaining the meaning of sawasdee to tourists with Orwellian zeal – while not spelling it as pronounced: *sawatdee*.

Spelling traps ensnare Thais, too. Place names with Pali spellings like Pathumwan and Chao Phaya interchange with the Sanskrit versions, Prathumwan and

right: **There's a language lesson in this converted canoe sign beside the Grand Palace in Bangkok. It's for a restaurant named after the letter** *Ror Reua* **- akin to 'B for Boat' - and the boat physically shows the word that symbolises the letter.** *PCS*

far right: **An inflatable Coke can shows how Thai letters are often adapted to resemble Western logos.** *PCS*

below: **The phone company Orange cleverly used Thai design to fit the 70 letters and marks of the Thai alphabet onto an SMS keypad. Vowel positions and the loop strokes of letters follow the cabalistic diagram drawn around the buttons.**

Chao Phraya. Dialects distort sounds further. Many Thais turns R into L or drop some Rs altogether.

"If we ask Thai people whether the writing system is a problem? 'Yes,'" Pracha says. "Children and foreigners often suggest things to simplify it, like adding spaces [as both Bradley and Phibun tried] or punctuation. But whether we should change it? 'Better not do that.'" After all, it works. It's ingenious that Thai can notate so many sounds plus five tones. It also enables witty wordplay.

Technology, however, drives change. When Edwin McFarland couldn't fit the two least-used Ks on the first Thai typewriter in 1892, they eventually ended up being officially discontinued. But like unwanted generals shifted to an inactive post, they remain at the top of the

table. As handwriting had done earlier, the modern fonts currently energising Thai graphics tend to streamline letters, for example truncating loops into serifs. Manop font even manages to match the West's sanserif Helvetica. Meanwhile, brands like Colgate and Coke distort script to resemble their corporate logotypes, at the cost of a Thai O resembling an English C.

Western numbers often displace swirly Thai numerals, headlines in English cap many Thai advertisements and articles, while both teens and ministers utter Anglo-American jargon to enhance both meaning and status. Blaming declining standards of Thai on absorption of English, the new Culture Ministry founded language clinics in 2003 and declared July 29 National Thai Language Day. This rearguard action is as much about power as grammar.

"The younger generation finds itself uncomfortable with the formality of the power-laden language of the past," William Klausner notices. "This verbal revolt is part of a social rebellion that takes many forms." E-mail, Internet, comics and indy magazines all simplify Thai pop-speak. Listings formats demand punctuation, and automatic translation software may force use of spaces or simpler spelling. While the 26 Western letters barely cram on the SMS keypad, how to fit the 70 letters and marks of Thai language onto buttons 0-9?

While some phone systems split them consecutively, Orange brilliantly drew a *yantra* cabalistic diagram around the buttons. The corner loops contain letters that start with the same looped stroke. Side buttons take vowels and marks that go above, below, before or after a consonant, leaving angled loops in the middle and non-looped letters on 0. Thus texting spawned the first new letter chart for a century. Orange had crafted calligraphy onto the keypad, humanising the SMS and turning every button-press into a reminder of how to write.

Potted Gardens
Portable plants for luck and lifestyle

below: **A typical potted garden where shophouse meets street. The spiny-stemmed 'Crown of Thorns' in the brown *mangkorn* (dragon) jar usually goes by doors, gates and steps, for luck, as does the auspicious fish pond.**

In a land where greenery effortlessly grows, where lies the challenge in gardening? With rice cultivation sculpting terrain, what impulse is there to landscape? When petals are considered most beautiful on a garland, need the flowerbed be more than a practical plantation? Given such conditions, experts like MR Kukrit Pramoj have doubted there is even such a thing as the Thai garden, finding few indigenous traits among the broad adoption of Chinese concepts, Japanese techniques, English lawns, French geometry, and colonial-style plantings of tropical flora. Judging by the mish-mash of styles encountered, Thai gardening seems a matter of pot luck. Pots and luck, to be precise.

"There is a tradition of growing plants in pots: Thai topiary (*mai dut*), and tray gardens (*khao maw*)," wrote Pimsai Amranand. Proof of pots dating from Ayutthayan times lies in the epic tale *Khun Chang Khun Phaen*, one of several literary sources that influence plant choice even today. "These traditions grew out of keeping plants portable, because annual floods made it necessary to carry them up to the open verandah. They were not the usual house plants, but fruit trees and scented flowers essential to Thai housewives to adorn their person, to scent water, food and clothes, and to offer to the Buddha image… Modern owners of old-style Thai houses have consequently been hard put when trying to make a garden go with the house."

Most public and private spaces still favour pots over beds for flowers, herbs, bushes, entire trees. Even clinging plants get potted – orchids spring from a slatted wooden basket, creepers are bound to a dangling coconut husk. Lining a balcony, dangling from eaves, bursting through a caged-in roof garden, potted plants are the hobby of the house-proud. When flanking an entrance, garlanding a stage or massed to depict imagery, pot plants express a sense of strict control over nature. The spectacular banks of flowers and turf along Bangkok's Ratchadamnoen Avenue turn out to be made from thousands of tessellated pots where you can barely spot the joins.

Amid barren concrete environments, pot plants become an understandable effort at beauty and civility. Hence the foliage sprouting from plastic cups, bottles, and even old light bulbs tied to lamp posts at some motorcycle taxi ranks. Yet the urge to pot is not just urban but rural, canalside and coastal. Looking closer, patterns emerge. Most of the ceramic pots follow a few standard styles. Certain plants pop up in the same position in different gardens. You can barely enter any premises without passing the eight-bloomed Crown

of Thorns, known to Thais by its Chinese name *poi sian*, meaning eight divinities. That's where the luck comes in.

"Poi Sian is a lucky plant among Chinese traders. It is like eight divine beings dwell in the eight flowers to protect the owner," enthuses Preecha Thipwet of the Poi Sian Club of Thailand, one of some hundred clubs dedicated to the cactus-like flower. With its petalled pink crown atop a stem of spines, a fine specimen might fetch 100,000 baht as advertised in one of the collectors' magazines. "It first came via Chinese junks in the 16th to 17th century, and spread among plant lovers, most of them well-educated people like governmental officers and merchants. Later, it became widespread among middle and lower class gardeners. Plants are like the arts and so reflect some sense of luxury. I think plants can show someone's economic background."

Nevertheless, few tastes unite Thailand's classes like *poi sian*. In Samut Songkhram, it graces both the balconies of King Rama II's palace and teetering canal homes. On

Phuket, *poi sian* signals fortune at Sino-Portuguese shop-houses and high hopes at the beach shacks of sea gypsies out fishing. Thriving as easily at gated mansions as by the briar thicket of an Isaan farm, the plant requires little more than sunlight. Hence the practical origin to its placement by gate, path or stair.

Despite its lack of visual appeal to Western eyes, the traditional Thai garden was not quite as haphazard in design as it might seem," William Warren muses. "There were strong beliefs regarding the placement of some plants and the exclusion of others – even in cosmopolitan Bangkok." These are most pronounced in the Central Plains, where quadrants of a compound suited particular species. "To the east of the house, bamboo and coconut… bring happiness and good health. To the northeast, *yor* and *saraphee* will ward off misfortune," writes Ruethai Chaichongrak. "In the North, *phutsa* and a variety of sedges, hemp and herbs are recommended to ward off black magic."

Considered lucky, fruit-bearing trees beginning 'ma-', like *ma-muang* (mango), were interpreted as harbingers of wealth. It's not surprising since fruit, vegetables and spices dominated household plots for the sensible reasons of consumption and trade, along with herbs, barks and blooms to heal maladies. Other species were prized for symbolism (especially the lotus), or scent. Fragrant shrubs, trees and climbers like *mali* (jasmine), *dok kaew* (gem flower) or *laddawan* still lend their names to girls in the hope they'll be as sweet.

Plant names prove decisive. Since *noon* means support, *khanoon* (jackfruit) goes behind a house, while *ma-yom* (star gooseberry) goes in front. *Yom* sounds like *niyom* (admiration), according to Warren. Beliefs can, of course, contradict. Ruethai's research positions *ma-yom* in the West, "to ward off ill intentioned people and evil spirits", since monks use its twigs to sprinkle holy water. Yet, points out Phya Anuman Rajadhon, "because of the name sounds like Phya Yom (the god of death), it is not grown near the houses of some people." Other trees are haunted by spirits, like the *yang*, *takian*, and the *thanee* banana. Despite glorious orange blossoms, *ngiew* prompts a double shudder: it features in the Buddhist Hell, plus its wood is suited for hollowing out for coffins.

To overcome ingrained taboos, some simply change the meaning. The cursed necklace of a prisoner trudging to execution, strings of *rak* (love) flowers now entwine bride and groom, who emphasise the positive name. Sheer beauty unbanished the Hibiscus. Worn behind the ears, it had been the brand of a condemned criminal (or adulteress), to the chagrin of Gauguin fans. Today's gardeners also ignore the limiting of certain plants to monks or royals. *Lanthom* (frangipani) simply looks and smells too good to be confined to temple grounds merely because its name sounds vaguely akin to *rathom* (agony). So Princess Sirindhorn recently renamed it *leelawadee* (prancing maiden). Though modern gardeners may reject some of the connotations of *bad* luck, curiously they still sow seeds to bring *good* fortune.

Behind superstitions often lurks a rationale based on utility. With mouths to feed, crops to sell and spirits to placate, plants needed justification. However, status over-rides wastefulness in the greediest kind of garden: golf course grass. In a clever recycling of resources, Tai Yuen tribes in the North grew gardens in the ground, but only where waste water splashed: around the well and the stair where feet got rinsed from a jar. Across the country, to prevent evaporation and flood-contamination, water was principally kept – like plants and lucky fish – in pots.

Often as not the pot bears the lucky likeness of a dragon (*mangkorn*), and comes in the distinctive shade of brown from the province of Ratchaburi. A century ago, an influx of Chinese encountered huge demand for high quality water containers and applied Chinese pottery techniques to the delicate, water retentive clay from Ratchaburi. "We don't dye the pot, but paint the dragon in *din khao* (white earth), glaze it with wood ash solution then fire," reveals Khun Lahn of Rattanakosin Ratchaburi Pottery. "The dragon is an auspicious creature. Chinese believe it has protective power."

Ample hipped and wide of rim, *mangkorn* jars are shaped for frequent moving. Pots enable the Thai garden to change. Plant beds require long-term planning and abstract visualisation. Cuttings take time to mature, while pruning must factor-in future shape. What's planted in the ground remains semi-permanent, with errors reveal-ing themselves only over time. Aside from patient, green-thumbed enthusiasts, gardeners with fickle tastes – or a Buddhist grasp of impermanence – prefer to rearrange pots, toss out tired greenery, bring in ready-nurtured foliage. Plants also need repotting as they grow, though restraining the roots keeps them a manageable size, something essential for another Thai passion: dwarfing.

Often kept in Chinese-style blue and white ceramic, Bonsai-sized *mai dut* and *khao maw* caught on partly since miniaturised detail resonates throughout Thai arts. Exquisitely *riab roi* (tidy) presentation gains face, since it requires time, wealth and skills most folk cannot spare.

Says Warren of the gracious, topiary-lined lawn at the Grand Palace: "If this is a Thai garden, does it perhaps express one aspect of the Thai character, the love of neatness, the need to keep strict control over oneself and one's feelings? Or is it just an idea from the Chinese?" From *poi sian* to topiary to rockeries, the Chinese aesthetic of man commanding nature proved compatible with believers in cool-hearted Buddhism needing to restrain tropical passions – and tropical foliage.

Upwardly mobile Thai have warmed to Western land-scaping, with a special fondness for fluted pots and Greek statues atop scalloped fountains to match neo-classical mansions. Thailand's first deliberately landscaped grounds were laid out in palaces by Chao Phraya Worabhong as one of the Westernisations King Rama V encouraged. For commoners, however, husbanding an entire property takes too much energy in this climate, hence the focus on frontal display: forecourts get primped, gates garlanded, doors festooned. With disorder held at bay, pots become

left: **The hanging gardens of Honda. A vendor's moped at Wat Don Wai acts as a plant display, with a Crown of Thorns in the front basket.**

below: **Who would know? A rock garden with bubbling fountain hidden on the roof of shops near the Montien Hotel in Bangkok.**

bottom: **Fish at doorways bring good fortune. Here, plants and ponds come in terra cotta pots and a classic *mangkorn* dragon jar, which come in many sizes, also with lids for fresh water storage.**

the sufficient gesture.

Commercial land use has reshaped Thai towns at the expense of trees, hiding how Thais had earlier used greenery for their benefit. "Ancestors built houses amid clusters of trees because of the shade and protection from the elements that this afforded," writes Nithinand Yorsaengrat. "It may seem strange today, but our ancestors were taught to treat trees with the same consideration they would show for any other living creature. It was thought improper to damage a tree and if one wanted to use its wood for some purpose, the tree had to be cut down in a 'caring' way." That served to moderate over-exploitation in the past, so blessing big trees with multi-coloured sashes has recently been revived as a protest strategy against logging. While spirits in large trees draw respect, Thais prefer not to live among them.

Until recent decades the jungle was a close, insatiable threat. In this fertile climate whatever is not in a pot, quickly goes to pot. At the fringes of a garden, canopies tangle, creepers strangle, ferns sprout, weeds propagate. Like wild forest, this encroachment isn't progressively tended, but left unkempt until periodically slashed back. Asking why someone denudes the undergrowth often gets the answer: snakes. "We found a one baby python a day, one under my bed," relates Dr Anucha Thirakanont from his home on Bangkok Noi canal. "We know there'll be more because a nest can have up to 40 hatchlings." People often kill cobras and vipers, but may take them to the venom farm. The snake centre in Lad Prao collects up to 600 constrictors a year. Putting them in national parks, however, can upset the ecology. Hundreds of snakes dumped just inside one park caused farm animals and pets to vanish from an adjacent village.

The previous abundance of common land in which to potter – and the historic lack of formal gardens – partly explains the paucity of city parks, or even slivers of shade where a bench might be nice. Urban green space was taken for granted until decimated by development. Many lines of shophouses actually stand in gardens they abruptly halved. Lumphini Park remained unique in Bangkok for decades after its founding in 1925. Despite the recent sprouting of parks big and small, many 'Pocket Parks' will be temporary. The Bangkok Metropolitan Authority adopts a vacant lot – like the long-delayed site of Bangkok's contemporary art museum – and buys a bunch of trees. Voila! Pathumwan Park.

Trees literally can be bought in bunches from markets, with several trunks strapped to a pick-up truck for under $20 each. A viable park can take root within a year. By the time it's mature, the owner probably wants the land back, so the trees disappear. It's that nonchalant. Local developers hardly ever preserve big trees, preferring to obliterate all vegetation from a site before covering it

above: **No pots? No terrace? No problem. This enterprising house in Bangkok Noi hangs plants from the eaves in old radios.**

Poodle Bushes
Fanciful topiary and tiny rock gardens

From the urban Thai jungle of dusty shrubs, hacked branches, and plants kept more for luck or scent than visual harmony, suddenly out pops a meticulously coiffed tree — although one might not at first recognise it as a tree. Twist-trunked *mai dut* (trained trees) brandish globes of manicured foliage to create an oddly beautiful profile. A pedigree poodle among soi dogs, *mai dut* stands apart from other potted plants, not just in artistry and order, but sheer whimsy.

The origin is well-known, though not how it later took on bizarre proportions in Thailand. "There had been interest in clipped and knotted trees since Sukhothai days when the influence was clearly Chinese, and later in Ayutthaya days when the Siamese tried to imitate Japanese bonsais," Pimsai Amranand explains. Both Chinese and Japanese sought to arrange miniature versions of idealised landscape painting, with wizened pines, pebbles coursing like streams around mounds of moss, evocative rocks jutting just so. They were yin-yang compositions of what nature should look like under man's command — compressed into a container.

Thais still place *mai dut* in tray gardens called *khao maw* (miniature mountain), typically in a tray of blue and white ceramic. Symbolising sacred Mount Meru or resembling some auspicious animal, the rock may be made by cementing vari-shaped pebbles, preferably from the Thai Gulf. Most prized is petrified wood, mined from the (fast diminishing) stone forests of Isaan. Many *khao maw* feature Chinese pavilions, tiny figures, faux waterfalls, reaching it's zenith in the giant *khao maw* at Wat Prayoon in Bangkok – with its gothic arbours and sub-urban toy houses.

Just as Thai rock gardens are styled after mythology, *mai dut* looks like no earthly tree. "Whereas the Japanese tried to imitate nature, the Siamese tried to make their trees into odd, fantastic shapes," Pimsai says. "The idea was clearly derived from the gnarled old pine trees, but the symbolism must have been lost because they look anything but natural."

But few Thai arts *do* look 'natural'. Dance, painting, sculpture, costume, architecture – all stylise natural forms into formulas. The visual language of *lai thai* (traditional patterns) abstracts the contours of flames and flora, gods and fauna, often in a manner to indicate a divine message. It might be another import that catalysed the transformation of the Sino-Japanese bonsai bush into the extravagant *mai dut* bauble. Following Ayutthaya's first diplomatic mission to France, ceilings styled after Versailles Palace found their way into the *wat*. So it's

possible that the gnarled pine got its globular makeover from the geometric topiary of King Louis XIV. Still, *mai dut* is far less mechanical than the cubes, cones, domes and drums of the hedges at Versailles.

"The art of *mai dut* strikes a delicate balance between nature and artifice," Alongkorn Parivudhiphongs says. "Often, groomers have to adapt their designs to accommodate the 'will' of the tree." Dwarfed to anywhere between three inches and three metres (the bigger ones grown in the ground rather than in pots), the branches must undergo repeated breaks to achieve the angular 'elbow' look. To improve the chances, connoisseurs train several trees at once. Some go awry or die, hence the demand for saplings, best found in Western Thailand, with branches already in 'starter positions'. Others relish the challenge of coaxing branches from a smooth trunk.

Despite their innate unpredictability, *mai dut* became subject, like many Thai arts, to bureaucratic rigidity. Luang Mongkhonrat, a courtier of King Rama V,

clockwise from top left: A *mai dut* bush in need of a manicure at Wat Amarinthara, Bangkok Noi. Weird shapes are categorised as an official kind of *mai dut*, here seen at Wat Buppharam, Trat. Temples, are often decorated with poodle bushes, like this one in a pot at Wat Kalayanamit, Thonburi. Adopting Western topiary style, this sprouting elephant stands guard at King Narai's Palace, Lopburi (*PCS*).

below: The Grand Palace grounds have magnificent topiary, such as this one in the form of Garuda, the auspicious man-bird emblem of Thai royalty.

right: *Khao maw* rockeries are auspicious, but open to ideas. A flock of faux storks roosts with cherubs at this temple fountain.

right inset: A dinosaur and a ladybird wander this funky streetside *Khao maw* rockery at Wat Gate in Chiang Mai.

committed to poetry the Ayutthaya-era stipulations that seven approved species could produce nine styles with three, five, seven or nine pom-poms on three levels, the upper level symmetrical with the lower. That standard endures despite efforts to experiment.

Easiest of the nine styles is *mai khen*, whereby three bushes resemble a rearward glancing deer; *mai khabuan* forms a carousel of evenly spaced branches; step-like *mai chak* evokes a Chinese screen; *mai kamalor* bends downwards – and back up again to form *mai hok hien*, twisting around its own trunk as if in t'ai chi pose; the nine bushes on *mai pa khom* gather at the top; *mai enchai*, often found in *khao maw* trays, inclines as if on a riverbank; *mai talok*, a hybrid of tangled roots, outsize

leaves and odd proportions, gets dubbed the 'clown tree'; and most other dwarf designs get named *mai yipun* after the Japanese bonsai.

Once the subject of beauty contests among aristocrats, *mai dut* fits best in a face-gaining context: courtyards, temples, mansions, palaces. But it crops up anywhere from shophouse to office desk. Making *mai dut* into street décor, however, usually backfires, because they soon become straggly. The trimming skills are too scarce. And expensive – good tree costs many thousands of baht.

"Unlike Japanese bonsai, the art of *mai dut* has only a small core of practitioners and there are no organisations or publications devoted to it," Alongkorn laments. "Today, fewer and fewer of them are grooming new trees, since the process is so time-consuming and they might not be around long enough to see the full beauty." *Mai dut* typically match man in lifespan, taking a third of that to mature. But in these faddish times, teens are hardly likely to invest in a hobby that won't show full results until their middle age.

Some prefer topiary as a toy. Cute topiary caricatures of an animal, bird or person arrived from the West at the same time as the technique of guiding branches along wires, which is now being applied to *mai dut*. Hence the

outbreak of foliated elephants herding across hotel lawns and planted peacocks preening their leaves in parks.

Beyond fun and aesthetics, the topiary hobby helps sculpt personality. "Both *mai dut* and *khao maw* can serve as rehabilitation tools for the hot-tempered," Alongkorn believes.

Yet *mai dut*'s survival may depend more on reviving the spirit of one-upmanship through competitions, Kennel Club style. Interest might increase if innovation took hold, perhaps by adopting shapes from *lai thai*, or by varying the kinds of plants trained. Chiang Mai's approach roads already feature Casuarina Pines sculpted into lotus buds. Imagine what breed of poodle bush might win 'Best in Show'?

Cute
The subculture of cartoon mascots

In this fabled 'land of smiles', smiles beam not only from people – everyone, most of the time – but from utensils, notebooks, pencils, hair grips, microwave ovens. Smiling is the Thai way to get things done. So the pleasantry's extended to machines, screens, instruction manuals and warning signs.

If Disney wrote the recipe of contemporary cute, and Japan baked it as a cupcake called *kawaii*, Thailand iced it with pink sugar. *Kawaii* intrigues social commentators because it seems to contradict supposedly sober Japanese culture. "Societies such as Japan's, which put such emphasis on social harmony, actually require a lot of repression and self-control on the part of citizens," explains Asian arts authority Alex Kerr. "So the primal innocence of childhood is immensely appealing."

Thailand, too, values a smooth surface and cherishes the same bright, happy, pretty, cuddly, giggly, passive, innocent, non-aggressive playthings. More than that, *na rak* (cute) resonates with several core Thai values: *sanuk* (fun sensibility), *suay* (beauty), *sabai* (contentment) and *kreng jai* (deferential consideration). It is also urban, plastic and commercial, and thus pop. That suits another aspiration: looking *dern* (modern).

Cute is loaded with meanings, while appearing normal to those who unquestioningly consume it. After all, hearts and baby animals cover TV, colonise the Internet, riddle advertising and brand even the blandest products. Plus comics are the principal pop literature. Bought or rented for a few baht, inch-thick books of Japanese *manga* with speech bubbles in Thai take students, drivers and professionals into realms of adventure and violence, sex and soppiness, school and superheroes.

Cute imposes inane uniformity, yet cartoon characters with limited expressions convey messages as nuanced as the Thai smile. Each *yim* (smile) has a name. *Yim thak thaai* greet strangers, *yim yae-yae* preempt a clash, *yim soo* supply fortitude when all seems lost. Given modern stress, cute companions provide comfort and a happy face. Hence notebooks flutter with hearts, flowers and a cuddly creature, winsomely cooing: "Perfect life", or "Funny life: what do you want? Something to make your life happy." Is this sweet, sad or sinister?

One dictionary definition of things cute, "affectedly attractive", implies calculation, especially commercial calculation. "The implication would seem to be that we are all as harmless as children," writes pundit Donald Richie of cute's role in the billion-dollar 'image factory', which spreads from clothes and food to advertising and fancy goods like figurines. "Look at us: we make fools

of ourselves, we invite you to laugh at us, and yet we are so harmless that your laughter cannot but be indulgent, that your hand cannot but reach into your billfold."

Like the Japanese, the Thai defer in junior-senior relationships. Well into maturity, the Thai plays *nong* (younger sibling) to a *phi* (older sibling, even a minutes-older twin) or parent, uncle, grandparent, submitting to employers, teachers and social seniors as if relatives. Plastering a lunchbox, car or counter with photostickers and fluffy mascots is an affirmation. As Richie says, collecting cute things enables disempowered people to surround themselves with something submissive. Hello Kitty can't answer back. She has no mouth.

Cute links heavily to fashion, group affinity, and the teenage search for identity. It's a tribal badge lasting till as late as parenthood, and beyond. On the body, cute arises in pictorial nail covers, while even people without dental problems get multi-coloured tooth braces to feel they belong. Itself a proof of having friends, the mobile phone is cute-central: screens display smiley faces, messages animate LED teddies, customised cases express your taste, ringtones turn hit songs into nursery jingles, gossip services have names like 'Na Rak Chat' (cute chat).

left: Thai crafts go cute in this popular genre of chubby pottery figures with extra-large head, babyish expression, and a soft stylisation of traditional clothing and top-knot hair.

right: Comics are Thailand's most popular leisure reading matter, whether as re-captioned Japanese *manga* or home-drawn cartoon strips. Stalls and shops stock countless editions for rent or sale-and-return.

left: At this stall in a temple fair, the face of Hanuman – monkey warrior from the *Ramayana* epic, – goes from the exquisite, hand-painted mask of *khon* court dance to flimsy moulded plastic. Around him are masks styled after characters from Ultraman, the Japanese superhero that Thais have adopted as their own – but not without a fight over copyright! *PCS*

Group photos create community, especially as photo-stickers or shoots in teen photo studios get divided between friends and put where others can see. Amid make-believe scenes in space, gardens, fantasy lands, the friends pose with V 'peace' signs, sometimes behind heads as bunny ears. Similarly, boys cup their chin with thumb and forefinger at right angles to make the 'handsome' gesture. Taking a naturalistic group portrait has become near-impossible, even among many adults.

Slogans about friendship riddle cute stuff, often printed in Thainglish to show sophistication. "Freshly & happy all day all night. Friends share stuff with you. They're funny. Sometimes they give good jokes," an exercise book advises. "Feel at ease: it's nice to be nice to someone. Always stick with a friend even when he is sick or in a bad mood. Never let him down," preaches a mauve plastic briefcase.

The saccharine sentiments echo the *paak waan* (sweet talk) that decorates Thai conversation, though some mottoes admonish like a Buddhist homily. As if a spoilt child, cute demands attention and is prone to tantrums. "Oh! Mae jao! A good friend is someone who does his or her homework with me," reads a pencil case dotted with flowers and hearts. Woe betide the bad friend who resists such passive-aggressive blackmail.

Cute also banishes seriousness. Pretty images soften anything perceived as difficult, dutiful or unpleasant: school supplies, workstations, public notices. The state has learned that a spoonful of sugar makes the medicine

go down. Official instructions are increasingly related by smiling cartoon ciphers, projecting a nicer reality. The police love cute. Mannequins and cut-outs of cops oversee traffic. Officers direct the cars from a fiberglass shelter shaped like a huge police helmet, complete with badge. Stickers and fridge magnets of cartoon police spread the law with a smile. The tactic is 'tell you nicely first' to avoid confrontation and minimise threat. As Richie says, it's not that the people themselves are childish, just the image they wish to project, which is ultimately conciliatory.

But some men feel cute is an emasculating retreat from the serious, competitive world and a symbol of feminine values overtaking the workplace. The greatest adult collectors of cute seem to be office girls, who seek a distinctive identity in the workplace, yet wish to appear passive and conformist. In a fast changing society, cute also reflects a newly extended childhood, unlike macho 'cool', which feigns accelerated growing up. Freed from having to help the extended family to farm or trade, teens and young adults suddenly have more time for play, while new industries feed their fascination for cute.

It first appears that most Thai cute derives from Japan or Disney. But beyond Pokemon and Ultraman, a local genre has evolved: cute handicrafts. Ancient Siamese arts were primed for turning into toons. Rather than paintings with shading, nuance, shadow and perspective, temple murals are series of panels using outlines, solid bright colours and non-realistic foreshortening. Murals relate scripture, folklore and village tales in cartoon strip form, often with captions. The divinities get generic

top: **Hello Kitty themed dim-sum buns being steamed in Trat.**

upper right: **Pangpond is the first Thai toon to adorn 'character products'. Not only is the big-eyed boy on postage stamps, but now also SkyTrain tickets.**

right: **Cute wisdom to live by, adorning just a few of the note-book covers on a shop shelf. The one called 'Funny Story' has a bell on its cloth bookmark and the slogan: 'Don't frown, because you never know who's falling in love with your smile!'** *PCS*

angelic faces, impassive smiles and gentle manners, with attributes expressed through the colour-coding, costume and gestures. Also found in shadow puppets, these traits translate into 3-D as classical dance, with its white face make-up and masks, which are half-way to the fixed expressions of *manga*.

Another thread is the delight in diminutive crafts. From puppets and tiny engravings to candies shaped like fruits, miniature collectibles have grown so widespread they've spawned a trade fair and museums. The spirit house resembles a doll's house with toy servants and animals sharing the hand-painted plastic finesse of figurines from fast-food outlets.

Now Thai crafts have gone pop: fruit carving evolved into soap carving, Buddhist rock gardens into table-top fountains with dinky figurines. The shortage of timber forced wood carvings smaller, which suited the booming demand in souvenirs and knick-knacks for tourists and locals with spare cash. Youngsters cruise markets with friends wanting to buy something, anything, under 200 baht, which invariably ends up being small and cute.

Often the inspiration is fantasies of village idylls or visions of the American West. As Erik Cohen reports of wood-carving trends: "A new family of styles unrelated to any past religious traditions, or local culture, or environment [was] adopted… expressed in copies of objects from Western or Asian models, such as dogs, ducks, frogs with umbrellas, masks, golf players and Disney characters." All are winsome and simplified – perhaps inevitable now that 'wood carvings' might actually be cast in resin!

Handicrafts now aim mainly to please, to be affectedly attractive. Thus they become 'infantile biomorphs' – a scary term for the eye-enlarging, mouth pursing, nose-reducing distortion that started in teddy bears, and grew stronger through Disney then Doraemon. Now eyes fill half the face of Pangpond, the first Thai toon to become a hit. This alien gaze now emanates from statues of angels, dolls of dancers, stuffed elephants, and pottery children with top-knots. Gilt carvings of novices seated

in supplication went doe-eyed and finally morphed into chubby kids reclining in a blissful doze. The ultimate caricature of heritage greets you in restaurants and shops: a *wai*-ing, smiling, wide-eyed woman – in wood.

"Two epithets characterise our culture today: either it is 'naïve' or 'cute'," wrote Kukrit Pramoj, citing popular misconceptions about both Thai traditions and cultural imports. "If there is anything we still strictly adhere to, we do it without knowing the philosophy behind it, we do it because it is cute. For other forms of art, we are still rather naïve." But perhaps cute *is* a philosophy. "It's never too late to have a happy childhood," assures one notebook motto, while another reflects on the reason: "Be happy… it's one way of being wise."

The Thai Dream

Siamese lifestyle went to the mall, the suburb, the golf course

A Bangkok boy in hip-hop cut-off jeans, sneakers and baseball cap ambles across Emporium shopping centre. He could be any copycat mall rat in Asia, Europe or America. His T-shirt blares the Thainglish catchphrase "Same same". On turning to exit onto the SkyTrain, his back reads "but different".

He may not consider the meaning of this slogan so beloved by vendors of copy goods, but the metaphor gives pause. He looks Thai, but feels (mo)*dern* and *inter*(national); at the same time, he appears globalised but remains deeply Thai. The same goes for urban Thailand. It looks like the American Dream filtered via Japan with a Siamese customisation of aspirational icons: brand names, housing estates, private vehicles, mobile phones, golf.

Long before the urge to look cool, came the urge to be cool. Though the humid climate helped create traditional culture, escaping it underpins the air-conditioned lifestyle of mall-car-condominium. Many malls enclose more shops, restaurants and entertainments than a provincial town. Just before the 1997 economic crash curtailed such gigantism, Bangkok boasted two of the world's four biggest malls. Several had roof-top funfairs, water parks and laser shows to rival Las Vegas. These theme parks

evoked fairy tale imagery from the West, rather than Disneyfying Thai folk tales. Other pastimes go West too, with football overtaking *takraw* and badminton as the sport of choice for a late-afternoon street knockabout.

Initially a non-place devoid of history or context, a mall swiftly comes to resemble the haphazard markets it replaces. Habitually, any open space, path or plaza congests with hawkers, thus marble concourses soon clog with stalls and bargain bins. A maze of tiny booths fill Mah Boon Krong Centre, Bangkok's epicentre of youth fads. Trade fairs, too, end up as mammoth discount sales. Even in the airport, fliers must steer luggage around vendor carts – official ones hawking Duty Free.

Malls routinely trumpet their qualifications in foreign terms, typically using flamboyant words in English: New World, Miracle Mall, Fashion Island, Future Park, Young Place. Some borrow prestige identities: Wall Street Tower, Times Square, World Trade Centre. Exemplifying the syndrome of 'status anxiety' coined by Daniel J Boorstin, the often justified phrase 'world class' recurs in speeches, signs and the company self-congratulation pamphlets depicting bouquets, that get inserted into newspapers.

Urbanites affirm their identity through addresses like Modern Town, Fortune Town, Town-in-Town. Strategic

left: **Tapping the Thai instinct to sing, karaoke boxes in malls fill with teens, while their elders frequent more discrete private karaoke rooms in nightclubs with hostesses.** *PCS*

facing page, clockwise from top left: **Siamese suburbia beckons through scale models of middle class housing projects, a newspaper ad for a luxury mansion that's evidently a work of art, and memorial shrines of real estate property in the next life, as seen at the** *khao maw* **mystical rockery in Wat Prayoonwong, Thonburi.** *PCS*

dropping of English sorts sophisticates from bumpkins, both in conversation and in print. Magazines with names like *Image, Lips* or *a day weekly* pepper their contents with English. So do advertisements, menus, posters and namecards. Nowhere is this flashing of bilingual face more enthusiastic than in the housing estates lining suburb and coast.

"On top of Your Achievement," reads an ad in 2004 for 18-80 million baht houses. "Luxury Elegance Prominence… the finest portrait of Beverly Hill. Splendid, with our world-class standards… on par with the presidential White House. Clubhouse's extravaganza to dazzle not only your guests but also yourself…" There are many ways to dazzle oneself. One might live in Silver Heritage, Belle Park, Prime Mansion, Elite Residence or Noble Aura. Hampton Residence and Madison evoke the American elite, and what could be more *elegante* than Château de Bangkok, or more posh than Windsor, The Colony or British Town?

While modern mansions evoke a courtly Thai fantasy through an auspicious Sanskrit name, few upwardly mobile Thais invest in a traditional teak home – a romantic idea to which many foreign residents aspire. Instead, estates offer a medley of adobe, neo-classical, neo-gothic and generic suburban chic with stone cladding. Inside, florid mouldings in varnished wood compete with pink ruched curtains and gilt-encrusted furniture in a florid French style vaguely dubbed *Louis*.

Younger buyers, however, increasingly prefer downtown condos like Urbana, City Smart and The Lofts. These yuppies follow the minimalist credo of 'less is more', whereby less usually costs more. Room sizes shrink due to property prices and the Thai extended family dwindling to a nuclear 2+2 or less.

Forbidding gates and apartment corridors prevent the former engagement with neighbours and nature. Airbrushing eyesores from their lushly vegetated ads, most developments nurture scant ornamental greenery, proving comedian Bill Vaughan's observation: "Suburbia is where the developer bulldozes out the trees, then names the streets after them." Hence we get Natural Park, Lake Green, Ficus Lane, The Trees and Grand Canal.

Buried down narrow, circuitous *soi* (lanes), often without adequate planning or amenities, both upmarket

and budget housing require private wheels. In artists' impressions of estates, everyone drives at least one Porsche or Benz. Realistically, the average urbanite parks an Isuzu beneath their one-bedroom flat or shophouse. If they have a car. When ramshackle downtown communities get dubbed slums, their residents may get shifted to sanitary, simple housing beyond the city fringes and public transport in state schemes called Ua Arthorn (We Care). Critical to their suburban dream is a motorcycle like the aptly named Honda Dream.

Thailand depends much on motorbikes. Domestically, it gets kids to school and relatives to work. Bikes aid errands, and enable young people to cruise with friends or meet sweethearts in private. Three or four can cram on one saddle, babies wedged in between, children perched on the fuel tank. Often the only work vehicle available, it gets overloaded with towering cargo or delivers anything from papers and pizzas to gas canisters. So its loss through an accident (or repossession, since many are bought on installments) has deep repercussions.

Increasingly, riders graduate to practical pick-ups, which make up about half of all car traffic. Playing bus or truck, the flatbed gets filled with cargo or people, often without protection from the CarryBoy cover that many drivers install. Otherwise, despite hefty duties, Thailand remains a leading market for luxury cars.

There's nowhere more impressive to be valet-parked than a country club. Golf appeals to the upwardly mobile and Thailand has several of Asia's best courses. Fairway fever has impacted society, economy, environment and government, though not in a fair way. Private talks on private greens suit the monopolistic deal-making of tycoon, bureaucrat, general. Thus foreign minister Surin Pitsuwan raised eyebrows by refusing to negotiate over golf. A startling headline reported that policemen were publicly ordered to stop playing golf while on duty.

Other imports fuse with Thai ways. Elaborate bridal emporia organise Western-garbed weddings, held in addition to local rites. International-style restaurants, pubs and clubs adapt to the needs of face, especially whereby a host shares the premium whisky he keeps behind the bar. Recent fads – wine, pasta, cigars, pizza, espresso, green tea, spas, juice bars – have spawned hybrids. Thus it's very Thai to order spicy spaghetti, green tea cake, durian milkshake, ketchup on pizza, beer on the rocks, or red wine served from an ice bucket.

Standard procedure at trendy bars is for each customer to place their wallet on the table, and on top of that their mobile phone. Thais were early-adopters of this portable status marker. Even the poor run up huge cellphone bills to keep constantly in touch with their group. In a 2003 Bangkok survey, usage was 49% friends, 25% family, 20% lovers and just 6% business, with 54% playing games on their handset. Over half change their model due to gimmicks or fashion, some monthly.

Brand one-upmanship extends from dames dripping with monogrammes to university bag racks being a roll-call of luxury labels. High-profile shopping doesn't always indicate living standards, however. Faces from the society pages may dwell in surprisingly normal digs.

For those who can't afford the import (and many who can) the fake entices. Many forgeries are as finessed as the original, and might be run-ons from the brand's own Thai factory. While the West lionises originality, Thai tradition dictates you shouldn't alter a master's template, whether a dancer's mask or a Prada purse. With free market frankness, many Thais don't see why they can't

left: **There's no refuge from labels in the totally sponsored environment. At some of Bangkok's SkyTrain stations, where TVs blare continuous advertisements, the only seat on the concourse is afforded by a pot of imported-brand yoghurt shampoo.** *PCS*

emulate something that works. Income disparity with the West makes patents look like a conspiracy not to share – until Thai products started being ripped off.

Local firms have now joined Western governments and companies in strong-arming the authorities to punish pirates. One music insider estimates that 80-90 per cent of CDs sold here are counterfeit, which earns so much money that the industry may be a net gain to the Thai economy. Despite increased raids and public crushings of counterfeit watches and DVDs, stalls get re-supplied and pirate kingpins elude capture. At the stalls, customers order from flipbooks of covers from movies and music, software and porn. Discs later appear from a hidden stash to be bagged in opaque plastic. Of the crackdown, a mall software vendor shrugs: "No problem. We go to lunch while they raid at 12.30pm every Tuesday."

In his 1985 rock anthem 'Made in Thailand', Add Carabao lambasted the cultural cringe in label mania. "What the Thai do themselves… the *farang* love it, but the Thai don't see the value. Afraid to lose face, worried their taste isn't modern enough," he sang, deploring the face gained by export goods re-imported as 'Made in Japan'. "We can tell ourselves it's foreign-made… Nobody has to cheat us, we cheat ourselves."

Thai brands became more popular after the 1997 crash, by which time Thainess itself became a brand: "Banks, beer, paint, and fish sauce were all advertised in terms of their Thainess," comments Craig Reynolds. "So successful were these campaigns at rooting consumer

products in the local culture that some Thai shoppers could regard Lux soap as Thai rather than foreign."

The way Thailand has interpreted Western things has much to do with the taste of Sino-Thai. Their paler features – and those of *luuk khreung* (half Western) celebrities – dominate advertising, media, entertainment, business and high society – and comprise the biggest-spending consumers and main arbiters of style.

This isn't new, but continues eons of cultural fusion. It's historically been policy to select fashions from the power of the day, all the while remaining independent and distinct. While the Western and Japanese influences sweeping Thailand today appear to be different, the situation remains same same.

Ritual

****

Royal Portraits
Pictures of kings past and present express the Thai sense of identity

Across the Kingdom, every home, office, business and public building displays at least one royal portrait. Thais identify their monarchs with good fortune, development and pride in nation and Thainess. Thus royal portraits are objects of deep reverence. As well as paintings and photographs of monarchs past and present, royal portraits may take other forms, such as the display of banknotes, coins and amulets bearing a royal image.

The face of the revered King Bhumibol Adulyadej (Rama IX) is omnipresent and given pride of place. His Majesty's picture is frequently paired with the beautiful visage of Queen Sirikit. Among other members of the royal family, Crown Prince Vachiralongkorn is often shown in military uniform, and Princess Sirindhorn is widely pictured engaged in good works and cultural endeavours. The late Somdej Ya (the Princess Mother who bore Kings Rama VIII and IX) is depicted in many homes. So are two great former rulers, Rama IV (King Mongkut) and Rama V (King Chulalongkorn), in tribute for securing Siam's independence and development. Thais show particular veneration for Rama V, placing offerings on many altars showing his pictures, statues and amulets, and also at his equestrian statue in Bangkok every Tuesday night, and on his birthday, October 23.

There is great variety of styles and themes in royal portraiture and people choose to show themes with which they identify. Some show royalty working, engaging in hobbies, visiting development projects, or conducting rituals. Oft-seen images depict King Rama IX with his camera, Rama VI acting in plays, and Rama V in the *rajapataen* suit he designed or, in one famous image, while cooking. Queen Sirikit has championed the refined Thai crafts, especially silk, that feature in most images of her.

Specialist shops and stalls stock a broad range, whether photographic, sculptural, or an artist's impression. The frame may be elaborate, simple, or, like many family photos, sealed in lacquer upon a board with wood grain and a spangled margin. Particularly grand examples incorporate detailing in gold leaf, glitter or mother of pearl. The prestige of an artist's original creates high demand for portraitists to create hand-crafted replicas of famous royal portraits in pastel or paint.

For all the sense of tradition, royal portraiture is a modern development. Bronzes and oils of the first three Chakri kings are subsequent artists' impressions, since historically it was a capital offence for all but a small coterie to look at the monarch's face. The first accurate likenesses of a Thai king, Rama IV in the mid 19th

facing page: **Oil paintings of King Bhumibol and Queen Sirikit, with Garuda emblems on each frame. Buildings kingdomwide give pride of place to pictures of royalty, as in this roti café at Phra Arthit Road.** *PCS*

previous spread: **7-Eleven's sign echoes the spirit house roof colours at Silom Road, Bangkok.**

clockwise from left: **Postcards depicting Thai kings. At royal birthdays, ornate displays adorn Bangkok's Ratchadamnoen Road; this portrait of Queen Sirikit has her entwined initials in her birthday colours. King Rama V is widely venerated and depicted in buildings, such as this restaurant in Prachuab Khiri Khan.**

century, were photographs. Cameras took little time to reach Siam and royals were among the first Thais to use them. Indeed, many of the painted portraits from each subsequent reign are based on photographs.

Portraits of royals from history incorporate the likeness with symbolic representations of kingship itself. These images can be 'read' for motifs and messages pertaining to that reign, right up to today's pictures of King Bhumibol. The camera he often carries displays his vision and artistry, the maps he holds imply the charting of his country's course, depictions of the inventions he patented demonstrate Thai creativity and development.

Historical pictures, too, serve a present purpose. After the economic crash of 1997, the theme was duty to one's country, embodied in images of King Naresuan and several regal women who sacrificed themselves for Siam, such as Queen Suriyothai and Princess Suphankalaya.

As in all art, the way these figures are portrayed has much to do with aesthetic taste in the era they were made. Proud postures of a square-jawed King Naresuan and pastel impressions of his demurely dressed sister Princess Suphankalaya tell much about standards of beauty, manhood and womanliness four centuries after they lived. Likewise, ancient kings now have tunics politely painted over the chests that archives record as historically bared. Costuming is particularly sumptuous in the film *Suriyothai* (2001), a cinematic royal portrait that recounted warfare with Burma and ancient court intrigue involving another strong-willed queen, Thao Srisudachan, highlighting the perils of disunity.

In the print media, protocol rules. A full page portrait of the King or the Queen precedes any magazine content in the issue of their birthdays. Year round, publications report royal events in front of any other society coverage,

top: **Thais revere historical royal heroines, such as Princess Suphankalaya, depicted with her brother, King Naresuan, at a shrine at Pai in the North.** *PCS*

above: **A celebratory billboard for Crown Princess Maha Chakri Sirindhorn near her residence in downtown Bangkok.** *PCS*

right: **Every neighbourhood has a shop supplying approved images of royalty past and present, from paintings to photographs. This one is in Chiang Mai.**

with royals and commoners placed in order of seniority. Rank influences the look of each page. As far as possible, the more senior person shown appears at the top and any facing images must show decorum. In Thai graphic design, etiquette overrides other considerations.

These conventions apply to each new medium. In the West, mass media has helped to undermine the special status of monarchy, yet in Thailand new technology has extended the royal portrait's reach. The king's face is ever present on television, in film and now on the Internet.

Before a movie screens any cinema, everyone without exception stops munching popcorn or rustling bags, and stands up to show respect to His Majesty. On comes a melody every Thai and foreign resident knows by heart. Penned by King Rama IX, the King's Anthem precedes any performance – music, dance, theatre – whether live or recorded. Dance-drama was typically performed in palaces and always dedicated to deities, and the Thai monarch has for centuries been regarded as the *devaraja* (god-king). A different anthem before a performance announces the presence of other royalty.

Each cinema theatre chain commissions its own audio-visual rendition of the King's Anthem. These have evolved from a sequence of slides, though animated stills to full special effects, all concluding with the phrase 'Song Phra Charoen', an equivalent to 'Long Live the King'. Apex theatres show images of the King slotting into place to form 'puzzlepieces' of a bigger pointillist portrait that's revealed only as the anthem culminates. United Artists theatres indicate the lyrics karaoke-style, while Major Cineplex shows the royal portraits in homes and businesses. At 8am and 6pm daily, another tune, the official National Anthem, is broadcast in television clips with royalty joined by state and military imagery. At those times, people stop activity if possible, and stand while it is relayed via loudspeakers across the country.

The King's Birthday on December 5, and the Queen's Birthday on August 12, see the ultimate profusion of royal portraits. Royal pictures adorn gates, doorways, eaves and purpose-built shrines with an altar for royal offerings, whether on a modest abode or covering a smart edifice. The greatest concentration of imagery lines Ratchadamnoen Road between the Grand Palace and the royal residence, Chitrlada Palace. Swathed in fairy lights, potted flowers and coloured ribbons, the huge picture frames exhibit gilded sculptings laden with iconography and the intwined insignia of each royal depicted.

In the era of globalisation, royal portraiture keeps in tune with changing trends. In the 1990s, when post-modernism set in, retro images of royalty appealed to the younger generation, encouraged by fashion magazines that display their high society connections creatively,

such as *Ploy Kaem Phet*, *Hi!* or *Lips*, which ran a mono-chrome cover photograph of the young King Rama IX that was hand-tinted using a Pop Art palette. Lifestyle magazines often select images of royal family members engaging with popular culture, particularly King Bhumibol's passions for jazz, boating, photography and painting. Other editors choose scenes from the royal couple's gilded youth, when they were photographed with the likes of Elvis Presley and Duke Ellington.

Women's magazines increasingly commission royal portfolio features, often involving younger members of the royal family. In place of official photographers, top fashion lensmen and stylists further diversify the range of regal imagery in the public domain. Modernity and the tabloid press haven't affected the Thais' deep respect for their royal family, which retains the affection and mystique that European houses have somewhat lost. The royal presence in every home, publication, performance and business inspires daily reverence.

Garuda

The mythic man-bird adorns bank, business and power pole – by royal appointment

Banks look like no other Thai building. Spotted from afar by its logo atop a scaffold, each bank juts proudly from the shophouses jostling at its shoulders. Like some architectural transplant from Brasilia, the bold cement geometry – parabolic arches, angular porticos, geometric sunshades – creates a futuristic gateway.

Emblazoned upon this modernist visage is a vision of ancient tradition: the Garuda (*Phra Khrut*). Man-eagle mount of Vishnu, this mythological creature cuts a daunting figure in red and gold. Sculpted from wood, metal or fibreglass, each relief image is a work of art, the finer carvings collected as antiques. Wings end in bent-back fingers, feathers flare from rippling biceps, talons splay from powerful feathered legs, the pointed beak opens in a fearsome squawk. Judging by his abdominal six-pack, flying is an effective workout for this fittest of fabulous creatures. An embodiment of power in action, Garuda has many jobs to do.

"It is very prestigious and the personal emblem of the king, who is considered a reincarnation of Vishnu," Trilok Chandra Majupuria explains of *Khrut*'s role as an indicator of divine kingship. "Seen as a motif on royal buildings and as the royal insignia and official seal, Garuda is also the throne carrier." Hence each vehicle of

above: **Garuda with a crown, all outlined in wrought iron on the entrance to Pratunam Market, Bangkok** *PCS*

right: **Garuda incorporated into the Royal Seal upon the Bangkok headquarters of Sri Ayutthaya Bank.**

the king – from Rolls-Royce and royal barge to trains and boats and planes – becomes Garuda, its anthropomorphic features projecting from prow, fuselage, carriage or grille. Rama V had a man-sized Narai riding man-sized Garuda's shoulders on the bonnet of a motorcar.

Garuda activates the King's orders through his image appearing in the Royal Seal since Ayutthayan times and in a standardised design since 1912. Embroidered into throne cushions, ceremonial monks' fans and the cloths hanging from the king's podium, *Khrut* also flutters upon the yellow *maharat* flag indicating the king's presence. Unconquered by even Vishnu, Garuda signifies supreme command of the armed forces when strident atop every sceptre, yet has a caring Buddhist side too. "*Khrut* are often found standing in a row supporting the weight of the massive wall of the ceremonial hall in a monastery under the king's patronage," writes Wisut Busayakul.

As a day-to-day presence, you see him upon the Office of the Counter Corruption Commission logo, for *Khrut* can't be corrupted. Military and civil servant badge bear his insignia, as do district offices, the Immigration Bureau and the Post Office. With wings splayed around the bow of every battleship, he plays figurehead. "As *Khrut* is invincible in war, he becomes an emblem for victory, and is depicted on the war standard for psychological purposes," says Wisut, citing a bird-shaped battle deployment called the *Khrut* formation.

His 12,800 kilometre wingspan (according to the 14th century text *Triphoom Phra Ruang*) literally covers the Kingdom. Garuda images physically mark that domain, and everything within that the state owns. You can't miss his likeness stamped in red over forms, printed on title deeds, pressed into telegraph poles, moulded as milestones, enamelled atop highway signs, in bas relief on bridges and tunnels, perched on bureaucrat office gables, engraved into medals, embossed upon passports and ID, and validating banknotes and coinage since Sukhothai days. Used to certify authenticity, *Khrut* evolved into the letterhead of all official documents, and the validating rubber stamp, as seen on visas and wedding certificates.

Garuda can take several stances, but King Rama VI favoured his sprung-legged dancing posture. That became the standard till today, though King Rama VII preferred *Khrut* flying. Garuda's rounder, fuller-breasted physique has generally tightened into a more defined human musculature since the 1920s, when the art deco Central Post Office bas reliefs of Garuda were carved.

Private companies, even individuals, get to brandish this most official of symbols, too. Like the crown insignia of the British Queen consort and heir, the State Seal has indicated the Royal Warrant since 1889. "The State Seal may be used by royal artisans, such as royal goldsmiths and royal photographers… strictly for their honour, and not as the logo or trademark of their business", says the law, though they can use the wording 'By Appointment to His Majesty the King'. Aside from several banks, he gives kudos to facades and labels like Siam Cement, Osotspa pharmaceuticals, Boon Rawd brewery, Thai Life Assurance, ESSO, Tang To Kang Goldsmith and the East Asiatic Company.

With Garuda so exclusive, some organisations and firms adopt other creatures of the mythical Himaphan Forest fringing sacred Mount Meru. Scholars deduce this domain to be the jungles skirting the Himalayas, with Garuda living in a silk-cotton tree possibly in the Tenasserim Mountains of Southern Thailand. Himaphan harbours many curious cross-breeds, like *mareukontii* (deer-fish), *ngeuak* (mermaid) and *nok hasadeeling*, an elephant-headed bird still constructed in the north as a funereal vehicle for taking late abbots to their pyre.

Thai Airways adopted the *kinnaree* (bird-woman) as the name for its domestic magazine and she's often seen *wai*-ing tourist arrivals. *Singha* the lion roars upon the beer of that name, and the *vayuphak* (phoenix) signifies the Finance Ministry and Krung Thai Bank. Himaphan's *kalapapruek* tree – seen at festivals as a money-tree decked with donated banknotes – was adopted as the name of a restaurant chain. Many more firms utilise the *naga* water serpent. It fears only Garuda, who's often shown with *naga* flailing in its talons. Some experts equate the Garuda with griffins and the *naga* with dragons, while both may have been inspired by dinosaur fossils, which are plentiful in Isaan.

"*Khrut* has in later times gained more popularity with the general public," Wisut writes. "Thus in Bangkok there

is a small shrine San Chao Pho Khrut built around 1942 by a small community to house a Garuda figure found drifting along the Chao Phraya River. At its annual worship day in April or May… compatible birth day animals are sold claiming they would bring the owner good luck, such as the Garuda for those born on Saturdays, a dragon for Sundays, a tiger for Mondays."

Among the many deities Thais adopted from the Hindu pantheon, Garuda remains most pervasive, having evolved from ancient symbol to modern motif. Banks may have relaxed design-wise since recent deregulation, offering coffee and trendy décor, but Garuda remains on the remodelled façades. In similar vein, his winged statue graces shop counters as a trade talisman. The key to Garuda's longevity may lie one of his roles in scripture: the stealer of *amarit*, elixir of immortality.

top and above: **Garuda stenciled upon a utility pole and outlined in relief upon a kilometre stone, showing his territorial reach.**

right: **Other mythical beasts living in the Himaphan Forest with Garuda include** *nok hasadeeling*, **an elephant-headed bird. Such creatures often appear on floats in festive processions; this one at a Northern funeral.**

Day Themes

A colour-coded guide to surviving the eight-day week

Ever wondered why Thais wear yellow on Mondays? Hunted in vain for a haircut on a Wednesday? Found that opening parties seem to clash every Thursday? Noticed how the Buddha postures for each day of the week total eight? In the Thai diary, each day doesn't start blank, but comes colour coded and pre-loaded with premonitions, taboos, and auspicious advice.

Thai day names relate to the gods of the planets in ancient Indian astronomy, each of which has a colour:

Sunday is coloured red for the sun god *Phra Arthit.*
Monday is yellow or cream for the moon god *Phra Chan.*
Tuesday is pink for the Mars god *Phra Angkarn.*
Wednesday is green for the Mercury god *Phra Phut.*
Thursday is orange for the Jupiter god *Phra Pareuhat.*
Friday is sky blue for the Venus god *Phra Suk.*
Saturday is violet for the Saturn god *Phra Sao.*
But what about that eighth weekday?

Conceiving the sun and moon as divine brothers – the oldest ruling by light, the second by night – the ancients reasoned there must be a resentful sibling who literally eclipses his brothers from time to time. The god of eclipses, Phra Rahu, is black, has a dark personality and rules Wednesday night.

Originating with astrologically-divined battle tunics, day colours became a sartorial trait of nobility, reflected in the costume of a colour-themed court dance. Poet Sunthorn Phu eulogised the concept two centuries ago in *Sawasdi Raksa,* a guide to princely conduct still taught in school for its poetry and behavioural rectitude. Today, regal insignia and flags incorporate royal birth colours, such as yellow for King Bhumibol, blue for Queen Sirikit and violet for Princess Sirindhorn. King Chulalongkorn was known for favouring the pink of his Tuesday birth. Devotees at his shrines make pink offerings and wear pink clothes, while the Chulalongkorn University football team dons pink strip.

"Everything pertained to colours, for one's inclination was to select the colour of one's birth day or the colour of the day," wrote cultural guru Phya Anuman Rajadhorn just before Phibun's repression of tradition. The sartorial rainbow declined as Western fashion took hold, but survived in formalwear. "Usually you can tell by the colour in the office what day it is," quipped scholar Vithi Phanichpant, wearing Friday blue. "When wondering what to wear, it's easy for me to think: 'what day is it?'"

Vithi was speaking before millions of Thais started wearing yellow in 2005 to honour King Bhumibol's

Diamond Jubilee and his role as a unifier during the anti-Thaksin protests and 2006 coup. Yellow polo shirts became a worshipful, yet casual uniform, along with yellow rubber wrist bands emblazoned 'We Love the King'.

Children are taught the days by their colours, and absorb constant reminders. The scarves tied around trees, boat prows, spirit house pedestals, and sacred posts are selected from the seven lucky hues (never black). For the prime pillar of a house, this might be the colours of the husband and wife and of the installation day.

Many Thais visit the temple on their weekday of birth. Instead of people lighting the generic joss sticks the *wat* provides, companies now market incense in the days' designated colours – and scents. The packets come printed with the spell of that day, which should be repeated according to that day's astrologically determined 'power number', which also determines how many years each planet rules over your life. Another astrological reason for having an eighth day lies in each day being assigned allotted a compass direction around sacred Mount Meru.

In this gem-mining land, precious stones unite all these concepts, whether adorning the rich or enhancing the cosmic power of amulets and regalia. Each day has a gem the colour of its planet. "For countless centuries, the cultures of India and Southeast Asia have revered the beautiful talisman known as Nava-Ratna... combining the gem stones representing each of the nine planets in sidereal astrology," writes Richard S Brown, who mounts auspicious 'Astral Gemstone Talismans' for affluent luckseekers to brandish. Diamonds are indeed a girl's best friend, but only on a Monday.

Each day was fraught with animistic and Brahmanic taboos in past eras when activities like farming, journeys, building, trade and hunting were subject to portentous interpretations of both predictable phenomena and chance events. Saturday's lucky for washing hair, but unlucky for cutting nails. Sunday's good for entertaining, but bad for sewing. You can cut cloth on Monday, but don't wear new clothes that day. Tuesday's good for blade-making, but not for showing off belongings.

Despite commercial pressures, some Thais observe the saying: "Don't cut things on Wednesday, don't demolish on Thursday, don't cremate on Friday." Barbers may close on Wednesdays, funerals involve many taboos, and black clothing has negative connotations. Since Thursdays's god, Phra Pareuhat, governs teaching, that is the day to hold *wai khru* – homages to masters of an art. Since Thursday symbolises creativity, socialites' diaries fill up that day with bar and restaurant openings, exhibition receptions and product launches.

As Thailand modernised, new day fads emerged. For the past century or so, eight of the Buddha's poses have been paired with days of birth, and the principle recently extended to the ancient practice of releasing trapped animals like birds, fish or eels as a mark of Buddhist compassion. "Vendors outside famous temples like Wat

Rakhang have unofficially categorised animals into days of birth," observes Anucha Thirakanont, a vice dean at Thammasat University. "When I was young there were no categories, but because I was a weak baby, my dad believed that I had to release turtles every month, to get a hard shell. I did that until I was fully grown."

Even modern-minded Thais consult astrologers, monks, shamans or Brahmins to glean the auspicious day (and time) for initiating anything, from a new house or business to marriage or changing their name. Problems may arise if your name omits any consonants and vowels designated for your day of birth. The alphabet's divided between the days, so you can often tell someone's day of birth by how their name is spelled.

top: **Clear resin Buddha images in the colours of the days, which are also matched to particular planets and gems.**

above: **The convenience store chain 7-Eleven adopts day colours in this promotional leaflet for sticking coloured discount tokens.**

Other day themes arise with the increased celebration of birthdays. "The whole idea of birthdays is very un-Thai," Vithi contends. "The calendar is Western and the Thai Zodiac is very Chinese, with the same animals." Some very old folk knows the year and month of their birth, but not the calendar date. To divine fate, all they need know is the day – and its colour.

Bright pigments typify all tropical environments, but in Thailand the meaning of certain colours led to the habit of using these particular hues in much design and decoration. The same intense, usually solid shades of red, yellow, pink, green, orange, cyan or violet recur time after time. This palette is no accident of light, dyes and a cheerful outlook. Colours are a key to the culture.

Monk Baskets
Shopping for offerings in the sacred aisle of the supermarket

After chanting at a ceremony, each monk gets a donation of products. This may be offered on a pedestal tray, but more often comes in a bucket. Coloured saffron like their robes, the bucket has become a symbol of practical faith today. It contains all the monks need, which is proscribed by their vows: things like a robe, soap, incense, candles, matches and flip-flops. If donated before the monks' last mealtime at noon, this *khreuang sangha than* package may contain food; if not it's called a *khreuang tai ya than.*

Monastic retreat is a simple life, a model one in fact. Everything else is surplus, the stuff of craving. Monks stop craving on behalf of everyone else, so it's incumbent on lay people to support their noble poverty. Do that and you *tham boon* (make merit). These karmic air miles improve prospects in the next life, so *tham boon* is popular. Thais often make merit by financial donations, releasing captive animals, or giving food on the monks' morning alms round, but also in rites at festivals, weddings, business blessings or overnight bus pilgrimages to sacred sites.

Thais never unwrap gifts in front of the giver, and the same goes for monks. On opening the orange plastic covering back at the wat, the monk must accept what he gets with equanimity, as with the mixture of food scooped into his alms bowl. Luxuries, adornments and intoxicants are taboo.

Tham boon is meant to be humble supplication. And a bucket's considered more useful than the metal offering pedestal used for such rites as holding the protective white string that monks tie around wrists and places being blessed. In theory, monks shouldn't handle gold, silver or money. Yet senior monks often get better products. After all, donating to novices accrues less merit. Monk lifestyle increasingly reflects secular tastes. In some notorious cases, abbots may be seen in Mercedes, while in 2003, the National Buddhism Office saw the need to stress a ban on monks drinking alcohol, having dinner, walking on beaches, cheering at boxing matches, publicly using a mobile phone, or browsing department stores.

right: **A monk unloads baskets of everyday supplies donated as offerings by hosts of blessings and ceremonies.**

facing page, clockwise from top left: **A monk supply shop near a temple. Ritual paraphernalia stocked with saffron coloured monk baskets in a Tesco-Lotus hypermarket** (*PCS*). **A miniature monk basket. Monk buckets printed with the** *mantra* **chanted during the offering ceremony.**

While the gifts are good and practical, the intent isn't always selfless. With karma in mind, Thais seek to get back in kind what they offer. Give candles, become enlightened. Give medicine, gain health. Give food, never starve. Give flowers, gain beauty. Give money, gain wealth. To donate a Buddha image brings future wisdom, while financing a *viharn* chapel gains sanctuary from harm. These come only in your next life, unfortunately.

But do the math. One package per monk. Several blessings a week. Multiple monks per event (at birthdays they number the celebrant's age plus one, to ensure longevity). That's an awful lot of buckets. And soap. And incense. Monks do keep very clean, but they limit their robes to two and just how much toothpaste can a mouth take? Where does the bucket surplus go?

What's not required goes into temple storage, or may go to charity, a poorer wat, or the local needy. Anything left may be given to a nearby shopkeeper, who in turn makes equivalent monetary merit to the temple fund. This ad hoc market operates informally, and isn't a fixed system with dealers. As for where the fund surplus goes, some wonder, and scandals do get reported.

The point of *khreuang sangha than* is not the gift, giver or receiver, but the sincere act of giving. *Tham boon* oils the wheel of life. "To me giving without taking something back is real happiness," said Sunee Tuampuemphol at the Pithee Kong Khao spirit appeasing ceremony in Sri Racha. "This tradition helps me understand the genuine concept of merit making."

Supporting monks in their mission to live without possessions or ego has, however, been commodified into a standardised ritual by secular lifestyles in which the gaining of possessions and boosting of ego seem to get more attention than following Buddhist moderation. As society gets more materialist, *khreuang sangha than* has flourished as a tangible token of faith. Not only does it contain consumer products, the monk bucket is itself a consumer product.

There's now no need to assemble the supplies your-self. Since the coming of chainstores, ready-made packs get sold from shops near a temple. Any foods are dried or tinned, not fresh, as was the norm until recent decades. A huge range of baskets fills supermarket aisles, alongside sacred powders, cloths, and spirit house dancer offerings. Plastic cups, plates and tubs come moulded in shades of saffron. Tesco-Lotus superstores even stock sachets of gold leaf, regalia for sprinkling holy water, and urns for your loved one's ashes. Packages cater to every budget and taste, from 99 baht lunchboxes to 999 baht buckets and innovative designs like saffron-hued first aid kits. At funerals, instead of wreaths (a Western import), you can offer blankets folded into animals, or towels shaped as gibbons, for re-use by the monks. The latest idea is to give satchels of study materials for temple school pupils.

Some people forget the *sangha than* prayer to recite on giving the basket. Conveniently, supermarket monk buckets contain the text – printed on the checkout label alongside the price and bar code.

Amulet Collectors
Lucky charms as a lifestyle

When 443 Thai troops deployed on humanitarian duty to Iraq in 2003 they were heavily protected; not just by armour, but by over 6,000 amulets. In an ancient rite, army commander General Sarayud gave each recruit clay Buddha images wrapped in sacred cloth depicting cabalistic *yantra* diagrams and inscriptions in *khom* (archaic Khmer). Many of the soldiers already bore magic tattoos, amulets or a hem from their mother's skirt, which is believed to disable weapons. Among the 46 amulets Staff Sgt Phetchai Srikhem carried to Iraq is one of only eight golden Garuda images issued by King Rama IX. It's the centerpiece of eleven amulets slung around his neck. He's not unusual. Amulet collection is a hobby and also an industry worth ten billion baht ($250 million) a year.

Pre-Buddhist inhabitants carried animistic charms to ward off harm – or to win riches, luck or ladies. But the business in amulets, particularly in mass-produced Buddhist tablets, boomed only in the past half century. They're traded from approximately 10,000 stalls and shops across the land, some fetching huge prices.

According to Phya Anuman Rajadhon, amulets come in four classes. The first are natural oddities: cat's eye stones; peculiar seeds; antlers; teeth or tusks found lodged in trees; transformed metals like quicksilver; and

khot stones found in animals or plants. Class II are images of the Buddha or monks; Class III need a spell to be activated and encompass trade talismans, folded palm leaf charms, phallic *palad khik* and *yantra* diagrams on cloth, jackets or tattoos. Another, *takrud*, is an embossed or engraved metal foil that's rolled onto a chord or, in a miniscule form called *salika*, inserted under the skin. Class IV are *waan yaa*, plant roots used in shamanic medicine, black magic and the making of amulets.

The Buddha amulet may come in cast bronze, carved wood, stone or tiger tooth, or most commonly as *phra phim*, clay votive tablets in rectangular, pointed, oval or bell shape. "Originally it was not meant for protection of the wearer, but for perpetuating Buddhism," says scholar Vithi Phanichphant of the unfired votive tablets moulded by early Mahayana Buddhists. Those were uncertain times of constant warfare and forced migration, when the Buddhist message might conceivably be lost. "They buried these amulets of the Buddha and inscriptions of his preachings in *chedi* (pagodas) so that Buddhism would survive for eternity." Now excavated and widely distributed in a time of materialism, these Buddhist time capsules to some degree fulfill their intended purpose to preserve faith.

Phra phim are made of more than clay. They may contain gold, pollen, insects, dried garlands, gem dust, powdered *waan* herbs, or ashes of palm leaf scriptures, bound together with banana paste or betel chewed by a respected monk. Primaeval cave tablets were moulded from the ashes of ancestors and shamans, though tablets today can veer towards novelty. Some are encrusted with gems. Newspapers have reported tablets pressed from methamphetamine as a blasphemous means to smuggle. "The latest substances are fossilised dinosaur bone or mammoth tusk. So it's the oldest Buddhist image in the world," Vithi chuckles. "Older than the Buddha!"

Ingredients influence the price, along with aesthetics, age, condition, number of pressings, purported powers, and the stature of the sponsoring monk. All classes gain potency from ritual blessing. Amulets made by the king, such as those King Rama IX crafted from sacred substances including his own hair, need no further blessing.

No living monk dispenses more charms than the venerable Luang Phor (Respected Father) Khoon of Wat Baan Rai, Nakhon Ratchasima. Aside from blessing politicians to use his image, words, taped sermons and amulets for electioneering, he issues millions of clay self-portraits in lucky series titled *goo hai mueng* (I give to you), *goo rak mueng* (I love you) and *goo hai mueng ruay* (I hope you get rich). "The abbot does not give special favour to particular candidates. Locals just assume the monk likes that candidate so they give him support,"

above: **Amulets are often strung in auspicious groupings on chains, as seen on the stand of an amulet case and chain maker in Khorat.**

left: **A sidewalk vendor with wares carefully organised and ready for inspection with an eyeglass.**

assures Chamlong Krutkhunthod of the Thai Rak Thai party. Coachloads of devotees line up before dawn to receive his blessing via a tap on the head with his rolled-up newspaper. Most of the thousand-plus visitors per day buy amulets like plastic bodhi leaves and faux banknotes bearing the Abbot's likeness. The proceeds have funded 400 million baht worth of social projects as well as his temple's multi-million baht *viharn*. Paying for good works is the justification monks cite for selling amulets.

Luang Phor Khoon's innovative amulets typify changes in how people want their luck. "In days past, charms usually boasted only one particular magical power. Today's talismans must offer a hodge-podge of magic, like the 7-Eleven one-stop-shop," writes Sanitsuda Ekachai of a mammoth tusk coin devised by a jewellery importer. "Responding to clients' varied needs, the anti-harm symbol offers safety while the mammoth ivory gives a sense of sanctity and uniqueness. The image of King Chulalongkorn, apart from promising business success, helps the coin owners feel closer to the centre of prestige and status."

Revered for its AK-47 repelling charms, one design from Bangkok's Wat Pak Nam was produced in huge quantities, from 84,000 in 1950 to three million in 1984. Though sales were slower of the five million released in 1992, at 100 baht a pop the income is enormous.

Attracted by the profits, laymen are edging monks out of amulet production and earnings. As with artists' paintings, death of a reputed monk gives a special boost to dealers' margins. Five particular amulets earn the most reverence, and may fetch from half a million baht up. Of these the most prized 'emperor of amulets', the Phra Somdet Wat Rakhang, was created in the late 19th century ago by Luang Phor Toh, the occult master who reputedly exorcised the ghost Nang Nak. At the first ever auction of amulets in 2002, one reaped a record 86.3 million baht.

The amulet market was then recovering from the 1997 economic crash, which briefly halved its volume, value and vending outlets. Content was also debased, with cheaper tablets being produced using less gold. Founder of the post-crash 'Market For The Former Rich', Wasun Potipimpanon innovated further in 2003. He barters amulets for Mercedes Benz cars, paying or receiving the price difference in cash. "Diversification into popular amulets is profitable for long-term investment," says Wasun of this lucky liquid asset.

Livelihoods depend on telling an original from a reprint or those stolen, copied or faked. Hence the

above left: **Amulets arrayed upon a sacred yantra cloth bearing cabalistic designs.**

above: **This vendor treats the phone as a modern talisman.**

left: **Magazines on the multi-billion baht amulet trade also relate tales of the supernatural.**

certification of amulets and noting of buyers' ID. Experts rove amulet markets with microscopes to test their authenticity for a 20 baht fee. Half a dozen magazines advertise prime pieces, swap gossip on discoveries, print going rates and recount miraculous tales of amulet-assisted escapes, often with bloody photos of near-death incidents. The first thing asked of an accident survivor is "*khao sai phra arai*" – "What amulet does he wear?" Mass market newspapers, especially *Khao Sod*, devote pages to the trade, though the government threatens a clamp-down on far-fetched claims.

Vendors, however, bristle at accusations of 'trading' in religious artifacts. They claim to 'rent' amulets, much as monks shouldn't 'handle money' but graciously 'accept donations' for amulets they don't, technically, 'sell'. Their latest term of art is 'worship fee'.

No qualms, though, about the case and chain being cash-convertible. Long a means of portable wealth and face-gaining display, yellowish high-carat gold is the container of choice, though silver or gilt-effect plastic does the job. Neck chains, however, are an import from barely a century ago. Thais wore sacred threads on the crown, wrist, ankle, bicep or waist, or from right shoulder to left hip like the Brahmin sash. "Wearing it round the neck is very Western. You don't find it in Ayutthaya, or even in the early Bangkok period," explains Vithi. "I think it grew from the Western fashion for wearing a cross. Faced with that missionary symbol, what do you wear as a protection and expression of your Buddhism?"

Along with every enthusiasm, though, come addicts. Necks sag with a lucky nine amulets on heavy chains; hips bristle with *palad khik* and *takrud* on auspiciously knotted chord; tablets almost hide the dials of a car. While it seems you can't have too much luck, you can show too much face. Thais mock such show offs as a "*too thong klueanthee*" (portable gold cabinet), and may regard those brandishing excessive amulets as hoodlums in activities requiring extra protection. Other collectors may revel in the aesthetics, the piety or the profits.

At some point these protective charms themselves need protecting. Choochart Marksamphan acquired so many outstanding pieces that he turned his home at Phutthamonthon into the Lord Buddha Images Museum. "These amulets do not belong to me alone but to all Thais," he says. "I am but the custodian for posterity."

As to whether they work, deaths of a wearer would often be put down to the spell having been negated. Not observing the monk's moral instructions could undo it, as would ducking under a clothesline that held women's underwear. Or they left on their amulet while draining bodily fluids, whether in the toilet or during sex.

In any case, karma works in mysterious ways. In February 2004, *Thai Rath* newspaper luridly reported a soldier non-fatally shot by a southern separatist as being saved by his Luang Phor Thuad amulet. The *Bangkok Post* simply reported the officer's terrible injuries. So, was he lucky or unlucky? Either way, his tale enters the folklore that keeps amulets at the heart of the culture.

Taxi Altars
The colourful world
of spiritual road insurance

Riding a Thai taxi is a religious experience. Some might suggest it's a near-death experience. For the driver, it's literally tempting fate. Particularly when he lifts both hands off the wheel to *wai* a shrine while cornering.

Spinning a steering wheel wrapped in sacred scarves, dials obscured by amulets, he hurtles his taxi inches behind a similarly bedecked pick-up, comfortable in the protection of the supernatural powers he's summoned. That is, until his time is up. "Accidents, in the Thai scheme of things, don't just happen," observes pundit Mont Redmond. "They are hatched in the past, and it is only the suddenness with which they fly up in your face that leaves you breathless."

Breathless from even the shortest journey defying the rules of the road, foreigners riding a taxi take an inadvertent tour through the byways of Thai culture. A wheel determines this path, though it's not the steering wheel, but the Buddhist wheel of fortune. And the driver is on auto-pilot, otherwise known as karma. Taking on board a stranger's karma throws the driver's fate awry. To cover eventualities, spirit offerings in a taxi tend to end up greater than in a private car, like the public transport premium on motor insurance.

"The strength of the Thais' belief in their talismans is reflected in their expressionistic driving styles," Philip Blenkinsop observes in *The Cars That Ate Bangkok*. "Their seemingly total disregard of street signs, traffic lights, lanes and other motorists can of course be viewed two different ways: the Western way, irresponsible and negligent with an almost blatant disregard for human life, or the Thai way, as sort of subconscious poetic blend of technology and karma on wheels at high speed where only the dead deserve to die." In which event, a shrine at the scene – replenished with garlands from other devout drivers – turns a death experience into an ongoing religious one.

"There are two different ways to go about avoiding death on Bangkok streets," Blenkinsop identifies: "*Pok pong*, being magic or spiritual protection to guard against all perils, and *pong gun*, steps taken to prevent accidents such as the wearing of seat-belts and helmets. Not surprisingly, *pong gun* takes a back seat to *pok pong*." Behind this lurks an historical anomaly.

The taxi is culturally still a boat. The steering column doubles as the prow, the vehicle's sacred 'head' where offerings go. Hawked by gangster-run kids for 20 baht at intersections, the long, ribboned garland looped around the taxi mirror is not the kind presented to a Buddha image. Since Thai culture is aquatic, the garland, sacred

below: Garland offerings to the journey goddess, *Mae Yanang*, typically hang with amulets from the rearview mirror.

right: Currency bears the King's head, so it's also auspicious to cover the dashboard in coins, here with banknotes lining the ceiling and amulets on the taxi license and pillars. *PP*

strings and tricolour scarves honour *Mae Yanang*, the protective spirit of the boat, and by extension, any kind of vehicle: car, motorcycle, bus, *tuk-tuk*, train or plane.

Traffic jams, too, have a long history in Thailand. Name a thoroughfare more freeform than the floating market. Boat traffic, followed by rickshaw jams, were no less chaotic than today's car congestion, past journals report. Thai road manners typify the commotion caused when the linear, rule-governed, first-come-first-served egalitarian Western ways contradict the circular, con-forming, hierarchical mandala of Thai culture, where the biggest vehicle, like the biggest face, goes first. And goes anywhere it likes.

Powered by technology, the habits of slower times turned lethal, particularly when fuelled by caffeine drinks and *yaa baa* amphetamines. In the past, the limits of human strength prevented a boat or rickshaw from speeding, and the watery highway meant collisions harm-lessly glanced, with no lanes determining their course. Taxis behave as if nothing's changed. They tailgate and overtake at high speed with inches to spare; they blithely straddle white lines without indicating, or cut across three lanes and screech to a halt at the merest hint of a hand politely beckoning palm down. With driving lessons an affront to face and licenses easily bought, many Thais intuitively steer their car as if on water.

Boats, trucks and buses display ritual charms for all to see, while taxis internalise the talismans. Blessed by a monk at an auspicious date and time, the taxi cabin accumulates layers of propitious paraphernalia. The inaugural blessing – gold leaf and daubed powder, topped by the *unalom* (a looping, flamelike flourish from the Buddha's forehead) – may last for years on the ceiling above the handbrake, or soon flake from a fluffy velour lining. Vinyl ceilings provide a more adhesive panel, also for stickers and plastic-sheathed pictures. From the sun visors rearward, cabs display the faces of kings, monks and deities gazing benevolently down upon driver and passenger, while others paste up news clippings, foreign

banknotes, or snapshots of their family and youthful exploits. Stickers of the amulet-making monk Luang Phor Khun bear the slogan "*yaa khap raeo*" (don't drive fast).

If that weren't reassuring enough, more such faces festoon the windscreen, sharing pane-space with stickers of bodhi leaves or faux banknotes bearing a venerable monk's face. Bronze or plaster images of monks, the Buddha or Kings Rama V and IX sit on the dashboard or dangle from the rearview mirror, in a red and gold plastic case trailing a red tassel. A string of Chinese Mahayana Buddhist meditation beads clatters against a magic *yantra* cloth of red, white or saffron bearing cabbalistic text and diagrams. Because these pendulous charms tend to swing, the driver often grabs them at just the moment he needs to change gear, causing a hazard to navigation, no matter how lucky they are for business.

As the taxi is a sales space, you may find common trade talismans like bottle gourds, fish traps, *palad khik* or string coiled in the shape of an *unalom*. "Red is lucky color for Chinese, and 9 is a lucky number for Thai," says driver Wichai of his red 100 baht with serial number ending in 9. "Maybe it'll bring me fortune." Nine is also lucky on number plates, where the two letters may also happen to spell a word, though authorities don't issue ones that read *chon* (crash), *tok* (fall) or *dot* (fart).

At Bangkok's cheap metered fares Wichai must earn at least B1,200-B1,400 per day to cover liquid petroleum gas and car rental for an eight-our shift to take-home B400-B600. Rented taxis bear the body colours of the company (red/blue, burgundy/white, green), while owner-driver taxis are green and yellow. The latter reap B1,600-B1800 a day due to their flexible hours, plus B500-B600 from subletting the taxi, minus the cost of the car. It's always a Japanese brand, though Honda doesn't allow taxi use.

Having a captive audience, the driver may turn into a tout. Ads hang from the headrests or peep from map pockets, inviting you to tourist traps, massage parlours or gem shops with prices you wouldn't (and shouldn't) believe. Some drivers prefer to rip-off passengers by tampering with the meter or refusing to use it. Inflated fares may, however, be passing on the cost of taxis having to pay bribes to wait at tourist or nightlife areas. Safety is another concern after a spate of taxi rapes. There was a scheme to fence in the driver, but it proved impractical. Besides, that would interrupt driver-passenger patter.

"Where you come from?" "Are you married yet?" "Do you have children?" For *farang*, this holy trinity of questions in the taxi inquisition leads relentlessly to "Do you like Thailand", "How much do you earn?" and, crucially, "Which you like: Liverpool or Manchester United?" Conversation also reveals one of the reasons why drivers often don't know the way; many are fresh off the bus from Buriram with very little training. Once largely Chinese, drivers now hail mostly from Isaan.

Passing the hours scouring the streets, drivers tune into the folk music station, Luuk Thung FM, or the talk shows, phone-ins, traffic reports and lost property announcements on one of the taxi community stations, Jor Sor 100, Ruam Duay Chuay Kun (Let's Help Each Other), or the less general-interest police frequency Sor Wor Por. Devout drivers may even listen to Buddhist radio sermons, though the accent is usually on *sanuk*.

"I sometimes get passengers who want an absolutely quite taxi, without even the radio on. That annoys me," remarks Suwit Thongthim, who converted his taxi into a karaoke lounge, complete with pulsating green light. The microphone connects to a micro-TV, so at no extra cost passengers can croon Chinese, Japanese or Western hits, but mostly Thai love songs. Another driver did his cab out as a disco, with glitter ball, blue neon bulb and silver foiled condoms, presumably for passengers to take rather than use on the back seat.

Taxis exude many aromas. Vinyl seat covers emit heady esters, garlands emanate jasmine, pyramidal 'air fresheners' sweat chemicals, and on the back shelf lie pandanus palm leaves – a natural deodoriser. Often these help mask a whiff from beneath the driver's seat, where lurks the Comfort 2000 – a urinal for relief in traffic jams.

The dashboard plays host to assemblages of souvenirs, cute cartoon mascots, model cars, wax fruit, heart shaped stickers or toy helicopters with blades whirring at the air vents. The dash may also be carpeted to stop overheating.

Vying for attention, the vinyl seat covers in pink, blue, green, red or yellow, have piping in a clashing colours. On the rear parcel shelf sit round spangled neon-hued *noon* (cushions). Provided partly for practical comfort, these cushions are another amulet, for *noon* also means support.

An example of folk art, the customised taxi inspired Thai artist Navin Rawanchaikul to create the Navin Taxi Gallery. In the late 1990s, he commissioned artists to make installations inside a taxi that people could hail at random. One year saw seats padded with monosodium glutamate, the next a Buddhist mural covered the ceiling. Looped video from a camera on a model car speeding round a race track struck a chord with people stuck in traffic. As taxi décor shows, when the vehicle can't move, the Thai driver explores his imagination.

top and left: **Dashboards host assemblages of Buddha, monk and royal images. A miniature of King Rama V stands beside a banknote portrait of King Rama IX.**

above: **Back shelves of cars often feature glittery round cushions as their name, *noon*, also means support. Like many offerings, this pair comes in gold and silver, meaning sun and moon.** *PCS*

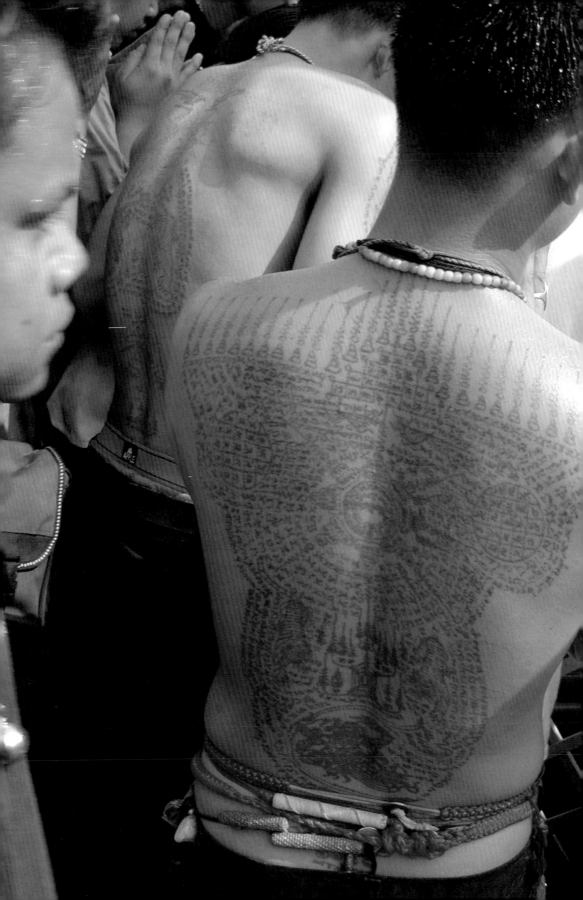

Magical Tattoos
Spells on skin make the wearer invincible – except against fashion

You are what you wear. While apt in fashion, the saying is literally true if it's a Thai tattoo in which you're clad. Imbued with magical powers, the arcane *roi sak* (tattoos) possess their owners – mostly men – at intense moments like combat, love or ritual. The full menagerie of tattooed creatures comes alive at February's *wai khru* (teacher honouring ceremony) at Wat Bang Phra in Nakhon Chaisri. The late abbot, Luang Phor Phoem, was a tattoo master with a cult following.

A tiger inscribed across his chest, one inexhaustible man repeatedly hurtles barefoot towards soldiers braced around the outdoor altar. Incisor teeth flaring, fingers ricked like claws, he pounces. Eyes rolled back after vomiting into a bag, a downy chinned youth flings himself from meditation posture to the ground. Slinking like the *naga* serpent across his shoulder, he's oblivious to the gravel nicking his dusty flesh. A whoop and out from the hundreds of seated devotees scampers a nimble monkey medium. Channelling Hanuman – the *Ramayana* epic's simian warrior pricked upon his back – he trails one arm like a tail. In quick succession they come: hopping frogs belch, a phoenix glides with arms outstretched, a hefty elephant man waddles deftly, his arm impersonating a trunk, amulets jangling upon his belly.

The soldiers scoop each flailing creature off the ground while attendants stroke his ears to dispel the trance. Dizzied, the possessed men drift back into the throng. After a few hours, the tattoo festival culminates in a mass surge to the altar, calmed only by holy water, pumped from vat sized alms bowls through a hose along the abbot's broom-length sprinkling brush.

All Thai arts feature annual *wai khru* ceremonies, and *khrob khru* rites, when a master's disciple is initiated by having the mask of the art's presiding deity placed on his head. In *khon* dance, the mask is of a character from the *Ramayana*, whereas mediums don the mask of the spirit they channel. The tattoo master, who may be a monk or a layman, would place on a student's head the gap-tooth gold mask of *ruesii* (the wise old hermit). Surrounded by occult artifacts, the master may also wear a *ruesii* mask and tiger skin robe while tattooing mythical creatures, cabalistic diagrams and *khathaa* (Vedic spells) upon skin stretched taut by tattooed followers.

The script is *khom*, used by the ancient Khmer, who Chinese visitors report wore tattoos in hand-combat two millennia ago. Like all amulets, it requires activation by the tattooist, who murmurs incantations in *khom* while he wields a two-foot steel needle, which might not be sterilised for the next supplicant. The ink, derived from charcoal, lampblack or Indian sepia, has historically been mixed with herbs, sap, lizard skins or buffalo bile, but many of today's practitioners claim to add a disturbing special ingredient, *nam mun phrai* – the chin fat of cadavers from violent deaths.

The first mark is the personal symbol of the master, who keeps secret the location of the tattoo's all-powerful 'heart' and may disguise the full version of the spell by omitting, abbreviating or swapping letters. Through such ploys, he can weaken a tattoo requested by someone untrustworthy. An unintentional mistake, however, brings very bad luck. Since most customers are poor, the price is low, and typically is divisible by or ends in a six.

One design may take weeks of 20 minute sessions to complete, each requiring an ordeal to activate the charm. This he does by blowing air or hot oil upon the bleeding weal, then slapping and rubbing it while muttering incantations. An effective tattoo should withstand a blow from a pretty sharp 'spirit sword'. To renew a weakened

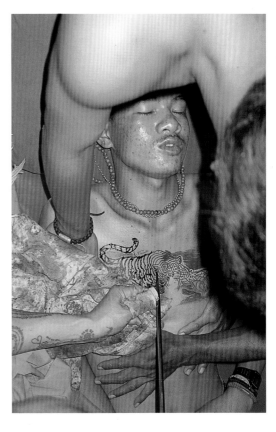

anti-clockwise from left:
Entranced devotees of the late abbot of Wat Bang Phra in Nakhon Chaisri enact the spirits depicted in their tattoos: *ruesii* **the hermit; an elephant; a lizard; and another** *ruesii***. The temple's annual** *wai khru* **rite is now known as the Tattoo Festival.** *PCS*

spell he may incise a further image atop the original. Tattoos jabbed in jail may pack macho pride, but would wield no magic power if the tattooist isn't qualified to activate the spell.

Supplicants might choose the image – either drawn freehand, traced on rice paper, or block-printed – though it's more likely to be determined by the tattoo master according to personality type and needs. "A dragon represents strength and wisdom, a wild boar is fierce, an eel can slip away from danger, a lion has both dignity and strength," writes Marlane Guelden. "Traditional Thai kick boxers favour the magical monkey for his supernatural leaps and powerful legs."

So where to place which image? Just as traditional costumes are a representation of sacred mythical Mount Meru, so *roi sak* conform to appropriate places on the body. Being most sacred, the head may host Buddha images or the *unalom* on the third eye, where Lord Buddha had a tuft of hair. Angels and mythical beasts

populate chest and back, lesser subjects and charms adorn arms, hands and abdomen, with cabalistic diagrams and inscriptions found throughout, including on the legs, feet and even penis.

"Sexual and animal tattoos, particularly when drawn between the waist and knees, are considered dangerous and aggressive," Guelden discovers. "Like other phallic symbols in Thailand, these tattoos are not necessarily related to sex but instead may connote power. One favourite sexual tattoo shows a penis with semen while another depicts a naked woman with an enlarged vulva. The penis drawing sometimes has legs and a tail, similar in design to some common amulets. A special tattoo can be applied to a man's sexual organ. Surprisingly, the procedure isn't considered especially painful among the tattoo cognoscenti."

Heavily tattooed men are considered vain or addicts, because a minimal symbol would suffice. It's the spells that matter. Call it spiritual insurance, for most seek *roi sak* for invincibility. As to whether they work, cynics might concede that reciting the spell at moments of peril might conceivably bestow sufficient clarity of mind to survive.

Aside from protection, some get tattooed to gain business or lure women, for certain images project *metta* – the Buddhist principle of loving kindness that Thais believe can defeat hostile energy. *Metta* is often embodied by the gecko, whose call kindly heralds danger in what you were about to do – a taboo some Thais still observe. Until a century ago most men, even nobles and earlier royalty, sported tattoos just in case, as Phya Anuman Rajadhon recalled. "Travel in the old days outside ones village was an adventure with danger from both human beings and the *phii* (evil spirits). One had to be a law unto oneself in some outlying places."

Those who goes under the needle now, tend to have dangerous professions. Bare-chested labourers display their decorated musculatures while heaving boxes onto trucks, steering baskets through markets, toting bricks upon teetering bamboo scaffolds. Inked curlicues stretch across the flexed fingers of motorcycle taxi drivers, who are confident that they need fear no threat to life, limb, or the passenger's kneecaps. Calligraphic *unalom* peep beyond the pressed collar of the security guard. Police and the military officially avoid tattooed recruits, though some subsequently get inked.

Society most identifies the tattoo's bullet-stopping, knife-rebuffing acumen powers, however, with hooligans, hitmen, gangsters. Increasingly bourgeois Thailand looks down on the culture of laborers, seeing it as déclassé at best, criminal at worst. "Why else wear a tattoo unless you're in a dodgy line of work?" they shudder.

Their visceral fear of tattoos is so widespread it's marketable. Oxide Pang's ethnic action movie *Maha-Ut* (2003) is named after the most venerated protective *roi sak*, which emphasises the vows made to the tattoo master to use its spell only for good or in defence. Break those vows and the tattoo becomes powerless – the usual explanation when an inked man gets wounded or dies. "The tattoo's power is also in jeopardy when a man urinates or has intercourse," Guelden writes. "Because of the threatening magical properties of women, tattooed men must remain in the top position during intercourse. They must also avoid contact with women's underwear and menstrual blood." Women, however may be tattooed, though by a lay master not a monk.

Historically the source of Buddhist tattoos, monks face increasing pressure from authorities to relinquish such superstitions. The squeamish Thai bourgeoisie would rather see *roi sak* projected on movie screens than injected on skins.

When a monk tattooed several pre-pubescent boys in 2002 to protect them from the endemic fights between vocational school gangs, the public was aghast. It was thought that boys curious to test their 'invincibility' would perpetuate the cycle of violence. At issue was not the tattoos' supernatural power, but social stigma. "How would they get decent jobs?" wailed the families, pointing to the tattoo removal scars on their sons. Tattoos have become a scapegoat for social ills. And in a culture emphasising surface, as Guelden points out, "simply taking off a shirt and exposing a ferocious animal tattoo is considered provocation for a fight in some quarters."

In Japan, full-body tattoos became so identified with *yakuza* gangsters, that the art became anathema, banned in public baths. With Thailand's government pledging to bar monks from performing tattooing rituals, *roi sak* is another tradition on the wane. Changes have been coming for a long time. Tattoos for marking slaves and corvee labourers were abolished by King Rama V and the non-magical Lanna tattoo is almost extinct. In the north, Lanna men wore skimpy loincloths in order to display the indigo patterns covering all but a few inches around waist and thigh. "Fish scale patterns predominated around the Mekong, a caged tiger motif to the west," Lanna specialist Vithi Phanichphant explains of a style that spread across Laos and Burma's Shan State, too.

"At one time a teenage boy was not considered mature or attractive to the opposite sex until he had undergone the pain of tattooing as a rite of passage – sometimes eased with the help of opium," says Guelden. "A northern proverb says, 'ten or even twenty blankets are not equal to the warmth of the tattooed leg of my beloved'." As a statement of manliness it's no longer in tune with the times. Fopping like a winsome boy band is now a more effective babe magnet.

The respectable aficionado does still have options. Aside from hiding them beneath clothing, they can get an invisible tattoo. That seems a contradiction in terms if you think of tattoos as essentially for display, but not if you want to avoid ostracism without losing the magic powers. Use sesame oil instead of ink, and the design heals into a faint welt, the spell undiluted. Secretly, you may be a tiger. But in the office, who would know?

left: In the Tattoo Festival at Nakhon Chaisri, suppliants pray in the yard outside Wat Bang Phra during the abbot's sermon. Several wear multiple amulets. *PCS*

above: **Possessed followers charge the altar, hands ricked in trance, to be calmed by the abbot. He sprays holy water from huge vats through sacred sprinkling brushes fitted with hoses.** *PCS*

Palad Khik
The eternal power of phallic charms

A vendor rummages for change in a basket, where she keeps her mobile phone and a wooden phallus. A man strolls by with a little lingum looped to his belt. At the 'rain-seeding' rocket festivals in Isaan, revellers – men, women, children – tease each other with saucy, spring-loaded penis contraptions. Freud would have foundered in this land where the male member isn't suppressed into unconscious symbolism, but sculpted, worshipped for fertility or protection, and brandished as a lucky charm.

Phallic worship occurs in many ancient cultures and Thais blend two traditions: *palad khik*, an animistic fertility symbol; and *lingum*, the phallic form of the Hindu god Shiva. Lowland, water-borne Thai originally carved or tattooed images of male and female genitals for protection. Parents hung *palad khik* as amulets around a boy's waist, so the erect shape and red head would fool bad spirits that the vulnerable child was an adult.

"When we bathed in canals we believed in the water ghost *phrai nam*," explains Supakij Phukaeow, a trader in phallic antiques. "It pulls kids down and sucks their blood if they don't wear a *palad khik*. Girls wore *chaping*

(a decorative shield)." Female charms are very rare and fewer boys today wear what translates as an 'honorary deputy'. Still, many men – educated urbanites included – dangle one or more inside or outside their waistband, at a spirit-distracting distance from their real deputy.

Anatomically correct, though styled in some bizarre ways, *palad khik* come in many a substance, colour and texture. Originating probably as 2-D diagrams on cloth or tattoos, they may be cast in bronze, brass, plaster, steel or gold, moulded from clay, or carved from wood, bone, ivory, marble, horn or black coral. "The type of wood is important," Supakij stresses. Teak resists insects and its name evokes the word 'honour'. Dense, shiny black wood has strong power, while a knobbly, twisted parasite growth on mango trees is favoured for carved phallic trees with branches ending in male 'fruit'.

The more heads the better, especially in odd numbers. A wooden peacock fans a tail of penile plumes. Penises combine with penises in endless variety. Rearing up on hind legs, some sport animal riders or may boast a glans on each limb. Tattooed ones often have wings, while tales

Wearers often interpret their *palad khik* as a *lingum*, in a prestigious association with the Khmer royal heritage that the Thai adopted seven centuries ago. While Buddhist Thais worship Shiva usually as a figurative statue, Hindu-style prang towers like Bangkok's symbol, Wat Arun, are clearly phallic. Many see the *lak meuang* (city pillar) of each town as a *lingam*, having a stylised bulbed tip and being presided over by Brahmin priests. Not all agree. While *lingam* are typically standstone, city pillars are generally wooden and resemble the guardian spirit pillars typical of Southern China and still found in Tai tribes never Indianised by the Khmer. "When the Thai consider the *lak meuang* they do not find its shape obviously phallic," writes anthropologist BJ Terwiel. "There was no shame involved in mentioning what Firth calls 'the instruments of life'. What is 'obviously' a phallus in western Europe need not necessarily be so in Thailand." On the other hand, *palad khik* are unambiguously realistic.

Supakij admits that not everyone understands. "Many think its only a penis or dildo. The young ask why I trade them. Some, particularly women, complain it's dirty."

abound of carved *palad khik* that can swim. A popular form is the priapic monkey. "It's the most clever animal, always getting what it wants," says Supakij, noting how phalli with legs have mobility to find money, customers, luck, sex, offspring. "All monkeys are like *jao chuu* – lotharios – always wanting more wives."

And some people always want more *palad khik*. A few years ago, a man suspected of concealing weapons at Ngamwongwan in Bangkok was forced at police gun-point to open his bugling coat, only to reveal literally thousands of phallic charms. Like amulet aficionados, collectors relish the workmanship, wood grain and inscriptions in ancient Khmer. Bruno Friedman of UNESCO quotes a magazine comparison between ones made by revered monks, "stating those of Luang Phor Luer are superior, with a fine bend. Those accredited to Luang Phor Ee are cruder and straighter."

Size, of course, matters. Practicality aside, wealth and the offering's purpose can dictate the scale, which ranges from a centimetre to a metre long. Some say small ones are just as potent, since it's the spell that counts. "There are many kinds of *khathaa* (spell), which depend on the monk," says Supakij. "During an exorcism, a monk will press the *palad khik* to the forehead to remove the ghost. But for everyday use most don't need *khatha*; you just concentrate hard and wish." People buy them for *saneh haa* (attraction): of customers, luck, money, popularity, women, whatever. Others help in lottery divining or protection, perhaps against road accidents if swinging from the rearview mirror. If people giggle at a *palad khik* it supposedly means the spell's working, but Supakij says beware if it's not. "If bitten by a snake, put the *palad khik* on the fang holes and it feels like the venom is being sucked out. Of course, if it's not blessed you die!"

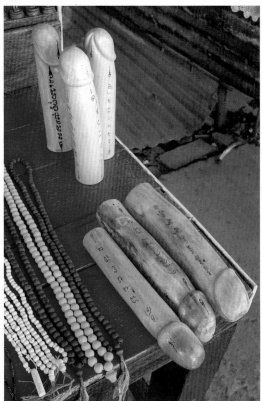

facing page: **Fishermen wish for a bounty and pray for protection by making phallic offerings to Phra Nang, the spirit of the princess cave at Ao Nang Beach, Krabi.**

left: *Palad khik* **inscribed with magical calligraphy on sale in Ayutthaya.**

below, clockwise from top left: **A phallic hybrid of the *nang kwak* beckoning lady charm; a boy at a Samut Songkhram canal, wears** *palad khik* **at his waist to guard against water spirits** (*PCS*); **lucky objects bring money to a Muang Boran vendor; for extra fortune, penis trees are crafted from a rare parasitic wood** (*PCS*).

Always considered slightly base, thus never worn above the waist, phallic charms are slowly succumbing to globalised prudery. Where missionaries previously failed, modernism is succeeding.

There are overtly sexual aspects of the *palad khik* that give grist to the critics. In some a carvings a woman lies spread-eagled across the shaft. The 'instructions' issued by renowned phallus-carving monk Phra Chawn dwell mostly on moral responsibility, but include advice to wear one in the left pocket if going to see a woman, in the right if going to a man. Similarly, a lay assistant told Supakij that his monk advised that "men going go to nightlife, massage parlours, go-go bars or call girls should carry a *palad khik* to bless her, so she has good earnings and a good life. They should touch it to the woman's genitals, not put it inside." Freidman's research found that some believe its powers increase if actually inserted.

While some deride phallus worship as gratuitous male power, women use *linga* too. For luck. As occult writer Marlene Guelden relates: "A Miss Thailand World beauty queen, who hid a phallic amulet in her hair to influence the judges, was chastised for unfair competition." Girls as well as boys wave phalluses at Isaan festivals, which loose pent-up pressures in a controlled breach of taboos on courting, sex, vulgarity, drunkenness, emotion. Would-be mothers may present *palad khik* in request or thanks to Phra Nang cave in Krabi or Chao Mae Tubtim Shrine in Bangkok. At the latter, *linga* of every size, colour and shape form a garden, complete with phallic fence.

Supakij expects *palad khik* to die out within a few decades, rendering them another antique curio. Barely ten abbots retain the lore to cast phallus spells. New ordainees are uninterested, embarrassed or even fear them as unlucky. Like the child's top-knot hair style, phallic charms can't withstand fashion, peer pressure and exposure to pop culture. Underwear ads don't feature *palad khik*, so nor will youths in bedrooms or locker rooms. Urban wearers often show such embarrassment that once the 'honoured deputy' has been spotted, it gets left at home, or dropped entirely.

History may be repeating itself. "In 1782, King Rama I ordered that all phallic representations of Shiva should be gathered together and burned," writes David Wyatt of an act of Buddhist reform partly intended "to avoid the ridicule of foreign visitors." It evidently didn't succeed, because *palad khik* are still very much with us. Today's puritanism might also fail erase the phallic charm. After all, it's a symbol of universal and eternal appeal.

Trade Talismans
Merchants use magic to make you spend

If shopping is the new religion, as many quip, then Thai shopkeepers are sitting pretty. They've long since enrolled religion in selling. The archetypal general store draws on the power of magic mascots. Few merchants seem to trust just one talisman, instead summoning a host of spirits positioned throughout the shophouse: front to back, floor to ceiling, and especially around the money. They display not just animist and Therevada Buddhist totems, but many charms of Chinese origin, indicating the ethnic lineage of many Thai merchants.

You can't get more Chinese than a red medallion of a gold character meaning 'good', 'longevity' or 'rich'. Such *huu* charms dangle over doorways or walls. Teens now take them into exams in satin pouches as a lucky mascot. Originally on cloth or paper, *huu* also come in carved wood or embossed plastic, many bearing the Thai word *dee* (good) instead of a Chinese character. Auspicious words in *khom* script also conjure spells around *yantra* diagrams on amulets of cloth, paper or palm leaf. To invoke protection or money-making benefit these must be blessed by a monk, medium or shaman before display.

Such inscriptions may lurk in the folds of *pla tapian*, a carp fish woven from strips of palm painted red, gold, black or yellow. Suspended on a string alone or as part of

a shoal in a fish mobile, it is increasingly popular in shops, and may be seen swinging from a car mirror or in its original location: over an infant's cradle.

Other animal spirits invoked include the spider – for snaring customers in the trader's web – and the gecko. By its cry heralding danger, this lizard embodies loving kindness, while a two-tailed one augurs luck.

Another Chinese emblem, *nam tao* (bottle gourds) dangle on lucky red chords, often alongside other fertility symbols like the phallic *palad khik* and the fish trap. Made from bamboo like the real thing, the model fish trap vaguely resembles a fish, tapering at the head, flared at its tail. In the family-run corner shop, you are its prey.

Like the fish trap, the shop entices with a splayed opening, this time an array of tempting treats: screw-topped cans of Hall's breath mints in colour-coded flavours; Krong Thip cigarettes rolled by the Thailand Tobacco Monopoly; gallon tins with windows showing the durian-jam biscuits inside that could take years to eat – and probably do. Thirst quenchers fill the generic steel cool-cabinet. Glass fronted upper shelves hold sodas, energy drinks and pots of Yakult yoghurt, while sliding doors in the top of the lower unit allow hands to plunge in to grab ice bags and bottles of beer and water.

left: **Dangling from shop altars, fish traps augur a good catch in any kind of trade.**

top right: **Every kind of luck-bringing talisman graces this furniture shop in Phuket, from monk portraits and mystical *yantra* cloth, to double-tailed lizards and a giant spider snaring a butterfly.**

middle right: **Fish are always good omens in doorways, whether in a pond, a pot or this charm, which is folded from 20 baht banknotes and inscribed with ancient Khmer letters.**

lower right: **Bird charms woven from reeds, akin to the woven fish mobiles hung over infants' cots.**

Once over the threshold of a general store, you face diversions from cannily placed obstacles: bags of peanuts stapled to cardboard brush the shoulder, racks of salted dried fruit jut into view; stacks of rice sacks entangle every step. In no time, Mom, Pop or their precocious children to assail you with a smiling sales pitch.

Inside, relics of deliveries past cram the shop. Stacks of water bottles, coiled hosepipe, and fairy lights force you to stretch for the heaving shelves. Cobwebs shroud tins of paint in any colour as long as it's white, red or grey. Out of dusty cardboard boxes spill pots of indigo blue fabric 'whitener' or sachets of Thipniyom herbal tooth powder. Atop a glass cabinet groaning under miscellaneous hardware, a basket offers sealed bags containing bread buns of indeterminate age. Faster selling are the ranks of cleaning supplies and kitchen staples: fish sauce, vegetable oil, instant Mama-brand noodles.

Being both shop and house, the shophouse merges trade into domesticity. A teen writes homework belly-down on patterned vinyl, while hysteric chatter blares from a television soap. Bathed in pale fluorescent light an emaciated granny slunk in a deckchair folds up her crepe-skinned limbs like a spider. The clatter of wok and spatula resounds from the lean-to kitchen erected in the rear alley. A limpid glow of red bulbs guides the eye up into the eaves to a red and gold shelf high on a wall. Facing anywhere but west, this altar displays the Buddha and below him bodhisattvas like *Kuan Im* (Guan Yin in Chinese) or *Phra Sang Khajjai*, the laughing fat man with

left: Bottle gourds are one of the Chinese charms adopted into Thai culture through the Sino-Thai involvement in business. This knot of multiple talismans hangs in a food stall in suburban Bangkok.

facing page, top: A door blessing *yantra* fringed by eight *unalom* marks and gold leaf; the Thai word *dii* (good), in very Chinese red-and-gold (*PCS*).

facing page, below: A shrine amidst clothing racks in Mah Boon Krong teen mall. *PCS*

wooden drawer, often behind a glazed display case on which the *nang kwak* lady talisman beckons or the equally potent *kumarn thong* (golden boy) stands at occult service. Amid the shop's money float might sit two kinds of special banknote. Shopkeepers typically retain any notes where the last digits of the serial number bear at least two 9s, read from the end like lottery winners. At collectors' markets, a 100 baht note with 99 sells for 200 baht, 300 baht for 999, much more for 9999 rarities. The other lucky banknote is fake; a virtual currency called *thanabat kwan thoong* and printed by a venerable monk like Luang Phor Khoon, bearing his face where the king's would be, plus a spell to attract further money.

In family businesses many relatives might dispense the change, though strict Sino-Thai patriarchs keep the till key on a chain or strap a moneybelt to their belly, both of which bulge in proportion to profits. Where a deep table of magazines, fruit or knick-knacks stretches beyond arm's length, the merchant wields a plastic basket upon a bamboo rod in which payment and change deftly shuttle. Upon the day's first sale, the vendor may flutter the earnings over unsold items in a lucky Southeast Asian practice here called *praderm* (opening sale).

Bargaining has been the norm here, though to smaller discounts of 10 to 20 per cent than in neighbouring countries like Indonesia, where a common 50 per cent knock-down would to Thai vendors be an insult. The recent growth in price labelling removes the gambling-style frisson of the opening bid. Canny buyers wring small discounts from the stated price, though not in malls or department stores, where fixed prices rule.

Obtaining a receipt from Mom or Pop is like pulling teeth, for to be valid it must note their tax number. Shops that submit to such an outrageous imposition make a demonstrative play of filling out an itemised receipt, as if you now owe them a favour. Busy stores make do with blotching the till printout in red with a self-inking stamp. Chopping documents with a red seal came with the Chinese. Customers seem to age visibly while sales staff proceed to stamp every last object's price label – a precaution against shoplifting long made redundant by the existence of till receipts.

On exiting from the shophouse gloom with purchase bagged in plastic, the buyer may inhale smoke wafting from three incense sticks. Symbolising the triple gem (Buddha, dharma, monkhood), they're lodged on a side pillar in a red burner shaped like a flat, inverted cone or a gourd, made gracious by a pair of peacock feathers from the mythic mount of a Chinese deity.

a hefty money bag. On the floor at a rear wall facing the front sits the Chinese equivalent to a spirit house. Styled after a red and gold Chinese pavilion and lit by a string of large bulbs, it often houses statues of a hermit flanked by a girl and boy.

"Chinese prefer assistance from people they can trust so they turn to relatives first," says a fourth-generation Sino-Thai, Chatchai Ngoenprakairat, of how the shrine reflects the all-hands-on-deck shophouse. "Thais feel that assistants should be of lower status, so servant effigies at a Thai spirit house sit outside and on a lower level." Typical offerings include oranges, chicken, duck, dried squid and Chinese foods like *khanom kheng* (flour cake in banana cup). "Chinese don't like to waste anything," Chatchai adds. "They offer foods they personally like so that after a few hours they can take it back to eat." Many Sino-Thais dedicate a showcase to the lucky trinity *Hok Lok Siew* in gilded, painted ceramic. *Hok* carries a bag for prosperity, *Lok* wears sword and armour to achieve power, and the bulb-headed elderly doctor *Siew* bears a bottle gourd, a staff and a long white beard to assure longevity.

The heart of the shophouse, the till is rarely a machine: that would leave a record. Instead the money sits in a

For charms to work, they should be propitiated daily by making the relevant incantation and offerings for that spirit. To accept that *kumarn thong* has a known taste for red and green soda requires a highly pragmatic faith. "Innumerable superstitions are founded on the assumption that the local population of ghosts and demons have the touchy pride and baseless malice of a spoiled child, as well as a level of gullibility that would make an idiot blush," observes Mont Redmond. "The very idea of Thai spirits and deities being so adeptly controlled by rituals and formulas, however, precludes the development of a grand, Olympian mythology. Thai gods are not to be explained, nor do they explain anything themselves. They are merely heightened reflections of the Thais' self-image… Heaven is a government lottery office staffed by spirits on the take and manning a rigged wheel."

Talismans seemed impotent, however, against the loss-leading prices and 'just-in-time ordering' of foreign superstores, which spread nationwide after the 1997 crash forced a liberalisation of trade. This sparked a nationalist backlash and the zoning of hypermarkets away from markets and corner shops. Yet Mom 'n' Pop face tougher competition from local convenience store franchises, many of which keep talismans near the till.

"[Franchisees] convert a lot of Mom 'n' Pop stores to 7-Eleven," says Korsak Chairasmisak whose company surrounds neighbourhoods with more than one new 7-Eleven a day, as if in a strategic game. It is. Korsak treats Thailand like the territorial game of Go, which isn't as cut-throat as chess. "The whole principle is to survive while tolerating your opponent. Even weak rival stores still survive after many years. We never try to stop them. If you're greedy, you'll lose. We have to adapt to the Thai way of life; we must sell what people really like."

Talismans, too, must adapt to the times. Content to treat amulets as mere mascots for emotional support, new-generation Thais are adopting Chinese and Japanese totems, and even mock African voodoo dolls for trend-oriented shops. Foreign fetish objects lend young traders and consumers confidence in being hip and up-to-date, while avoiding the hassle of rites and the spookiness of spells. "They might be sacred and magical, but they scare me," concedes Chutiya, a student, about Thai talismans. "They look too serious, as if there might really be some spirits in them." Now that shopping has indeed become a new religion, faith succumbs to fashion, the occult goes cute and the merchants' *mantra* turns into the scripted, corporate Thai equivalent of "have a nice day."

Nang Kwak
The beckoning lady brings business and love

"Those who don't ask don't get" runs the English proverb and Thai shopkeepers aren't shy to ask for more custom. Most unambiguous of all the trade talismans, *nang kwak* (beckoning lady) ushers in business at restaurants, shops and stalls. Often seen on counters near the till or door, she was originally kept in a money bag.

Dressed in traditional costume and crown, she sits Thai-style – legs tucked in to the right, left hand on floor or thigh – her right arm half-raised to beckon. In the courteous way that Thais summon taxis, waiters or social juniors, her palm faces down. Were *nang kwak*'s fingers pointing up, trade would suffer. Made by men, that rude gesture aggressively challenges; made by women, it's a raunchy signal to "come hither".

Actually, *nang kwak* does have a sexy side. Like many amulets, she doubles as a love charm, though in the form of leaves from the plant of the same name. It's among a class of *waan yaa* (herbal medicinal amulets). "Whoever desires a magnetic charm in himself or herself for love or

kindness, smears the face and body with *waan nang kwak* accompanied by the recitation of 'Namo Buddhaya' 108 times," wrote Phya Anuman Rajadhon of old lore.

Though arcane, the practice persists. "In junior high school half a dozen girls in my class would wrap *nang kwak* leaves in a handkerchief to place in their top pocket to find a boyfriend," recalls Chatchai Ngoenprakairat, 24. A few men likewise pocket a *waan sao long* ('infatuated girl' herb) leaf or wash in Waan Sao Long brand herbal soap to attract women.

Coloured red or green with a white centre, *nang kwak* leaves curl down – an auspicious trait seen as beckoning. Leaves have a limited life, so their power was extended by carving a beckoning figure from the herb's tuber root. It must be found in the wild and dug up only after offering liquor, betel and other goodies to the spirits.

Over time, the sculptures were enlarged and executed in ivory, bronze, clay or a particular wood (notably the fig tree). Most elegant in gold leafed black lacquer, they're often now plaster or plastic, moulded and painted with the same imprecision as spirit house attendant figures, among whom *nang kwak* sometimes sits.

"To carve *nang kwak* it is advisable to wear a white suit and finish within one day," Sombat Plainoi cautions. Shamanic medicine was inseparable from magic, hence the mystic letters engraved on the body: *bhogam* (left hand), *jana* (right hand), *du* (left breast), *sa* (right breast), *ma* (forehead) and *ni* (back), which combine into the spell "*bhogam jana du sa ma ni*" (meaning 'heart treasure') uttered in 108 incantations. Today, fewer *nang kwak* get inscribed, but they still require blessing by a monk, medium or shaman in order to turn the figurine into an amulet for enhancing public relations.

To show what people actually say when muttering a spell, here's a translation of her *Maha Ongkarn* mantra:

"Om, Maha Siddhi joga. Om, the great Phu Chao *(Lord Paternal Grandfather) of Blue Mountain with an only daughter named* Nang Kwak. *Women adore her, men love her. May luck be bestowed on me, and all people know me. Om! Traders, lead me to the* Maen *(god) country where I gain a thousand* thanan *(coconut shell measure for rice) full of ring gems. I trade in diverse wares and gain profit easily. I trade in silver, it comes to me brimful; I trade in gold, it comes to me brimful. Come friends and partake of food, for today I have much luck. I come home with baskets full. I am better in luck than those female traders, even surpassing the owners of junks. Om! Lord Phu Chao bestow good fortune on me alone."*

Just as leaves wither, so magic wears off. To top it up requires reciting *Maha Ongkarn* daily while offering popped rice, candles, garlands and scented paste. The hassle of all this leads many to adopt a similar Japanese talisman, the *maneki-neko*. A beckoning cat, it's happy with simple snacks and sweets and needs no invocations.

Adopting the same pose, purpose and position as *nang kwak*, the *maneki-neko* raises the right paw for luck in general, the left for financial fortune. "The *maneki-neko* had gone global by the end of the 20th century," Nicholas Bornoff writes. "Outside Japan you're more likely to see the *maneki-neko* in Chinese stores and restaurants than in their Japanese equivalent."

Like many Japanese imports, the cat's popular among the hip, globalised young, who spurn Thai traditions like *nang kwak*. "I'm selling trendy outfits for youngsters. She'd make the place look sort of old-fashioned, which might drive customers away instead of drawing them in. It wouldn't look cool," says Chanthorn, 25, who instead picked *maneki-neko* as the mascot of her Siam Square boutique. "It's cute. Displaying a Japanese charm makes my shop look modern and fashionable; it speaks to my young customers more than any other sort of talisman."

Nor do these believers want an old-fashioned *maneki-neko*. The original white pelt with brown tabby blotches makes way for all-white coats of papier-mâché or painted porcelain. Increasingly made of plastic, *maneki-neko* come in pink to solicit love, in red to banish bad luck or completely gold-coloured to bring riches. For hi-tech effect, many sport a battery-powered beckoning foreleg that swivels perpetually like a metronome.

Perhaps in response, *nang kwak* statuettes are getting less fussily detailed. It may only be a matter of time before an entrepreneur turns her into a cute toon girl. A bridal shop has already made one out of a mannequin.

The two talismans have become so interchangeable in Thailand that some may wonder if they are related or a total coincidence. Originating in a local herb, *nang kwak* evidently evolved through ancient indigenous shamanism. She's unlikely to have been inspired by *maneki-neko*, which first appeared in Edo in the early 17th century, just after Japan made contact with Thai traders at Ayutthaya. So it could well be that *maneki-neko* has come home, that the beckoning cat is a Nipponese *nang kwak*.

far left: **A Bangkok bridal shop reimagines the beckoning lady as a shop window dummy.** *PCS*

left: **Metal *nang kwak* in silver, gold and – in a rare two-handed gesture – bronze.**

top: **The Japanese beckoning cat *maneki-neko* is a growing fad among modern shopkeepers, though the *nang kwak* is older and authentically Thai.**

above: **A simpler, stylised stone *nang kwak* beckons customers to a carrot juice stall.** *PCS*

Lucky Number 9
Numerology enters the digital age

In 2003, a minister paid 4 million baht for the car plate 'S Ng 9999'. Thai bidders focus less on car plate letters than on lucky numbers, and no number is luckier than 9. Hence the new 09 mobile prefix excited an already dizzy market in premium phone numbers, with 09-999 9958 costing 58,000 baht and 09-999 9919 a cool 400,000 baht.

Nine is all around. Many ventures start on days that end in or total 9, banknotes ending in 9s act as talismans, and the luckiest month to marry is August, the ninth in the Thai horoscope. The first 99,999 riders on Bangkok's subway got souvenirs. Many prices (including fortune tellers' fees) end in 9 or 99, not just to make prices look cheaper, but to bless the vendor. Even the 2003 state budget was arranged into a total featuring many nines.

Nine is a *lek mongkhon* (auspicious number) partly due to the many nines in royal and religious heritage and ritual. A nine-tier parasol indicates the king. The Thai digit also resembles the mystical *unalom* symbol seen on blessings, tattoos and the Buddha's forehead. Nine's also seen as lucky because the word for it (*gao*) sounds like the word for progress. Thai number words come from southern Chinese, along with good and bad associations with words that rhyme or sound alike. Many Sino-Thai inherit the Chinese fear of four (meaning death) and favour of 8, widely seen in the Poi Sian plant with one bloom each for the 8 divinities. But language differences mean some Thai associate 8 with dirt and 6 with spills. Just as Chinese philosophy and politics tends to use

numbered lists, so is Buddhism: 3 gems, 4 noble truths, the eightfold path, odd numbers of monks at blessings. On the whole Thai believe odd numbers are luckier.

Another logic derives from Hindu astrology, seen in the horoscope diagram that crops up on taxi ceilings and tattooed chests. A 3-by-3 grid within a circle fringed by lotus petals, it symbolises 8 heavenly bodies revolving around a 9th, sacred Mount Meru. Many Thai ventures today are determined by fortuitous dates, times and numbers. These had roots in survival. Farmers needed a good facility with numbers to predict monsoons and new year. Since the 7th century AD, they didn't have to track stars because Indian tables were more accurate than any Western calendar before 1752. Inscribed in stone or palm leaf – and now in popular almanacs – these were legible not just to court Brahmins. "There was a lot of such numerical sophistication 'out there' in the countryside," insists David Wyatt, citing monastic education.

Mathematics helped manage the complex Thai blend of Chinese and Indian astrology. From China came the 13-moon lunar year, the 12-year animal cycle, 5 natural elements and the yin-yang power of 2. From India came the 12-month solar calendar and an 7+1 day week based on 7 planets, plus Rahu (god of eclipses), arrayed in 8 compass directions around a 9th world, Mount Meru. Ringed by 27 constellations, these planets each have a cosmic power – 6, 15, 8, 18, 19, 21, 10 and 12 – totaling 108, an oft-seen mystical number also derived from 9x12, which additionally makes the sum 1+0+8=9.

Crunching these numbers worked like a medieval Excel spreadsheet. Enter day, month and year of birth and each line total in a table indicates status, wealth, spouse, friends, whatever. Any remainder got factored into the next calculation. Applications were endless, such as predicting a baby's sex; an odd remainder meant a boy.

Most interest in lucky numbers has another motive: lotteries. Gamblers ask monks, pick digits associated with their life data, or discern number shapes from rubbing wax, wood, leaves, statues or *takian* tree bark.

Thai numerology may sometimes ascribe even good and bad news to the same number. "We cannot fail to note that the portent for the month of birth can often be virtually the opposite of that for the day," shrugs scholar HG Quaritch Wales. "And that is just what appeals to the Thai temperament, enabling one to be set off against the other, leaving a favourable balance of course."

Comfort with numerology has inoculated the Thai against the modern tyranny of serial numbers that Patrick McGoohan encapsulated in TV's *The Prisoner*: "I am not a number, I am a free man." What could appeal more to the Thai than digital technology? From phones and car plates to PIN codes and ID cards, the digital era isn't faceless at all, but new fodder for the number culture.

Fortune Tellers
Divine fate from your stars, cards and moles

One way to discern an impending coup, it's whispered, is to watch when generals visit their favoured soothsayers. They're seeking an auspicious time to seize power. From personal life to the fate of nations, divination guides most Thais at least some of the time. *Mor duu* (seeing doctors) advise on investing, building, lotteries, marital compatibility, installing spirit houses, averting danger. And they'll specify timings to the luckiest minute.

With karma deciding the Buddhist's fate, millions of Thais check their astral accounts with a *mor duu* twice a year. Fees average 300 baht a time, though a third of those pay 500-1,000 baht, and some 'donate' much higher sums. It's a lucrative industry that mirrors the fortunes of the wider economy, generating 1.5 billion baht in 2002.

At the respectable end of this futures market stand monks. Not supposed to interfere with karma or the public world, they typically prescribe merit-making, which may include a voluntary donation. Commercial *mor duu* act as counsellors, dispensing practical advice.

Though not bound by a professional code, they join associations for credibility or – when a prediction flops – self-defence. Half are female, as are most *khon song* (mediums), who channel predictions direct from the divine or the dead. The alpha-male branch of the occult, *mor phii* (spirit doctors or shamans) claim to relay the answers direct from the underworld.

While mediums and shamans shirk publicity, *mor duu* feature visibly at markets, malls, sidewalks, parks or near temple gates. Some adopt a studious, spectacled look, others go for outlandish, otherworldly trappings. Famous *mor duu* take private appointments from adherents. In addition to its annual fortune telling fair, Bangkok's luxury Montien Hotel hosts soothsayers favoured by *hi-so* matrons between hair and lunch appointments.

At their booths, palm and zodiac illustrations adorn the banners, signboards and decorated lids of boxes that contain cards, almanacs, astronomical wheels, notebooks and cabalistic diagrams. Other *mor duu* simply set up a

table or groundsheet, where their accoutrements and smaller signs spill out of a decorated briefcase. Usually this includes candles, incense and a Buddha image.

Many read the Thai horoscope, a complex hybrid of Chinese, Indian and Western systems. "It seems to give real meaning to the term Indo-china, in which the imports acquire a distinctly local character," says scholar HG Quaritch Wales of the myriad Thai zodiacs that use numerology and images from folklore.

While Western zodiac signs reduce to simple logos, Thai horoscope treatises look as hectic as a temple mural: gods, animals, buildings, and human activities like pounding rice, trading goods or fighting hand-to-hand. Charts for interpreting dreams adopt a similar style. By enabling people to 'read' their forecast like a cartoon strip, Thais turned astrology into art. Old zigzag folding books of horoscopes equate to illuminated manuscripts in medieval Europe. Now these fabulous images have migrated onto greeting cards and souvenir prints.

There are many kinds of imagery. Thais categorise each animal of the Chinese 12-year cycle into four kinds, thus a 'snake' born in June is a 'king cobra'. Also critical is the weekday of birth, a Hindu concept relating to colour-coded planetary gods, each riding a symbolic animal. The numbers of each day appear in the *chakra rasi* (zodiac wheel) seen on astrological charts and places such as taxi blessings and tattoos. A three-by-three grid in a circle, it's often fringed with lotus petals, looped curlicues or other *lai thai* patterns.

However beautifully drawn, number diagrams seem grimly final. Fate feels more manageable – and invites potential influence – if the day also has a deity, address and resumé. Thus for Friday: "At a gold house on Venus, Phra Suk guards the north. Coloured pale blue, he rides oxen, likes sapphires and fires arrows." Many zodiacs read like stories; one aligned the Chinese horoscope's 12 years with the *Jataka* (tales of the Buddha's lives). Others match *Ramayana* characters to compass points, with prophesies like: "If you go there will be trouble, for it was when Rama used Lak to fetch Sita." In another treatise, an omen about travelling at mid-morning on a Thursday reads like a soap opera: "If you go an enemy will cause you loss. It was when Mars committed adultery with the Moon. His relative, Jupiter, caught him." Yet another fits 12 zodiac signs into the *chakra rasi* by adding a diagonal cross. Its signs resemble tarot archetypes, with good images like a sorcerer, palace or golden umbrella or more ominous symbols of a prisoner or a decapitated man.

"Most people of any standing can show you their horoscope, and are careful to have the exact times of their children's births recorded," writes Quaritch Wales. A town's precise moment of inception, on erecting the city pillar, means they too have horoscopes. Bangkok's, made on 21 April 1782, is taken as Thailand's horoscope. Astrology's credibility from centuries of royal statecraft persists in political predictions and is part of national identity and ideas of Thainess, despite the rational views of Buddhism and science, as Nerida Cook explains.

"Fortune tellers can even be regarded as informal moral police," adds Cook. Readings provide a rare chance to reflect and confide, while a *mor duu*'s warnings uphold the idea of karma, and their upbeat advice urges calm, sociable behaviour. "Prognostications are left vague, intentionally it would seem," says Quaritch Wales. "So as to leave room for the soothsayer to exercise the psychological skill on which his reputation largely depends."

Many are trained at the Thai Astrologers Association (TAA), and the term 'doctor' earns status. Yet anyone can access the exotically illustrated *Phrommachat* (Brahmanic Birth) manual, found at markets in royal and commoner editions. Astrology was bigger among the elite, who had access to literacy and accurate timing, but has spread to the achievement-oriented middle classes, who relish its accent on personal choice. The *Phrommachat* also covers divination from omens favoured by more fatalistic rural folk, including ephemera like cloud shapes, dreams, knots in wood or rat bites in clothes.

When it comes to reading the body, the most popular method is palmistry. Some read the lines according to Indo-European methods, though most favour Chinese chiromancy. This technique dwells on the hand's fleshy mounds, temperature, colour, texture and clamminess, noting shapes like fish tails, letters or coffins.

Other *mor duu* divine the soul from the sole. Mod Daeng, a 42-year-old widow in Saraburi, reads a dozen feet a day. Though the feet are washed first, she doesn't touch them; she measures a man's right foot or a

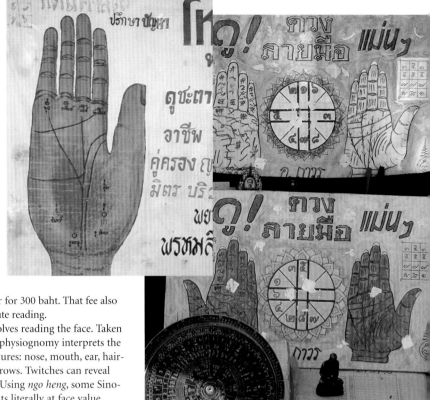

woman's left with a steel ruler for 300 baht. That fee also includes a tape of the 20 minute reading.

A greater risk to 'face' involves reading the face. Taken from Chinese *ngo heng*, Thai physiognomy interprets the shape of the face and five features: nose, mouth, ear, hairline, and eyes, including eyebrows. Twitches can reveal disturbed bodily energy, too. Using *ngo heng*, some Sino-Thai firms judge job applicants literally at face value.

Drawing on Indian and Chinese methods, fortunes can also be read from another unique trait: moles. Location, colour, size and grouping proving critical. Though seven black moles shaped like a W on the forehead portend luck, generally hidden moles are luckier, whether around armpit, elbow fold, sole, penis or the crease of a breast. Some visible moles curse their owner, which partly explains the boom in mole-removal surgery.

People tell seers other private matters. Work is the lead topic (26.3 per cent), then family (24.9%), finances (22%) and love (20.3%). Mediums take this consultant role further and offer specific remedies including herbs. "Fortune tellers are like psychiatrists. They make suggestions as to where to redirect one's life if it is going astray," says former TAA president Vorapan Lauhawilai. "We're the supporting, behind-the-scenes factor in a person's life. It's definitely an integral part of Thai life."

Most *mor duu* don't charge outright, but like monks they accept a donation – a way to exploit generosity and the anxiety to show face through wealth. It can get out of hand. A flamboyant young monk in Ayutthaya has apparently reaped 10 million baht from reading fortunes of disciples to a revered elderly abbot. An official thanked him for a predicted promotion with a mobile phone and an air-conditioner, while a factory owner gave a new car.

Recently, Western fortune telling has gained a trendy cachet. Lifestyle magazines and many astrologers tap a fashion for the European zodiac, which links to the names of Thai months: *Singhakhom* (August) means Leo the lion. Others throw dice, deal playing cards or read from a tarot deck, even via machines in Bangkok malls.

Again, imports get assimilated. One tarot deck matches archetypes from Thai literature, proving how myths are universal. The *Ramayana* villain Ravanna is 'The Devil', while 'Strength' is a tiger-riding goddess of Songkran.

With so many psychic options, the future can always be made more positive or tailored to aspirations. As Quaritch Wales concludes: "The Thai do not mind an unfavourable omen if they know they can make offerings to avert it. Or they can apply for a 'second opinion.'"

Mediums & Shamans
Psychic consultants peddle ancient
remedies to modern society

In what seems like a fantasy vision, King Taksin stands up on the throne, hoisting shield and sword aloft, before engaging in a martial dance with the elephant-headed god Ganesh. Yet this scene is typical of Asahna Bucha night each year in Wat Tum Phrathat, Lopburi. When reality resumes, Ganesh – an ex-policeman – crumples before the altar. On removing his gilded mask, he vomits into a bag. Puffing on three cigarettes, King Taksin retires to her throne. Yes, 'her'. The face beneath the black brimmed hat belongs to an elderly woman.

Like many *khon song* (mediums), she channels the two-century-dead king of Thonburi for a living. That full moon night, she slips into this character for an annual mediums convention with some hundred others, which include several embodiments of Shiva clad in leopard pelt, dagger clenched between teeth. From the seated throng, up pop mythical creatures like Garuda, then numerous incarnations of *kumarn thong*, the 'golden boy' spirit of a foetus sacrificed for magical rites. Worshipped in turn, each spirit infuses any medium able to channel it, hence the multiple manifestations.

What seems an unusual event is in fact quite usual. An estimated 100,000 *khon song* practice nationwide, parting anxious Thais with money in exchange for wise words from beyond this dimension. Countless *wai khru* (homages to masters) happen each year, though usually on a smaller scale and varying by region. Often in the hot season hundreds of shamans trance-dance at Pratu Pah cave shrine in Lampang, dressed in vivid wraps, wielding swords to a hypnotic Mon band. Publicised by word of mouth, the occult *wai khru* spectacle remains perhaps the country's biggest cultural secret.

Thai shamanism hasn't been marketed as a tourist sight like animistic rites in some countries. The Thai occult remains vital, private and personal, evoking the doctor-patient relationship. Just as well; with entranced mediums lurching, leaping and thrashing, the visitor feels an ominous sense of preternatural forces barely tamed. This is perhaps why the Tourist Authority of Thailand

doesn't include such events in its 'Unseen Thailand' promotion. Some things may be better left unseen.

Today's mediums multi-task. They thrive partly by combining attributes from rival spiritual consultants: clairvoyants, unorthodox monks, spirit doctors. *Khon song* claim to foretell the future and offer psychological insight, but by voicing an all-knowing spirit, rather than divining from stars, palms or cards. From the domain of charismatic monks, they may perform exorcisms and activate charms. Choodet, a fairly typical medium from Thonburi, donates the small entrancement fee (always ending in a lucky 9) to make merit. He earns his living by

charging 100 baht for services like holy water bathing, an auspicious name change, or spells cast for blessing or protection. In an industry worth 20 billion baht a year, fees escalate the more demanding the service, reputed the medium, or richer the customer.

This siphons off 'white witch' business from the spirit doctor (*mor phii*), who's left hawking mainly black magic with a capacity for force or harm that they naturally deny. Evolved from the shaman-cum-undertaker, the macho *mor phii* boasts a soul too 'strong' for possession. Not medium but middle man, he simply states what his spirit 'allies' confide. While similarly Faustian 'influential figures' may commission his potions, love philtres and voodoo-esque rites, mainstream Thais regard *mor phii* as amoral and un-Buddhist. Newspapers generally report their antics in terms of scandal.

The medium's *tamnak song* (divine house of possession) can feel as intimidating as the den of a *mor phii*. Both places brim with mystical paraphernalia, masks and eerie images. Ancient Khmer *khom* script lends a spooky frisson, much like gypsy clairvoyants evoke in the West. This helps credibility, since no one alive can verify, say, the voice of Shiva or King Chulalongkorn. Those who channel the revered reformist monarch also mimic his appreciation for brandy, cigars and the colour pink. Mediums of the cheery monk Chi Kong of Shaolin, China, adopt his foot-raised-upon-seat posture, laugh in his elderly voice and swig liquor from a bottle gourd.

To bolster their aura of divinity, mediums perform strange feats. Eyes rolled back in trance, they extinguish a handful of yellow candles with their mouth. Chin dripping with molten wax, they revert to fevered drags on a bunch of cheroots, glugs of rice wine and chewing of betel. The narcotics induce both altered senses and otherworldly detachment.

Skeptics point out that *khon song* never miss a chance to upgrade their rank, calling a grandfather 'son', talking in arcane jargon, aggrandising their host spirit with titles

like *phor phu* (great grandfather). The Golden Boy now has a grander incarnation: *kumarn phet* (Diamond Boy). Even the job description, *khon song* (chanelling person) gets elevated into the more mystical term *raang song* – possessed body. The pretension works; customers proffer the submissive language Thais reserve for the teacher, the doctor, the elder.

This guru-complex can lead to culthood. Charismatic *khon song* accumulate 'disciples', often by diagnosing someone as a past-life follower of a spirit they voice. Mediums claim a monopoly on recognising the chanelling gift in others and on recruitment. Helped by disciples they anoint an initiate's forehead in a rite called *perd ong* (opening the divine portal) and crown them with the gilded mask of a *ruesii*.

Possession requires a receptive soul. Since orthodoxy considers males to be spiritually strong, mediums have since ancient times typically been sensitive souls: women, *kathoey* (ladyboys) or those with infirmities believed caused by them denying their gift. Nor can you choose which spirit to host. Uncannily, the link is often visual: a jowly man ends up as Ganesh, a deep voiced girl with simian gait gets branded as monkey deity Hanuman.

Khon song also speak in tongues of the dead. While divinities act as general oracles for behaviour, goals and luck, the dearly departed undergo a more practical quiz during a séance. A family near Ayutthaya insist they learned from a voice "80% similar to Grandma's" where their late matriarch had hidden her valuables.

Some suspect a scam. Aside from impersonating gods, faith healers can come across like magicians using sleight of hand. One trick 'extracts' a harm-causing substance into an egg placed on the possessed body part. Some fraudulent *khon song* and *mor phii* have admitted to re-sealing an egg pre-inserted with a nail, thread, hair or blood that appears when the egg gets cracked.

As during the state regulation of Thai Buddhism in the early-Bangkok period, newly bourgeois Thailand

left: **A Hindu medium anoints the crowd with red paste at a festival in Bangkok's Silom financial district.** *PCS*

above: **A Lampang medium channels a spirit by holding and then spinning wildly upon a dangling sacred cloth to trance-inducing Mon music.** *PCS*

facing page, far left and left: **Mediums from Lampang dance for the spirits at a Chiang Mai business inauguration: a ladyboy medium induces possession with cheroots; a young man trance dances; and dozens of mediums bless the offerings with candles lit upon sword tips.** *PCS*

below: *Ruesii* **the hermit is the fount of all Thai knowledge. He is worshipped by performers and artisans as if they channel his wisdom.** *PCS*

an imported rarity and psychiatry associated with face-losing mental illness. So believers treat *khon song* and *mor phii* as psychic consultants.

Formerly, frazzled Thais sought solace at the temple, the core of the community. Now individuals find comfort in the mall, in karaoke, in online chat. Few males ordain for more than two weeks and the ranks of wise monks dwindle. The state's stern reaction to wayward monks and moral drift adds to the gap between religious and modern lifestyles. While mostly guided by Buddhist virtue and social hierarchy, Thais have historically sought diverse advice. The more ambiguous or urgent the matter, the more attractive the spirit world. It's a matter of what works. As Mont Redmond suggests, "Wisdom, no matter how hidden or holy, had better have some results to show for itself, or Thai won't have it."

resounds with moral purges. Politicians proposed bans on claims of supernatural powers in 2003, potentially threatening tattooists, amulet collectors and the para-normal's role in pop culture. Tales of mediums, ghosts and *mor phii* permeate tabloid newspapers, television soaps, movies and amulet magazines.

Since folk belief meets a need, it thrives underground. "State Buddhism has become dry and distant, unable to respond to the people's emotional needs for love and security," says Professor Nidhi Eoseewong. "What has followed is a burgeoning of commercialised cults and superstitions, since animism is no longer governed by Buddhist morality as before." Whereas the Buddhist Japanese made folk belief official through the parallel faith of Shinto, Thai officialdom marginalised it, thus also hampering a feminine role in religion.

"In the Northeast, women spiritual healers called *phii faa*, meaning spirit of the sky, still command high respect. In the North, ancestral spirits are worshipped along maternal lines," writes Sanitsuda Ekachai, who champions the re-ordination of nuns as one way to keep Buddhism relevant. "Given Thailand's traditional receptiveness to occult beliefs, the result is a phenomenal rise in spiritualism among the mobile-phone toting urban professionals who seek both to enhance their physical well-being and to fill what they experience as a spiritual void. Up until recently, fear of ridicule has kept many well-known professionals as closet believers."

Their concerns are universal. "All kinds come to us," Choodet divulges. "A woman whose husband has a minor wife, relatives of a suicide, people with incurable disease, the mentally troubled, bureaucrats missing promotion, students facing exams, people possessed by a ghost." Thailand is not a welfare state, with counselling

Ghost Stories
Haunted houses, restless souls and supernatural soap operas

Old wooden houses set the Westerner swooning with nostalgia, but cause many a Thai to freak. No wonder refined mansions are so readily demolished in Cement Age Thailand – they're presumed to be haunted. The same goes for beautiful old furniture. Suspicion that a stranger died horribly on the bed, or the chest belonged to a drowned aunt, sends exquisite teak heritage into the trash in favour of new plastic or chipboard replacements. Even the Prime Minister's residence Baan Phitsanuloke is believed haunted and few stay overnight there.

Haunted houses are hardly unique to Thailand. What's unusual is the number of them and how much *phii* (bad spirits) affect day-to-day perceptions. Ghosts are a mainstay of newspapers, magazines, soap operas and movies. Spine-chillers spin a major thread through Thai literature, from the mid-20th century ghost yarns by Hem Wejakorn and 'One Baht' pulp horror booklets through to today's comic strip ghouls.

Most potent remains the oral tradition. A purported 80% of Thai believe in the supernatural, taking seriously those who've experienced a visitation, or someone who

knows someone who has. Some believe that dogs howl at night on seeing a ghost, others that you can see a ghost's true form when looking back between one's legs. Even sophisticated urban Thai who poo-pooh superstition find themselves assuaging the *phii* "just in case", and uttering mantras at moments of fright.

The spirit house, is a relic of an age when specific environmental spirits guarded village, forest, mountain, field, path or pier. *Phii* included all incorporeal beings, good and bad, until the Hinduisation of Ayutthayan culture promoted good *phii* into *thep* (angels), relegating *phii* to describe mostly malevolent spirits.

Thai ghosts come in over 40 generic kinds, with regional variations, each conveying moral messages. Among the ecological spectres sensed today are *nang thanee*, a flirtatious lady poltergeist found in *thanee* banana plants, and *nang takian*. This beautiful nymph cries if anyone cuts her valuable *takian* tree abode, but relents if the log's made into the main pillar of a house.

Some evil spirits possess the living, typically ugly, anti-social old crones – the archetypal witch. *Phii porb*,

the suffering souls of the greedy, hang around reclusive old women, tearing apart livestock by night. Spread by spitting, *phii kraseu* consumes the 'host' woman's entrails. At night her disembodied head trails innards and a glowing heart while feeding on raw meat and waste in foetid places like kitchens and toilets, wiping her mouth on laundry. Her male equivalent *phii krahang* wields a pestle and glides with a winnowing basket on each arm.

Other spooks derive their form and habits from the way a person lived and died. When Thais expire their *winyaan* (soul) hovers around, sometimes spotted translucently near their body or past hangouts. After seven days in limbo, karma determines their fate, so that's the usual time for cremation. After exhausting karmic credit as a *thep* in heaven or slaving for parole in hell, the soul rebirths via a couple with commensurate merit. "During this interim the soul of a person who has died violently or has committed evil is likely to take the form of a *phii* that haunts and disturbs other people in its uneasy quest to right old wrongs," anthropologist Jasper Ingersoll explains. Evil doers and parent abusers end up as *phii prate*, a harmless translucent male as tall as a tree. This hungry ghost inspires compassion in festivals where the net-like Southern dish *la* is offered as the only food that can pass its wailing pinhole mouth.

Dying prematurely causes the resultant *phii tai hong* to hang around, worried about the loose ends they've left. A prompter cremation may avoid turning merely scary *phii tai hong* into vengeful *phii phrai*. On the other hand, the violently dead were buried to prevent angry souls being freed. Psychopathic *phii phrai* only find peace by luring a victim to an identical death. Hence the shrines at accident black spots like Sii Yaek Roi Sop (100 corpse junction) in Pathum Thani, or the house in Lad Prao Soi 106, Bangkok, where allegedly four women hung themselves in succession. Until the house was demolished, neighbours heard a chair fall each midnight.

Pregnant women (and/or their foetus) make the most virulent *phii phrai*, like Thailand's most enduring ghost, Mae Nak Phrakhanong. Named after a district in east Bangkok roughly two centuries ago, Mrs Nak died in childbirth while her husband Maak was at war. Mother and baby initially appeared normal on his return, only to turn vicious when exposed as spectres. In what some see as a moral about Buddhism overcoming craving and the animist impulse to offer sacrifices, Nak was reconciled to her loss through exorcism by a 12-year-old novice. He trapped her spirit in an earthen pot wrapped in sacred cloth and submerged it in a waterway, but her story lived on. Film and TV remakes have become as a lucrative a franchise as Dracula, while wary devotees and conscripts flock to her shrine in Phrakhanong's Wat Mahabut, donating dresses on hangars to please Nak and toys to placate the child, in return for lucky lottery numbers and protection during military service.

Exorcising a ghost once featured tests of evilness like medieval European witch trials, and people branded as being possessed by *phii porb* have been occasionally exiled from villages in modern times. In a rare, shocking case in 2004, a girl was slain as a bad spirit by her mother and aunts, all supposed mediums. Normally, exorcisms aren't violent and aim for a compassionate rebalancing of energy to right wrongs and begin again, like an audit clearing the books for a new financial year. Conducted by an unorthodox monk or a lay spirit doctor, exorcisms still happen. Two thousand people showed up for one in 2003 near Udon Thani. It took the monk and teams of 'ghost catchers' three hours and much of the village budget to snare 39 ghosts blamed for premature deaths. "Nine of them are strong willed *phii porb*," the monk said. "The rest are other ghosts and stray spirits."

Seeking answers in the occult has only increased with modernisation. In a culture governed by hierarchy and belief in karma, science and logic wilt before the unanswerable and at times arbitrary authority figures, both human and divine. Generic *phii* impart particular social messages, thus these spirits haunting each environment

above: **At the Phii Khon Phang Khone festival in Sakhon Nakhon, Isaan, young devotees don suits of old monks' robes and primitive masks of kapok wood and fibre, wielding phallic swords. They dance manically until coralled within sacred ropes in the temple grounds.** *PCS*

left: **Phi Ta Khon (ghosts with human eyes), a festival in Dan Sai, Loei, is a bit like a Thai answer to Halloween. Evil spirits come out to play for one day a year, giving youngsters a chance to be naughty pranksters.**

and activity formed part of early Thai law. Ghost stories helped sustain resources and social order, while instilling awareness of hygiene, safety and what to avoid: greed, faeces, spitting, uncooked innards, straying after dark, ruffians, the unsociable, the angry, the delusional. *Phii kraseu* were invoked partly to make practical tips like not leaving laundry out overnight. Ancient Thai medicine was also inseparable from ghost management, and some of that knowledge is migrating into modern therapies.

Bogeymen still work today. Shrines at dangerous bends correct reckless driving more effectively than any law, sign or fine. "Parents don't use scientific reasons to socialise children. They say things like 'don't play with knives or a ghost might push you,'" admits 24-year-old Chatchai Ngoenprakairat. "My grandfather warned me about *phii phrai* when I was young, so I didn't drown when swimming." Steeping young minds in scare stories, may however balloon suspicions into convictions.

Such is the power of auto-suggestion that one girl screaming at a school camp in Khorat in February 2001, sparked mass hysteria. Residents and monks ascribed it to possession by spirits from a graveyard. A 1980s bar strip in Bangkok lost custom once revellers realised it was built on a cemetery. Most widespread was the belief in 1990 that a rash of sleeping Isaan men suffering Sudden Unexplained Nocturnal Death Syndrome, as far afield as Singapore, was suffocation by a female *phii*. In response, many Isaan men wore sarongs to bed and painted their nails to fool her that they were female, as well as erecting *palad khik* outside their homes to distract her.

Though *phii* are generally considered dangerous only when provoked, some young people today challenge ghosts, perhaps emboldened by examples from Western media. Rather than wanting to resolve the spirit's angst, they seek cheap thrills. Gangs of teenage boys explore haunted places with courage from a night of drinking, though they may make merit afterwards. Legitimising this trend since the late 1990s, the radio show 'The Shock' has broadcast late-night ghostbusting expeditions live. Owned by the DJ, Kapol Thongphlub, two Bangkok bars of the same name are lined with 'spirit photographs'. He leads up to 20 Shock members (numbers limited by lucky draw) to secret locations, mostly in Bangkok. Afterwards listeners may independently explore, though he advises, "We don't want people to go there by themselves. Something bad may happen."

Long dominated by indigenous ghost stories, Thai films are starting to scare in the more perfunctory way of global movie clichés, particularly American collegiate gore-fests and possessed-technology flicks from Japan. *Takian* (2003) imitated the *Blair Witch Project* aesthetics, costume drama niceties de-clawed *Nang Nak*'s 1999 remake and the Thai puppet poltergeist in Three (2002) recalls Chucky the doll in *Child's Play*. The antics of *Bupha Ratree* (2003) descend the *Scary Movie* path into self-parody. Yet the generic nature of Thai ghosts make them ripe for export, as artist Navin Rawanchaikul showed in his *manga* comics pitting Japanese superheroes against an invasion of Tokyo by various Thai *phii*.

Whether or not *phii kraseu* is the new Godzilla, Thai ghosts continue to haunt both the psyche and pop culture. So you might think twice before buying that lovely old teak bed that's inexplicably selling for a song.

above: **Worshipped on many altars, *kumarn thong*, the golden boy, is the helpful assistant ghost believed to have been created from a sacrificed foetus.** *PCS*

Left: **One of the many generic ghosts, *phii porb*, lures temple fair goers into a haunted house sideshow.**

Modern Shrines
The spirits keep pace with modern trends

Contemporary shrines offer new styles, new uses and sometimes new deities. While Buddhism remains the consistent bedrock of Thai faith, Hindu gods, spirits and other god figures have their place in modern life.

Saan phra phum (spirit houses) are the defining note of places where Thais live or work. Having evolved from shrines to the village spirit, they reflect social change by marking ever-smaller family plots as Thais have urbanised. Some now stand on shophouse roofs. In ancient indigenous belief, spirits governed a location and needed to be placated to ensure a safe journey or activity. That survives most clearly today through spirit houses being tended daily with offerings and requests for things like the spirit's permission to build, marry or cut trees.

Spirit houses typically come in pairs. *Chao thii* – the animist 'spirit of the place' – occupies the lower one, a plain miniature home on four or six legs. Later Hindu influence on Thai culture means that the taller painted masonry shrine resembles an opulent Khmer sanctuary upon a pedestal. Inside, stands a gilded icon of the 'spirit of the land' holding a sword and money bag, who gets a prestigious Sanskrit name, *phra phum*.

"They are envisaged as an old man who lives in a traditional wooden house and an angel who lives in a

above: **A glass spirit house for an eye clinic on Ratchadaphisek Road in Bangkok.**

right and facing page, bottom: **Marble pyramid designs suit sophisticated spirits of the land in Bangkok's financial district. Note how the higher-ranking spirit lives in a modernist home; the lower-ranking one in a Thai-style house.**

facing page, top: **Old or broken shrines require a blessed site as a dumping ground.**

palace," Marlane Guelden explains. "Thais with Chinese heritage pay homage to an analogous earth god, who resides in a lighted red and gold shrine, often appropriately placed on a store floor." Most stand away from the residence, draped in fairy lights to induce the spirits to reside there and not cause mischief among the humans.

Illustrating the authority of *phra phum*, attendants flank the upper levels, male to the right, female left, while elephants, horses and female dancers cavort on the lower deck. These figurines are usually of moulded plastic. Offering tables in front support incense, candles and tiny bowls for whichever food and drinks that spirit prefers.

Yet old styles may look incongruous beside an edifice of stark modernity. The wooden spirit house fronting the blue-glass façade of Bangkok's Mah Boon Krong mall looks as comfortable as someone's Dad at a teen disco. The only concessions to the mall's faddish character are the swathes of garlands in colourful plastic. As architecture evolves, however, so does spirit house design.

For trend-literate spirits, downtown Bangkok showcases hip shrines to suit the sleek towers they guard. Hence the pyramidal stone and glass geometry *saan phra phum* of Tisco Tower, the bevelled slabs and skylights of the Harindhorn Building shrine, or the multi-faceted one

right: The earth goddess Mae Thoranee wrings water from her hair, often forming a fountain, as at this Siam Square spirit house in Bangkok.

far right: The Chinese goddess of mercy, Kuan Yin, has become an icon of middle class Thais.

below: In a new phenomenon, young trendies sporting red cloth make offerings to this Hindu shrine at Central World Plaza in Bangkok, which they erroneously believe depicts the god of love. The apparently hope to solve relationship problems and find partners. *PCS*

and glass, it preserves key components, such as the lower ledge reaching the owner's eye height, so it can't be overlooked, and the pillar being swathed in tricolour scarves.

"It's like I'm creating a new style of sculpture," says Nopadol Thithipongpanich, designer of Bangkok's Harindhorn shrine. "Before long, modernistic shrines in all kinds of innovative designs will be a common sight." While modernist *saan* have a niche boutique market, most spirits won't see their old-fashioned homes consigned to the sacred disposal sites any time soon.

Discarded shrines litter the feet of sacred trees swathed in tricolour scarves. Invariably under a Bodhi tree – site of Buddha's enlightenment – the *saan* cemetery may occupy a temple or roadside sanctuary. The date and time of removal is as critically auspicious as the moment of installation, divined and conducted by a Brahmin, or more likely a Buddhist monk.

Saan phra phum that stand prominently at the roadside, however, likely indicate danger spots. "Some believe accidents occurred because the dead took other lives to replace their duties, or the victims showed disrespect to *Chao Phor Khao Keow*," states an advertisement for the Disaster Hotline, about Nakhon Sawan bypass. Now many drivers slow down and honk as they pass the spirit houses at this uphill curve, or at other notorious black spots listed on www.disaster.go.th. "Thai belief in spirit houses can be positively defined as a sign of concern for safety on the highway," the ad asserts.

Thus shrine power overrides human control over destiny. Some drivers turning past the Erawan Shrine in Bangkok lift both hands off the wheel to *wai*. The modernity of a shrine lies not just in the architecture, but also in changes in usage, who gets worshipped, and the demographic of devotees.

"There are no gods for city people involved in commerce," writes cultural pundit Nidhi Eoseewong. "It can be said that Kwan Yin has become the goddess of trade." This rosebud-lipped Chinese goddess of mercy has recently been absorbed into Thai popular religion as

of Diethelm Tower. A fusion of hi-tech and high art, they hint how post-modern temples might evolve. Most new temples nationwide follow a generically Central Thai template, rare exceptions including the twin royal *chedi* atop Doi Inthanon mountain, the faceted new spire of Wat Sothon Wararam Worawihan in Chachoengsao, and the flying saucer-esque *chedi* of Wat Phra Dhammakaya, home of a populist Buddhist cult. While the mainstream has hesitated at embracing minimalist shrines, the spirits can be convinced to upgrade their abode.

"I was able to do my job without any worries because I was following the Brahmin priest's orders," assures Suluck Visavapattamawong, architect of the shrine at Oriflame Asoke Tower in Bangkok. A construct of granite

Kuan Im. A bodhisattva in Mahayana Buddhism, she's now also found in vividly painted porcelain at house and shop altars and even in Theravada temples. This helps reclaim the congregation who go to her shrines, like the massive complex at Chokchai Soi 4 in suburban Bangkok to which many of her supplicants annually parade.

"Over the last decade the Goddess cult has come back with a vengeance at a time when the Buddhist clergy – who have marginalised indigenous goddess worship and alienated women supporters through sexism – has begun to lose touch with the middle class," explains Sanitsuda Ekachai of a cult with an individualist accent focusing on meditation, vegetarianism, family and financial security.

"Paralleling the Kuan Yin cult is the worship of King Chulalongkorn as a father figure by city people," Sanitsuda adds. Always present, images of King Rama V have increased in line with the economy since the 1980s boom, as a symbol of progress, stability and prestige. His photograph appears on walls, miniatures form amulets, bronze busts sit on taxi dashboards, myriad images appear in indoor shrines to Rama V in restaurants, homes and businesses. Every Tuesday night, followers gather en masse at his statue in Bangkok's Royal Plaza, especially on his birthday, October 23.

The reform-minded look to Phra Mae Thoranee, an earth goddess shown drowning the demon army of Mara by wringing water – a symbol of Buddha's goodness – from her long hair. Hence she's a popular fountain in gardens. One installed at Sanam Luang park in 1917 doubled as Bangkok's first drinking fountain. Mae Thoranee is also the mascot of the Democrat Party. When the ponytail of her statue at party headquarters snapped in 2003, some saw it as an omen.

The most famous spirit house of all, Bangkok's Erawan Shrine, is actually dedicated to Brahma, rather than its namesake Erawan, the three-headed elephant mount of Indra. Brahma the Creator is part of the Hindu trinity with Vishnu the Preserver and Shiva the destroyer, and has a far bigger following here than in India. The shrine was erected to placate bad spirits troubling construction of the old Erawan Hotel. Today, its mirror-mosaic Khmer-style shelter protects the post-modern Grand Hyatt Erawan Hotel now looming behind. The Erawan Brahma is thought to have the invincible power to answer all wishes. If they're if granted, the wisher returns to donate more offerings and perhaps pay for the troupe of resident dancers to perform.

Since 2003, vendors have sold as many garlands across the intersection at Central World Plaza mall. Its suitably huge spirit house contains a gilt statue of the five-faced Panjaphak. Showing how fashion can transform faith, young trendies have come to believe it's Trimurti (the god combining Brahma, Vishnu and Shiva) and that he's the god of love. They mass here on Thursday nights wearing red and making red offerings in seeking answers about relationships, especially wishing for a foreign partner. "Love is something out of your control," explains twenty-something Nuttamon. "In fact I make my prayers at Buddhist temples and shrines of Chinese and Hindu gods and goddesses. I respect them all, but I choose to go to the one that is said to grant what I'm hoping for."

Given such diverse, pragmatic beliefs, it was only a matter of time before someone combined all Thai faiths in an all-purpose, one-stop shrine. Lek Viriyah, the late creator of the Ancient City museum, founded two multi-denominational centres. At his Erawan Museum in Samut Prakarn, a 150-tonne metal statue of the triple-headed elephant contains a chapel in its head, reached by a lift up the rear left leg. In Pattaya, Lek started the Sanctuary of Truth, an enormous carved wooden shrine depicting more gods from more religions than possibly any structure on earth. And this process will continue as cities and countryside develop at an ever-increasing pace. As the land changes, so will the spirits of the land.

right: **Populating spirit houses, miniature figurines of servants, dancers and auspicious animals keep the spirits of the land in trouble-free contentment.**

Sanuk

****

Temple Fairs
Where it all comes together

Thais go the temple for worship. And also for solace, shelter, or making merit. Others go for healing, learning, or lottery numbers. Or to party. As mural after frolicking mural shows, the sacred sanctuary was a venue where the Thai sought *sanuk* (fun) throughout history. Many still do.

The temple (*wat*) hosts the hottest happening parties in local Thailand. A fund-raising religious event buzzing with raucous energy, the *ngan wat* (temple fair) promotes reverence through fun, combining food fest and flea market, live performance and freak show, casino and courting ground. No wonder *ngan wat* memories make many Thais go misty eyed; each fair is a life episode.

From origins in the seasonal festive cycle, *ngan wat* gained their form through a half-century of development that brought mobile movie projectors, big bands and consumer goods to the Kingdom's remotest corners. Informal village gatherings grew into longer, bigger spectaculars on each temple's annual day, and at bumper festival times, like Thai new year (Songkran), the river-blessing rite Loy Krathong, and each end of the monks' rainy season retreat.

"Not only do Thai villagers commonly make merit in social situations, they enhance their merit by sharing it with others in the act of making it," writes anthropologist Jasper Ingersoll." Dancing then becomes a donation.

Devotion done, people throng the sideshows after dark, every few steps finding some speciality to eat. The agile fold into Dodgem cars or wrought iron gondolas on the neon-spoked Ferris wheel, philosophically dubbed *chingcha sawan* (heaven swing). Friends lark, sweethearts carouse, families treat toddlers to candy. Kids try to snare fish before their paper 'net' disintegrates. Teen sharp-shooters fire pop-guns at targets that, when hit, animate tableaux of motorised costumed dolls. Lads throw balls at levers to dunk a scantily clad girl into water.

So far so innocent, though the hallowed ground also hosts gaudier attractions. Banners of topless mermaids lure the curious to the freak show where mirrors and strategically positioned pink curtains conjure faux fish-women, Siamese twins, and winking, disembodied heads. They're a kitsch yet disturbing throwback to the original Siamese twins, Chang and Eng, who lived a Barnum and Bailey exhibit for real. From dark corners mannequins induce shock when suddenly they flinch. Unlike the hi-tech horror effects in theme parks, these haunted houses are lifelike – because what snatches your wrist, your ankle, your breath… is alive!

While able-bodied actors now play the freaks, dwarfs have migrated to the *talok* (comedy) stage. Another butt of slapstick humour – and source of swoons – *kathoey* (ladyboys) are integral to any Thai festival. Sashaying in flamboyant attire, they star in the parades and beauty contests. Female beauty queens also rehearse their smiles through village pageants.

Festival goers like to test their luck. *Muay thai* boxers hone their kicks at *wat*-side rings and cockfights often feature. *Ngan wat* stage further games of chance, from wheels of fortune and random prize dips to rinks where rats scurry into numbered holes. Some punters win a gamblers' kitty, others Hello Kitty.

Diverse as each district, fairs form a key circuit for touring shows of comedy, dance and music. Massed troupes from Khon Kaen and Udon shimmy in Day-Glo across Isaan, trilling *mor lam* songs to the churning throngs. Shamanistic *manohra* dancers flutter birdlike on festive Southern nights, while shadow puppeteers pass subtle social comment. Likewise in the Central Plains, *likay*, *lamtad* and *pleng choi* – folk opera, bawdy musical banter, and singalongs – bridge stage and audience with wry wordplays, saucy exclamations and exaggerated gestures. In the North, sword dances, long drum contests and *khantoke* floor-dining are as much a part of fairs as ground-level markets under red lacquer umbrellas.

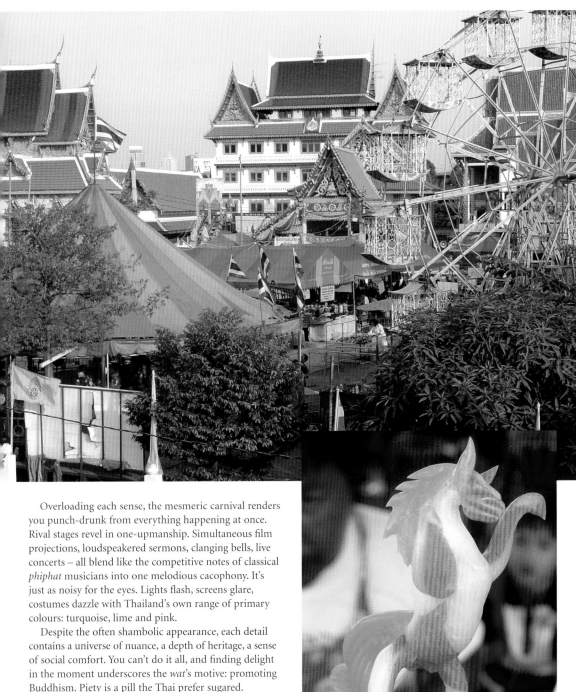

Overloading each sense, the mesmeric carnival renders you punch-drunk from everything happening at once. Rival stages revel in one-upmanship. Simultaneous film projections, loudspeakered sermons, clanging bells, live concerts – all blend like the competitive notes of classical *phiphat* musicians into one melodious cacophony. It's just as noisy for the eyes. Lights flash, screens glare, costumes dazzle with Thailand's own range of primary colours: turquoise, lime and pink.

Despite the often shambolic appearance, each detail contains a universe of nuance, a depth of heritage, a sense of social comfort. You can't do it all, and finding delight in the moment underscores the *wat*'s motive: promoting Buddhism. Piety is a pill the Thai prefer sugared.

The *sanuk* is like the 'hallelujahs!' in a gospel choir – a communal re-affirmation, a gentle way to proselytise. "We should invite others to make merit with us, which increases our own merit," villagers of Sakathiam, Nakhon Phanom, told Ingersoll. He found that most Thais prefer to make merit at their own temple, where it will be more visible to people who matter.

Hence, *ngan wat* happen in great numbers, even in Bangkok. They're so part of the cultural furniture, so local, that news of them only spreads by banners and

above: **Sweets swiftly sculpted from warm pearlescent sugar using metal shears, at a fair in Ayutthaya.**

word-of-mouth, not media listings. Those outside the loop must rely on serendipity. A succession of multi-colour fluorescent tubes hanging from trees indicates a fair's around the corner or hidden up a lane.

To draw custom, many *wat* offer garish attractions. "These days a fair is likely to include acrobats and other circus-like acts, even a 'wall of death' motorcycle stunt," writes Subhatra Bhumiprabhas. "People's reasons for coming have also changed. A temple fair used to be for all the family… but still attracts bargain hunters, the curious and the nostalgic. The main attraction for the younger generation has been the chance to catch their favourite *luuk thung* band and to enter amateur song contests." And, given the growth in stalls, to shop.

The 1940s Phibunsongkhram regime encouraged fairs to distribute local produce. The template of this trend towards trade was the Golden Mount fair, recalls Suthorn Sukphisit, the *Bangkok Post*'s festival-spotting columnist. "It set the style for many kinds of events, offering clothing for sale before the days of garments for export, household items before the advent of home shows, and amusement parks for children before anyone had thought of Dream World."

Today, the coming of the fair remains a novelty that villagers celebrate. As a portal to new horizons, it features as a primal moment in several recent Thai movies: the *muay thai* initiation in *Beautiful Boxer*, the *luuk thung* singing contest in *Mon Rak Transistor*, the renaissance of folk wisdom in the Isaan-dialect *Mekong Full Moon Party*. Urban trendies may wince at labelling this guileless *sanuk* as nightlife, but sophistication's at a premium when several provinces were, in 2002, declared "disco-free". The only way the youth of Sukhothai and Ang Thong get to bob to Techno is aboard a merry-go-round.

Some officials harrumph about the cheerful vulgarity of the *ngan wat*, and seek to sanitise it. Yet fairs thrive precisely because they cater to public mores. Fine arts decline faster the more rigidly they're defended, since any tone of compulsion alienates the potential audience. By contrast, folk arts remain viable because they're free to adapt, to remain 'pop'. Given many temples' declining social roles and attendance rolls, *ngan wat* committees, always secular, adopt mass-market tips from malls and television. Yet these rivals inherited their variety formats from the fair: garish colours, advertising, low humour, high jinks, celebrities, music and chatty MC duos, mixed with veneration. In some ways Thai TV resembles one continuously broadcast *ngan wat*.

With temples scarce in Bangkok suburbs, fairs often visit vacant lots. Among their biggest fans are migrants relishing a reminder of home. Thus fairs seem backward to some of the urban elite, who go to the *wat* largely for ritual, favour pubs and cinemas for entertainment, and

won't mix with the masses. "Although [Golden Mount Fair] is thought of as an event for people of the lower social classes, it is actually an authentic Thai cultural event that is never restricted or closed to any segment of society," Suthorn retorts. "In this way it is different from modern, specifically designed 'culture streets' like Phra Arthit Road, with its uninterrupted line of yuppy pubs."

Cultural 'Walking Streets' are one of the ways people reinvent *ngan wat*. It took the 1997 crash for the erosion of traditions and community to be noticed. The wave of nostalgia for things Thai found the fair format ideal. In 1998, the '1st Alternative Temple Fair' sold organic produce and herbal remedies, while promoting the Buddhist path to economic recovery. Bangkok Governor Bhichit Rattakul then instigated the Walking Street to galvanise communities and promote local products. Since applied upcountry, this marked the first time pedestrians reclaimed the roads from traffic.

The liberating Walking Street mood inspired *indy* youth to create truly alternative fairs with art, dance, music and handmade books. Out of this impromptu trend evolved the fair-like Bangkok Theatre Festival. "What makes us most happy is when the rich people sit in the audience with the poor people," enthuses its 2003 director, Pradit Prasartthong, whose troupe applies *likay* to current affairs in modern contexts.

Others took the *ngan wat* upmarket. The corporate-run Wat Arun Fair applied a Rama III-era theme, even in costumes, games and coins. Patravadi Theatre instead makes the *ngan wat* contemporary. It often hosts fringe acts, workshops, traditional masters and cross-cultural hybrids for the same audience at the same event. The open-air stage has a fairground ambiance, amid stalls, food, art, music and happenings. Founder Patravadi Mejudhon integrated old and new by working outside the establishment. The state stages Thai arts mainly for VIPs. To visitors' dismay, the National Theatre hosts ad hoc, occasional events with minimal publicity, rather than scheduling – as Tokyo's *kabuki* theatre does – daily shows with top artists, clear explanation and taped translation, so people can gain appreciation for the real thing.

Those interested must make do with lacklustre tourist dinner shows – or find a fair. "In a country where Westernisation is rapidly replacing traditional ways, the temple fair is one of the few places where you can still experience what is left of Thailand's traditional popular culture," says John Clewley, an expert on Thai music.

The most dynamic *ngan wat* movement is in the North. Subjected to Bangkokian standardisation for decades, Lanna culture has resurged since the late 1980s. Walking Streets have been most successful in Chiang Mai. Meanwhile, the cultural experts Vithi Phanichphant and Paothong Thongchua have helped re-energise Lanna festivities with both care for authenticity and fervent imagination. Their fair-style events fizz with wit and drama, drawing both locals and urban sophisticates.

For modern people to appreciate the *ngan wat*'s many attractions as exotic, rather than mundane, requires the rekindling of interest in festival-making. That process was always interactive and developing. At many northern fairs everyone present dons local fabric as a mark of respect and participation, as they do in many offices each Friday. Though the combined impact is stunning, some might consider this contrived. But traditions are merely an accumulation of contrived acts. *Ngan wat* result from the layering of innovations upon conventions over many generations. By mixing a diversity of popular culture, the folk fair remains a crucible of cultural change.

Festivals
Ancient rites, invented traditions and imported ways to party

Thailand doesn't just hold festivals – it turns everything into a festival. Few countries match its constant calendar of fun, the variety of excuses to have it, and the glee with which even the most sombre occasion bubbles. *Sanuk*, the sensibility for gaiety, gets fully unleashed at such times. Festivals run a wide spectrum. In those geared to Buddhist, royal or national days, the keynote is reverence, decorum and time-honoured form. At the other end is the 'Walking Street', where a neighbourhood turns a road into a stage for a day. In between, countless other festivals invent new rituals, adapt ancient rites or turn imported celebrations Thai.

Community involvement is total. At these moments, Thailand wistfully evokes Neverland, Fairyland, Disneyland – a realm of imagination and delight. Villages and urban parades take on a themepark feel, with fantasy sets, mythic creatures, infectious smiles. And entry is free.

New festivals apply a traditional formula so 'authentic' they seem to date from antiquity. First take a local product, animal, activity or historical happening. Then add contests, processions, costumes, concerts, stalls, beauty pageants and, crucially, food. Finally serve with a liberal dose of *sanuk* and two chattering MCs under the benevolent presence of an 'influential' VIP, typically with graduated shades and slicked-back hair.

Of course, the party should be profitable. All festivals feature markets, many with specialist dishes. Out of humble harvest rituals with produce to sell, a rainbow of fruit fairs exploded. Rambutan, durian, lychee, longan –

the promotions blossomed into festivals with heritage trappings and lots carvings in ice, fruit and Styrofoam. Similar salesmanship inspires Chiang Mai Flower Festival, Khon Kaen Silk Festival, Bo Sang Umbrella Fair, Saraburi Sunflower Festival, Pracha-Nareumit Furniture Fair. Often, the principal rite is the right to shop.

To attract tourists, new festivals may focus on wacky activities. Farmers turned casual water buffalo contests into the staged Chonburi Buffalo Races. Surin revived elephant corralling into an Elephant Round-Up, along with costumed 'battles' and elephant football. Even the scientific Elephant Conservation Centre in Lampang hosts an annual *satoke* (Northern feast) for pachyderms. Anantara resort in Hua Hin recently imported elephant polo, which will doubtless soon seem Thai all along. Thai trippers to Lopburi show more interest in feeding the monkey colony than in the town's landmarks. Hence the annual banquet for the monkeys. It feels like a primordial offering to the gods, who anyway should be placated.

above: Since the Songkran (Thai new year celebrations) have turned into a water fight, the authorities have tried to ban pump-action spray guns like this fired by a Northern man in Chiang Mai. *PCS*

left: Songkran's heartland is the north, where for up to ten days people douse each other. Tens of thousands of revellers flock to the moat of Chiang Mai for *sanuk* and unlimited water to toss. *PCS*

right: **Re-enactments of Siamese battles on elephant back are a staple of modern extravaganzas. This one at Samphran Elephant Ground marks the Miss Jumbo Queen beauty contest.** *SYL*

below: **For Loy Krathong festival, floats traditionally crafted from banana stem, leaves and flowers, have been created here using lottery ticket origami for extra luck.**

bottom: **To combat polluting polystyrene** *krathong,* **eco-friendly bread rafts not only keep the water clean and feed the fish, as here at Bangkok's Lumphini Park, but also offer cute new design potential.**

While new events try to look antique, old fiestas get a makeover. The Phi Ta Khon ghost festival in Dan Sai, Loei, centralised several villages' versions, and then morphed with new materials and modern themes. Ghost masks bear trendy slogans or even logos. The spontaneity can be spoiled, though, when mass tourism overwhelms local events, or when officials prioritise order over fun.

Where a festival involves national identity, like Loy Krathong and Songkran, the Thai new year, the moralists get into high gear. Loy Krathong implies continuity since the Sukhothai era, so this dainty water rite emphasises decorum and traditional dress. Reflected candlelight from the elaborate *krathong* floats sparks a national sigh of contentment at being Thai. No wonder the fad for kids to toss firecrackers drew reprimands and a neat solution: organised firework extravaganzas. Others violate this 'thank you' for clean water by turning the *krathong* – normally of banana trunk, flowers and banana leaf origami – into a polluting Styrofoam raft with plastic bunting. In a playful, ecological compromise, some are baked of bread with cute sugar decorations.

Festivals must balance two contradictory principles. "A combination of *sanuk* (fun) and *sa-ngob* (serenity) has brought about the outgoing personality of the Thai," columnist Thanong Khanthong writes about Songkran. "Yet *sanuk* can get out of hand in berserk-like fashion." A fertility rite adapted from India via Burma, Songkran involves sprinkling Buddha images, elders' hands and friends using water scented with petals and powdery *nam ob* liquid. But from this quintessence of quaintness, Songkran became a water fight.

For three days – up to ten in the North – strangers drench each other. Each gang out-crazes the next, using pump-action guns, buckets and home-made canons of blue plastic pipe to spray water that's chilled, dyed pink or from canals. Dancing revellers scoop water from vats on pick-up trucks while cruising around all day. Passers-by receive handfuls of paste in the face, clouds of prickly heat powder in the eye, and ice cubes slipped down neck or waistband. "Songkran has come to increasingly signify violence," Thanong laments. "But we rarely complain because nobody wants to stand in the way of *sanuk*." But the authorities do, inevitably, try.

Songkran had been suppressed in Bangkok as unruly in times of dictatorship. Today, government attempts to zone water throwing, ban spaghetti-strap blouses and arrest anyone dousing motorcyclists. Paradoxically, the *sanuk* surplus only highlights the extent of self-control in daily life by making drudgery bearable and acting as a social safety valve. Just as Christmas brightens the Western winter solstice, Songkran always enlivened the hottest, most barren season and was a rare chance to flirt.

Despite frequent festive days, workers have few other days leave. The massed rush of migrants to their home province adds to the horrific Songkran road toll – which in 2003 outstripped allied deaths in the Iraq invasion. People go wild. Enforcing any code becomes hard when the police themselves are drenched. It's the one time when people can freely get their own back.

To promote a 'return to a gentler golden age', the state dazzles the public and tourists with spectacle. Sound and light extravaganzas trumpet a nation-building script at historically sensitive locations: Sukhothai; Ayutthaya, razed by the Burmese; Bangkok's 'River of Kings'; Khmer sanctuaries in what is now Thailand; re-enactments of wartime horrors at the River Kwae Bridge. The dialogue many sound like a press release, though the staging can summon wit and whimsy.

Thai craftsmanship evolved in service to power, so state pageantry conveys meaning and magic through ornamented costumes, gateways and mythological tableaux. These are so detailed, delicate and finessed that Thai floats regularly win the Pasadena Rose Parade in California. At home, competition between proud groups keeps standards high and ensures diversity. Yet designs look coherent because artisans – though suffering the loss of masters, oral knowledge and everyday usage – use *lai thai* traditional patterns. This language of iconic shapes transfers well to modern materials and techniques.

The attempt to turn Bangkok's 2002 Songkran parade into a mardi gras felt more like a revival, with elaborate imaginings of folklore using foam, foil and gold aerosol – and that was just the costumes; the floats went really over the top. Though rather mannered, the annual 'River of Kings' extravaganza has witnessed astonishing sets by artist Chalermchai Kositphiphat and human puppet out-fits as ingenious as any in the musical *The Lion King*.

The country seems on permanent festival standby, primed since childhood to dance or garland flowers at a moment's notice. Sometimes that's all the notice that event 'planners' give. Knowledge must remain secret until selectively released just days ahead, foiling stated aims to boost tourism and often denying a willing audience the chance to attend.

That cliché of the impromptu Broadway musical – "hey, let's do the show right now!" – seems to be standard procedure. Festivals pop out of nowhere. Bureaucrats

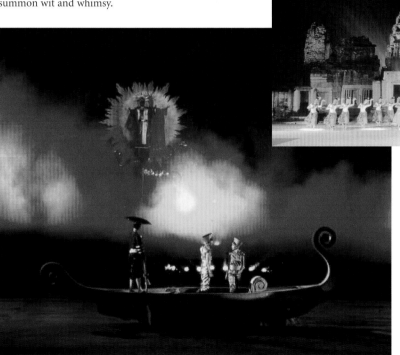

above: **Sound and light shows reimagine history at many ancient monuments, from Sukhothai and the River Kwae to Phimai, shown here.** *TAT*

left: **The annual River of Kings spectacular on the Chao Phraya in Bangkok has taken the staging of sound and light shows to Broadway standards.** *TAT*

right: **Sound and Light shows both revive Thai costume skills and serve diplomatic purposes. This temple show at Phi Ta Khon ghost festival in Loei dramatises a pact by Thai and Lao kings.** *PCS*

below: **The Khmer-era ruins at Lopburi are perhaps most famous for their colony of feral monkeys. So now a festive annual banquet is held in their honour.** *TAT*

may keep organisers hostage by granting last-minute approval, but a lot must always be done on the day. Make-up can be highly elaborate and dancers must be stitched individually into their costumes by an assistant, so that arms and torso fit tight. Moreover, much of the décor is perishable: folded banana-leaf offerings; miles of flower arrangements; ice and fruit carvings on a vast scale. While Sydney Mardi Gras plans a year ahead, Bangkok's gay pride parade must be thrown together in

36 hours after approval to use the road on condition the event conforms to Thai culture. Thus Lycra and lamé get transformed into loincloths and crowns. The average Lanna procession shows only marginally less skin.

One objection to the gay parade is that it is foreign, yet the calendar's full of ethnically alien parties, from new year countdowns to Christmas. Halloween plugs straight into the fetish for ghost stories. Though some regard St Valentine's Day as an affront to Thai (female) virtue, it has become a Thai festival through the Trang underwater massed wedding. Another import, the Guinness World Record attempt, is usually a group event in Thailand: largest buffet, longest catwalk, biggest mass aerobics. Record-breaking efforts turn into full-blown festivals while stoking local and national pride. What could be more Thai than filling a stadium with hundreds of metres of bamboo and banana leaf scaffolding to support the world's longest Thai sausage?

Chinese immigrants are now so assimilated that their culture no longer seems foreign. Since the rise to power of Sino-Thai businessmen in the 1990s, Chinese festivals have gone from a minority family affair to celebrations of a common heritage, particularly in Phuket, Bangkok and Nakhon Sawan. A few years ago, Chinatown fell silent at Chinese New Year. Now ministers in silk pajamas lead parades past Bangkok's opulent new Chinese gate.

The urge to make any activity festive goes beyond *sanuk*. Siamologist Neils Mulder puts it down to the animist-Buddhist mind's moment-to-moment need to feel *tham samai* – up-to-date, both with trends and in renewing short-term contracts with the spirits. Carnivals are also a chance to make merit, make money and attract tourists. And as villagers migrate, a yearning for carefree communal bonding shifts the revelry from field to stadium, temple fair to themepark. Likewise, imported modern activities like catwalk fashion become part of the culture by bringing them under festive control, making them fun, auspicious and Thai.

Gambling

The urge to bet on lotteries, hi-lo and half-goal

Anytime football is televised live, much of the country tunes in – at home or in bars, restaurants, shops, hotels, and even saunas. They're not watching Thai teams, but Spanish, Italian or German matches, and especially the English Premier League. Come the World Cup, attention is all-consuming. Football kits are worn by teens and mums alike. Soccer corners conversation and acts as an ice-breaker in talking to *farang*. The lure for fans is partly sporting, partly fashion, but also financial. Thais bet 100 billion baht a year on football – and it's all illegal.

Punters prefer handicap bets to figuring odds. In leisure as in politics, Thais hedge by backing favourites, with the margin of dominance – goal difference – being the deciding factor. The onus is on the favourite to win, though bets on underdogs get returns for wins, draws or limiting the defeat. Odds like 'half goal' mean the payout is halved if the favourite merely wins by one goal.

Yet football is just a fraction of a gaming economy in which 70 percent of Thais indulge. Originally betting on animal contests like cockfights, Thais came to wager on games of chance, lotteries, casinos and other sports. State lotto, plus totes on horse racing and *muay thai*, are the only legal flutters – though that may change.

The archetypal street-corner, drinking-buddy, honour-settling, gamer's game is *soong-tam* (high-low), better known as *hi-lo*. Simply toss three dice and count. A total above 11 rewards those calling 'high'; 11 or below wins for calls of 'low'. But 'low-high' might better describe the escalating stakes: bet coins, your shirt, your buffalo.

Dice games start young. Kids get weaned on *namtao-poo-pla* (gourd-crab-fish), named after a cubic cardboard box depicting prawn, goldfish, crab, cockerel, frog and bottle gourd on sides numbered 1 to 6. The die rattles with seeds that help it settle once tossed. Put money on a picture on the game board and hope it matches what lands face-up on the die. Frog-frog, you win.

Even simpler is the wheel of fortune. Fevered huddles of men at fairs place money on numbers matching those on a spinning wheel. If its spin stops at your digit, you collect. Of course, certain numbers are pre-determined as lucky, which is one reason gambling's integral to popular culture. The national psyche of fatalism tempered by luck propitiation – making offerings to spirits for big returns – applies directly when Thais seek lottery numbers from monks, mediums and fortune tellers. Ahead of draws on the 15th and end of each month, thousands flock to

'winning' shrines like the Erawan Museum. Some discern numerical shapes in natural oddities like waxed bark. In 2001, a monitor lizard 'possessed' by its owner's dead son suffered when hundreds of people rubbed it with powder to see numbers magically appear.

For all the superstition, figuring odds may sharpen the mathematical mind. "Gambling is a product of a society advanced in finance," says one Thammasat lecturer. "I believe it derives from China." While the chance of easy money may lure ethnic Thais, the Sino-Thai penchant for having a flutter mirrors their willingness to take risks in business. The top bookmakers hail from Chinatown and illegal casinos nearly all bear Chinese-Thai names.

Gambling naturally favours the bankers, who benefit further from the fact that staking ever more money gains face. Bankers often evolve into 'influential figures' (that's code, used in newspapers, for scary people you wouldn't want to argue with). Their fee might be as high as a quarter of a bet and the odds constantly shift. Doubts about fairness extend to scandal-hit official draws – one reason the National Lottery Office was immolated in the 1992 massed protests. Today, there are live TV broadcasts of the blind-sighted wheel-spinning and ball plucking.

Aside from illegality, debts are a reason bettors like anonymity. As gaming debts were endemic in old Siam, King Rama V criminalised gambling to stop people selling their children, wives or selves into slavery on failing to repay. Yet still today, loan sharks pray on the millions who can't resist frittering away their future.

Though gaming is half-hidden, the equipment's sold brazenly. Signposted by outsized dice, specialist shops in Bangkok's old town stock boards, dice, chips, cards and counting paraphernalia. Poker faced about their purpose, owners make like they are toy shops. "These games are obviously illegal, so there are not any licenses for selling them," admits a former retailer. "My dealer would pay the local police station a *suay* (periodic bribe), about 35,000-40,000 baht per year when I retired in 1995. That makes the shop go 'unseen', or else its stock is counted as leisure goods. Retailers who don't bribe instead sell out the back door for advance purchase orders."

Gambling is a very big business. Underground lotteries made 542 billion baht in 2001, up from 320 billion in 1995. In addition, surveys count casino turnover at 673 billion baht in Bangkok and 142 billion baht upcountry. Plus so much currency flows to foreign casinos that it may affect the baht exchange rate. Of casino proceeds, operators get 20 percent and police around 1.7 percent according to findings by Sangsidh Piriyarangsan. When Pol Lt Col Santhana Prayoonrat was dismissed in 2002 for resisting a casino raid, he revealed to the press – citing maps, names and videos – that "up to 10 gambling dens in Bangkok each pay up to 10 million baht a month for the police to turn a blind eye." The capital also has over a hundred smaller gambling dens.

Many feel the national interest lies in bringing the black economy out of gangsterism and into the regulated open, something that the state lottery has failed to do since its founding in 1939. Meanwhile, the state ponders how it too, while espousing morality, can make money from gambling through 'sin taxes'. Some ministers have advocated lifting bans on cockfighting, casinos and now soccer speculation. Who'd bet against it?

In 2003 the Government Lottery Office (GLO) started playing the illegal numbers racket at its own game: lots of draws of 2 and 3 digits for fixed prizes. As well as 12,000 online terminals, it says proceeds will go to good causes, and promises innovations like scratch cards, mobile phone bets and, possibly, Internet gambling. Though the GLO offers worse odds, it has not only turned many punters legit, but has, as feared, hooked additional, better educated customers. "I don't see new forms of online lotto as things that will make our society worse," rebuts GLO director general Chaiwat Pasokpuckdee. "On the contrary, I see these as ways to protect society."

Of course, powerful legislators would never frequent a gambling den. It's amazing how raids on these widely known institutions can arrest over 200,000 punters a year yet almost never net any *phu yai* (big shots), just warm seats, scattered mah jong tiles and a haughty matron threatening to sue. Yet some influential politicians readily admit, nay boast, of gambling abroad. In 2003, the first Thai minister convicted for corruption claimed his unusual wealth was winnings from Australia. Hence the baize tables in offshore liners, Thai-owned casinos across the Khmer and Burma borders, society photos of *phu yai* with Macao kingpins, and the Thai spirit house at Caesar's Palace, Las Vegas.

Repatriating lost currency, argue some, justifies a legit casino in Pattaya, Phuket or Koh Chang. It might help tourism, since Vegas is seen as a model for de-sleazing Pattaya. Still, many feel the benefits aren't worth the moral costs. As with decriminalising drugs – also floated by government – the frisson of what's left illegal persists.

Unregulated gambling appeals to several Thai traits: freedom, *sanuk*, sociability, courting luck, and delight in outwitting authority, in the manner of the sly folk hero Srithanonchai. "For many people who run it, and the punters, the underground lottery is a way of life," points out Preeyanat Panayanggoor, noting research by Professor Sangsit Piriyarangsan that it's been the habit of half of Thailand's adults for a century.

Given the gambling culture – and the ease of betting by cellphone – Thais will likely still wager in unofficial ways. There seems little to stop secretaries running sweepstakes, vendors issuing 'tax-free' lotto, or friends making a card game 'interesting'? The local bookie, and his musclebound mates, can always offer discounts, faxed bets and repayment schemes you simply can't refuse. So, to suppress or to legalise? Maybe they should decide with a toss of the *hi-lo* dice.

top: **Friends wager with bottle cap chips on a two-man game of checkers at Bobae Market, Bangkok.**

above: **A plastic playing surface for the dice game *hi-lo* can be rolled up quickly if need be.** *PCS*

left: **Football integrated fully into Thai culture when Wat Pariwat in Bangkok installed a sculpture of David Beckham into its altar. His then Manchester United strip even included the sponsor's logo, though Becks' hair has changed many times since. The mural shows a scene from hell. Soccer gamblers perhaps?** *PCS*

Animal Contests
Betting on buffaloes and beetles, cockerels and fish

When an opinion-former like rock star Add Carabao champions a cause, you can be sure it has huge support – and commercial potential. In espousing full legalisation of cockfighting Carabao taps a part of the Zeitgeist. Many animal fighting traditions remain popular despite being legally limited to just a few arenas due to cruelty, gambling and the impression that it's 'uncivilised'. Still, specialist magazines feature cock fancying and fighting fish, stag beetle duels symbolise resurgent Lanna regional pride, and bull fights draw Samui holidaymakers. One temple fair sideshow involves betting on which hole in a circular rink a rat will exit through. Enthralling to some, repugnant to others, pet pugilism never dies.

Yet such blood sports hardly reconcile with Buddhist compassion. "Thai people do contradictory things all the time," reflects cultural scholar Anucha Thirakanont. "They release animals at temples, trying to compensate for killing animals for food, yet they torture them in contests." Still, the aim is usually not to kill, but to see

which combatant's nerve holds. Southern Thais pit bull against bull not against man, with no spears, sword or ritual death. Horns lock, nostrils snort, hoofs pad the dirt bullring until one simply runs away.

Kwaang (stag or Hercules Beetles) lock horns on a very different arena – a stick of sugar cane or soft wood. The contested female is kept beneath it or in a carved niche. *Kwaang* can be trained using their taste for sweet things and a metal whirligig hums them into combat mood. It may take 15 minutes until one *kwaang* lifts another or flees twice. Eventually, the winner gets to breed. To stop them flying off during their five-month rainy-season lifespan, collectors tie their upper horn to a carved, toothpick-size stake. "The tether has to be beautiful – it's like a boxer's trunks," says Niyom Chuenjaidee. "If a beetle has an eye-catching outfit, it can intimidate his opponent." Many *kwaang* get named after politicians.

A common pastime for kids, *kwaang* contests remain a semi-covert adult sport at markets or gambling dens. A few are licensed, but police harass breeders. "Local entertainment treated as an offence! The authorities have never understood the people's way of living," argues Pairath Disthabamrung. He founded the Hercules Beetle Club of Thailand in 1996 to preserve both the tradition and beetles. With the head pulled off, *kwaang* make a tasty snack when fried. But with the drop in population through eating now being balanced by breeding, there are plans to export them as a trendy pet to Japan.

Gambling laws also affect *pla kud* (Siamese fighting fish). "The government allows breeding for conservation only. Fish fighting is illegal. We don't get backing because many people think we torture them," says the owner of Pla Kud Paa shop in Chatuchak Weekend Market, named after Isaan's favoured species. Central Thais prefer the *pla kud luuk mor*, Southerners raise a bigger cross-breed, while connoisseurs keep the less combative Chinese *pla kud jeen* in aquariums. Breeders rate aggression, as well as the number, colour and beauty of the fins that make the genus (aptly named *Betta splendens*) so collectable.

The fish can be trained, taking eight months to mature. "To make the fish fight we use its instinct," the vendor adds. "To toughen it or improve swimming skill, just stir the water. To make it more energetic, let it chase a female." A single parent, the male *pla kud* fights less over mating than to protect the fry at his nest, which he makes out of bubbles in still, shallow water. Other *pla kud*, even the mother, may cannibalise the young fish.

Remove the card between two narrow jars they're kept in, and they'll butt the glass and flare their fabulous fins.

left: Siamese fighting fish kept calm by a card inserted between each lovingly inscribed jar. On seeing a rival, the males flare and intensify the hues of their fins. Poured into the same jar they bite each other to submission or death.

right: A sign at Sukhothai's ruins appropriates the city's UNESCO World Heritage status. *PCS*

lower right and bottom: Prize birds peck, flail and stab in a *bon kai* (cock casino) ring. *TGC*

below: Between bouts, roosters get tended with herbal ointments to salve wounds, clear clots from their gullet and increase their fighting spirit. *TGC*

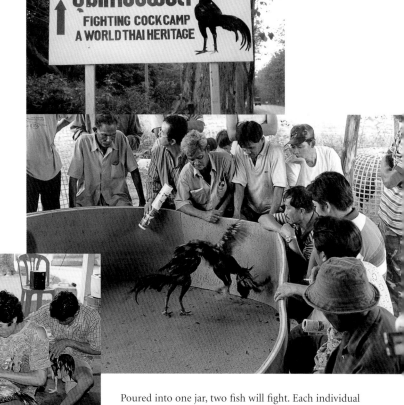

Poured into one jar, two fish will fight. Each individual nibbles it's favoured spot, whether fin, tail, body or cheek. When one flees they're separated and their wounds treated. "Mostly, we won't let it die. We preserve the fish with special formulae to make them stronger," says the vendor. The ingredients can include soil from a termite mound, or dried leaves of banana or deer's ear plant. And their favourite food: mosquito larvae.

In a scary development in 2004, enthusiasts illegally imported piranhas. Police seizures of the Amazonian flesh eater prompted fears they'd be released into waterways. Though the risk is low, Police Colonel Wichit Nanthawong warned: "Be careful going into the water. Especially men should cover themselves well, otherwise they could be sorry for the rest of their lives."

Centuries of breeding were also threatened when in 2004 bird flu swept camps of *kai chon* (fighting cock). Culls partly exempted the camps, which since 1982 have been limited to two per province. Tall and strong, patient yet fierce, this native species is reared separately in domed bamboo coups. The yellow necked, white-tailed *lueang hang khao* is the prized breed used by Prince Naresuan in the late 16th century. He gambled on cock fights with the Burmese viceroy while a hostage in Pegu before liberating Ayutthaya as king.

"We breed *kai chon* separate from other chickens," explains Boonrawd, an aficionado in Saraburi. "When one reaches eight months, we train it by bouts with one the same age. Good fighters we keep for breeding, others

last half of the ten possible rounds of 15 minutes. The birds start off clashing in mid-air, then scrap on the ground with boxer-like holds as they tire. "When a cock cannot keep fighting, it'll cry out and run. The referee then stops the fight," Boonrawd says. "Each owner bets equal money to the banker, the winner getting all the money minus 10 per cent for the casino fee."

Even cocks worth up to 100,000 baht look deceptively scrawny. That's because they're cooled with water in grooming and clinic regimens before the match and in the ten-minute gaps between bouts, as Sam Fang records. Swabbing with saline turmeric water, a 'doctor' will suck clots from swellings, stitch cuts, apply a heat compress, massage the stiffening legs and feed them rice laced with sugar, lemon and other ingredients. Blood and mucous gets removed from the gullet by twirling a feather, which then gets shoved up its rectum to induce an enema. As if that doesn't make them angry enough, smoke from burning herbs heightens their fighting spirit.

Though cock breeders dote on their brood, animal rights activists condemn what they see as cruel violence parading as entertainment. Yet official disapproval forces it underground and invites gangsterism. "Two *bon kai* in each province aren't enough because there are lots of small clubs," complains Uan, a breeder. "They go to *bon paa* (forest casinos) instead." You can still see roosters peeping out of motorcyclists' jackets in Bangkok.

The influential ex-interior minister Sanoh Thienthong also campaigns for full legalisation, citing its role in local culture and community. As a sign in Sukhothai declares: "Fighting Cock Camp: A World Thai Heritage." This highlights a dilemma that many countries face: whether fighting heritage should be kept intact, sanitised or banned. Who would like to bet on the outcome?

we use as meat." Its long thighs are particularly relished. A cock learns to leap, defend and recover from tumbles, as well as peck, flail and stab, though its spurs are usually sheathed. Some now pad treadmills, pop vitamins, ingest secret herbal nutrients, eat organic foods (including raw meat), endure skin-enriching turmeric baths, and wear powder (from rice water) against the heat. The constant handling accustoms them to human instructions.

Punters pack the *bon kai* (literally 'cock casino') arena, whether dirt pit or barn with ranks of bleechers. Amid frantic gestures of the odds, vast sums of money change hands. To audience cries of "Ao! Ao! Ao!", bouts usually

Muay Thai

Thai boxing kicks and punches its way from ringside ritual into global pop culture icon

Tony Ja aims to do for *muay thai* what Bruce Lee did for kung fu. In his hit movie *Ong Bak* (2003), the actor took Thai kick boxing into choreographed cinematic realms. *Beautiful Boxer*, the biopic of transgender pugilist Nong Toom, followed in a swift one-two. As this national icon goes global, *muay thai* faces a fight: how Thai can it stay?

International celebrity comes curiously late, since *muay thai* rates among the deadliest of martial arts. *Crouching Tiger*-esque special effects aren't required to make this brutal sport beautiful. Nimble swings, leaps and swivels display the grace of the dancer, the precision of the craftsman, the dignity of a warrior. "Such a mixture of gentleness and violence is characteristic of the Thai people and their culture," poet Montri Umavijani writes. "Thais were subject to a call to military duty at any moment. Military training was usually given to people, even children, in temple schools. Basic to this was a boxing skill."

The *nak muay* (Thai boxer) wields five weapons: fist, elbow, knee, kick and foot thrust. Linked by theatrical footwork, these can also act as armour. Strengths and vulnerabilities ensure that no weapon can dominate. As a student rule goes: "kick loses to punch, punch loses to knee, knee loses to elbow, elbow loses to kick". It takes years to master the 15 major and 15 minor tactics. Winners display their own flair, but strategy prevails over showmanship; a mundane thud to a thigh might sap more effectively than slamming elbows upon shoulders.

Muay thai connects many threads of folk culture: play, music, gambling, dance and respect for teachers, not to mention amulets, aromatherapy and the army. Underpinning this raw physical discipline lurks a very Thai weapon: modesty. Showbiz may yet compromise *muay thai*'s integrity, but polite, gigglesome Thai boxers are a welcome respite from boastful Ali or thuggish Tyson. To paraphrase the Olympic ideal, what counts is not the winning, nor even the taking part, but the respect for tradition. "No boxer wins ultimately," Montri insists. "He only wins when he knows where he stands. Out of the fight he becomes a gentleman and artist." Whatever the prize or glory, this sets *muay thai* – as well as Thai sword fighting and *krabi-krabong* stick-wielding – apart from most sports. Behind the punch lies prayer.

Before entering the ring, a fighter requests permission and protection from the spirits at his corner three times, tests which nostril breathes easiest and strides with that side's foot first to the ring, skipping the unlucky lowest step. Before leaping in, he'll *wai*, and may stroke the top rope, uttering incantations. Once inside, some *nak muay* circle the ring, touching the ropes to seal out evil. He may offer flowers to his corner. From the middle, he'll *wai* each side, a gesture that in tennis earns Paradorn Srichapan many fans.

Before each bout, boxers must perform the *wai khru ram muay* dance in homage to teachers past and present. From kneeling prostration – derived from when fighting

left: **A boxing poster in a café beside Bangkok's legendary Lumphini Stadium. Note the neck garlands, and two images from the Thai historical war movie** *Bangrajan*: **the water buffalo Boonlert, and the film's title in Thai lettering, which shows several** *unalom*, **an auspicious symbol closely resembling the Thai lucky number nine.** *PCS*

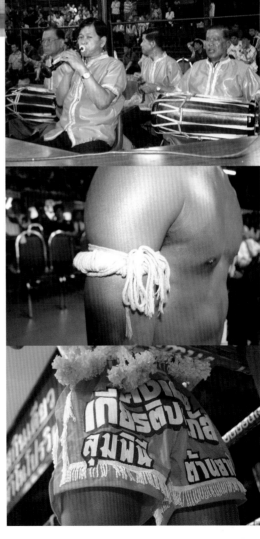

before royalty – he juts one leg out and the other back, rotates his hands paw-like, draws his arms out wide and thrusts them forward, rocking with precise rhythm. He pivots to repeat the rite in all four compass directions, never starting in unlucky west. Both then stand to mime the footwork they'll later use in the fight. Enhancing the trance-like moment, the band's cymbals ching, drums mutter and Javanese oboe rasps. A live soundtrack to the fight, this eerie cacophony builds during each round to a frantic crescendo until stopped by the bell.

These elegant motions help psyche-up the nerves, warm the muscles and focus the mind. A chance to assess the foe's prowess, it formerly enabled combatants in dirt arenas to scope out the sun glare and ground conditions. A boxer moving thumb from canvas to forehead echoes the placating of the earth goddess Mae Thoranee. Other ritual quirks may be personal. Nong Toom mimed hair brushing and checking his make-up in a compact mirror during the *ram muay*. Upon victory, he planted a kiss on the vanquished, adding blush to bloodied cheeks.

Oil slathered upon the boxer's taut skin helps deflect blows and prevents friction burns, but inevitably violence begets injury. Trainers apply an aromatherapeutic muscle soother of ancient origin that's migrated from the locker room to the medicine cabinet and massage parlour.

Knowledge passes down, as in all Thai arts, from master to pupil. Tradition and obedience permeate the learning process, which may start in servitude to a teacher – and his boxing camp. Prospective teachers must again submit to a guru and years of study. They can take on students only after initiation through the *khrob khru* ceremony, in which they're crowned with the Thai equivalent of a karate's black belt: a sacred *mongkhon* head circlet to be kept as a lifelong talisman.

The *mongkhon*, a ropelike loop with ends protruding behind, likely derived from the early Siamese soldier's bandanna. Removed in a solemn rite after the *ram muay*, *mongkhon* are compulsory attire, as are the blue and red *prajiad* armlets binding the biceps throughout. These tiny scarves originated as a *pha yantra* charm; many still are.

Most *nak muay* are walking amulet collections. A boxer may hide a Buddha tablet within the folds of a *mongkhon* or *prajiad*, or perhaps a hair from his father or a piece of his mother's skirt. Others thread amulets under the waistband of the Western-style shorts emblazoning the name of his camp across the front in Gothic Thai script. With the only armour being his genital cup, the last line of defence may be a magical tattoo, or a *waan* mystical herb root he chews or uses in solution as a pre-fight body wash.

As always, an amulet's potency depends on good conduct – and superstition: a woman may never touch a man's *mongkhon*. Women are, however, allowed to box – as apparently they did for self-defence in ancient times. They even wear *mongkhon* and *prajiad*, but must duck under the top ropes in rings designated for women. They're banned from men's rings on the grounds they'd curse male fighting ability.

Founded in 1995, the World Muay Thai Council makes it compulsory for even foreign fighters to do the *wai khru ram muay* and wear *mongkhon* and *prajiad*. This ethnically specific rule perhaps exceeds the coloured dan belts of karate, sumo or tae kwondo, yet Westerners have warmed to *muay*'s Thainess. Many choose to train here, some contesting for titles. The *wai khru* need not be religious; fighters can adapt the amulets and incantations to their own worship, or treat it simply as exotic.

Modern *muay thai* is relatively young. That title arose in the nationalistic 1920s to distinguish it from foreign boxing and its evolution from several regional variants. King Rama V had earlier honoured regional fighters, an act that galvanised the largely military activity into a sport – called *muay kaad cheuk* after the hand bindings – that preceded *muay thai* for a few decades. These ropelike wraps could be hardened and whorled with pain-inducing knots and – legend has it – glass shards.

Turning *muay thai* into a safe, consistent sport in the 1920s required a code. So from the Queensberry Rules of international boxing it adopted leather gloves, weight categories, mouth guards, reduced target areas, roped canvas rings of 24 square metres, red and blue corners, and five three-minute rounds with two-minute breaks.

The first arena, Suan Gularb, opened in 1920. Later came the major Bangkok stadia; Ratchadamnoen opened in 1945 and Lumphini in 1956, the latter moving to Nang Linchee in 2005. But as *muay thai* went professional, some standards declined. The boxer's status slid from knight to gladiator. Promoters, sharks and gamblers took notice of the profits, and the low social clout of those who saw boxing as a path out of poverty. The boxers' submission to a stable's 'ownership' is most evident in the boxer being given the camp's title as his public surname. Boxing also now feeds the celebrity industry. Potential to act, sing or model keeps some careers short to avoid any blemishes. Asanee Suwan gave up his top ranking in order to play Nong Toom in *Beautiful Boxer*.

With *muay thai* reaching over 100 countries since the 1970s' martial arts boom, it will likely stray farther from its roots. Olympic recognition would require dropping 'Thai' from the sport's name. So just when *muay thai* gets global recognition, it risks squandering its heritage. "We have a priceless property… it is the art of the survivor," says Amornrit Pramorn of Siamyuth Gym, who trains in the pre-1920s style, in which strategy, locks, throws and bound fists ensure a strategic nuance and unpredictable pace that the modern game lacks. "The original Thai boxing is wilder and more complicated, tricky and deep, which I want to pass on. It's a work of art."

Yet commercialism – and debasements like foul play, betting and throwing of matches – in turn spurs interest in the earlier forms, now collectively dubbed *muay boran* (ancient boxing). Exponents of these graceful styles pop up at festivals and stadia, complete with drawn tattoos, bound wrists and *thok khamen,* a short, tightly wrapped loincloth derived from what warriors once wore. A trove of wisdom resides in their diverse stances, techniques and philosophies. Solemn and mannered, yet teasing, they require lengthier spiritual training.

Out of possessiveness, authorities and masters have fossilised many Thai crafts and dances into endangered shadows of once thriving arts. By contrast, folk music and *muay thai* evolved into vibrant living traditions with vast appeal. An interested minority will likely continue to demand the authentic original. Meanwhile, the majority will watch *muay thai* go Hollywood.

left: **The foot thrust is one of five** *muay thai* **weapons, including kick, punch, elbow jab and knee thrust.** *PCS*

above: **While fighters trade punches; gamblers wave hand signals in the stands as judges keep score at the ringside .** *PCS*

right: **Boxers show the acrobatic** *muay boran* **style, combining kick, hold, knee-thrust and flying leap, all as if lightly dancing on tip-toes.** *PCS*

Beauty Queens
At more than one pageant per day, beauty is serious business

A popular measure of female beauty, Apasara Hongsakul won Miss Universe 1965. Her victory then launched the modern era of Thai beauty contests, which peaked after Pornthip Narkhirunkanok clinched the country's second Miss Universe title in 1988. LA-schooled, and with an American accent, Pornthip heralded a new standard of beauty: forthright, professionally educated in the West, and often only half-Thai.

Pornthip fever swept the land, with around 700 Miss Somethings crowned per year. Pageant-fatigue has since seen contests drop below 500. With just nine every week, that's like Bill Gates being reduced to $50 billion. Beauty being such a priority in 'face' culture, the country remains enthralled by demure maidens parading gowns, grins and virtue. Though many do pageants for fun, half enter the circuit for fame and fortune – or as a way to pay for further education. Contests aren't only for women; men out-beautify men to win Mr titles, while Thai ladyboys out-beautify everybody.

Pageants power the fantasy business. Until the recent boom in media, fashion and photo studios, they've been the main way to harvest a new crop of celebrities. Today, the genres can merge, as in male and female supermodel contests voted by readers of women's magazines.

Whether managed by agencies or coached by pageant organisers, hopefuls learn how to be products in the image industry. Think of the sash as a brand name. Miss Dutchie Girl does. Her crowning glory is to advertise DutchMill yoghurt with Mr Dutchie Boy. Commercial pageants compete for trade, whether they promote fruit (Miss Durian), cars (Miss Motor Show), underwear (Domon's Man of the Year), herbal whisky (Miss Drunk) or hangover tonics (Miss Hang). Such commercial events require designer hair with clothes far more fashionable than the pageant cliché in which the provinces revel.

Many contests are held outdoors, where every feature must be accentuated and weather resistant. Hair gets built to withstand monsoon gales, either piled into a lacquered helmet called *phom klao* (gathered-up hair) or aerosolled into a *faraa* wreath – named after Farrah Fawcett. Faces are caked with make-up to look ultra-white and stay intact under sun, rain or the inevitable tears. By night, vivid costumes must out-shine the day-glo backdrop. The winner's prizes must scream even louder: boldly printed sashes, poster-sized cheques, and trophies of gold coloured plastic a metre high. Now thanks to air-conditioning, glam staging and camera close-ups, major commercial pageants allow for softer hair, more natural

make-up and subtler traditional fabrics, along with the Western staples: crowns, gowns and swimwear.

Provincial and fruit festival contests may be limited to locals, but they often act as practice heats for national contests, which are riven by schisms among organisers and sponsors. Devotees of beauty worship a trinity of goddesses: Miss Thailand, Miss Thailand World and Miss Thailand Universe. Each contest aligns with a TV channel (iTV, Channel 3 and Channel 7, respectively), plus a

far left: *Benjarong* pots and national costumes for Miss Songkran 2001 winners at Wat Bang Ping, Samut Sakhon. *PJ*

above: **Crowning Miss Thailand 2003, Chalisa Boonkrongsap.** *PJ*

left: **Miss Tiffany 2004 and runners up. Born men, they out-beautify many female beauty queens.** *TIF*

below: **Miss Thailand 2002, Patiporn Sitipong, enthroned.** *PJ*

global pageant such as Miss World and Miss Universe. Though national contests take sequinned international shape, local pageants reveal the ancient Thai tradition to pick the prettiest person.

Festivals often involve the appeasing of spirits or gods. Judging by the angelic faces on murals, comeliness is next to godliness, so processions and rites require actors to embody these supernatural beings. As the good-looking presumably have good karma, they get picked for parades and for dozens of contests at two national festivals: Songkran and Loy Krathong. Nang Songkran (Miss Thai New Year) represents one of the seven daughters of the Brahmin god Kabila, who take yearly turns to lead the mid-April parade. At Loy Krathong in November, Nang Noppamas evokes the princess of Sukhothai credited with starting observance of this rite to honour the water goddess Phra Mae Khongkha (Mother Ganges). Perhaps because beauties have long conveyed social messages, few object to them endorsing products, promoting tourism, advocating causes or even playing politics.

"The national beauty contest was first held by the government on 10 December 1934 in order to honour Constitution Day so the people could understand democracy better," reveals Prasert Jermjuthitham, an organiser and historian of beauty pageants. After that it was a stop-start process, reflecting the political climate, with Miss Thailand contests suspended during wars, dictatorships and royal mourning. Now Miss Thailand plays cultural ambassador for the tourist authority.

The public service role requires contestants to fit a conservative image of femininity: virgins yet to be sullied by real-life womanhood. Miss Thailand World Second Runner-up 2003 was vilified and stripped of her sash for lying about having been married. But the beauty queen demographic has changed. Formerly a route out of poverty for country girls, pageants led into a world of entertainment scorned by middle and upper classes. Now that celebrityhood has become a career for *hi-so* women, too, rich material girls monopolise the crowns. To cope with the clamour for glamour, many contests add extra titles like the media's Miss Photogenic, Miss Confidence, or a people's choice.

"In the past, they didn't need to have any skills. A beautiful face was enough," says Prasert. "Modern beauty queens always come as a package; beauty, high education and a good family play crucial roles. Judges now look for brains equally with beauty. This upgrades the image, but it's almost impossible for a provincial girl to become a star these days." Because many entrants are now urban students or graduates, less educated beauties daren't enter due to the tougher interview round. Universities themselves often hold 'Miss & Mr Student' contests with titles like 'Smart Freshy Boy & Girl & Talent'.

Intelligent, professional role models like 'Mr & Ms Scientists' or 'Miss Mobile IT & Smart' draw approval, but not everyone delights in mixing beauty with brains. When psychiatrist 'Dr Bird' won Miss Thailand in 1999, fears her swimsuit appearance could provoke erotomania in patients led to calls for her to be banned from her job. "Beauty contests in our country are closely identified with sexuality and the contestants are viewed as sex objects," Professor Dr Nongpa-nga Limsuwan insists. "A beauty queen cannot be a good psychiatrist as patients can relate to her in an inappropriate way."

Another barrier to country girls is their ethnic look. Though models with golden skin can do well in foreign markets, pale skin has long been favoured over dark. Also Sino-Thais, dominant in the economy and media, have become major arbiters of taste. Today, entrants, judges and audience favour dainty Chinese features and the taller, *luuk khreung* (half-Thai) look. Part-Western accents and looks have become a pageant fixture ever since lots of offspring fathered by foreigners in the 1960s and 70s came of age in the 1980s, along with returning daughters of the elite who'd studied abroad. Often more forthright, they emanated the success that boom-era women professionals seek to emulate.

Career girls, however, don't conform to the old early-marriage ideal. A 2003 contest for singleton professionals over 28 was named Miss Khan Thong (Miss Spinster). It attracted women from some prominent families, though the winner now says men with fragile egos are afraid to date her. Also not to be excluded are Ms Memai (Ms Divorceé), nor women over 64 contesting Senior Miss Songkran. The 2004 winner was 90.

Further expanding the definition of beauty, Miss Jumbo Queen has since 1999 selected women over 80kg who display the grace of the elephant. Contestants shimmy through song and dance numbers in outfits also judged for their novelty, and get weighed on stage. The heaviest wins a topical title like Miss WTO (Weight Top Over) or Miss IMF (I'm Fat), with a record scales tip of 187kg. It aims to promote elephant conservation and increase self-esteem among large women. Now Miss Jumbo Queen Junior targets hefty kids and Miss Payoon (Miss Dugong) enables women over 100kg to help the endangered mammal by wearing a mermaid fish tail.

above: **The weigh-in on stage at Miss Jumbo Queen, at which prizes go to not only the most beautiful woman over 80kg, but the most photogenic, best dressed and, yes, heaviest.** *SYL*

right: **Hosted by Samphran Elephant Ground, Miss Jumbo Queen promotes pachyderms by finding the woman who most match their outsize but delicate grace.** *SYL*

Empowerment is a buzzword in pageants. Miss Malee Confidence promotes personal development – and sells Malee fruit juice. That argument was used by the 2004 Miss Sexy Body contest, in which children aged 3-12 dressed up like Britney Spears. An outraged ministry of education resurrected a dictatorship rule from 1961 that bans schoolgirls and teachers from beauty contests. Thailand's new puritanism has consigned the swimsuit behind closed doors in Miss Thailand and banned it in Miss Thailand World, though some think this deprives Thai girls of preparation for competing abroad.

While fame from winning lingers throughout a career, so do expectations. The higher class the title-holder, the further they may fall. Despite close supervision, incidents like saucy fashion shoots stir controversy. The Miss Thailand cliché was revised most dramatically by Areeya 'Pop' Sirisopha, who went back to her journalism career and also joined the army. Donning khaki fatigues, 2nd Lieutenant Pop taught English at the Chulachomklao officer academy.

The last word in beauty, naturally, goes to *kathoey* – transgender queens. While they're barred from most women's contests, women have had to be screened out from hugely popular contests held to bolster the chorus lines of the Pattaya's Alcazar and Tiffany cabarets. Played for fun and charity, events like Sao Praphet Song (Miss Second Kind of Woman) send up the whole process. Miss ACDC (formerly Miss BBC: Beauty Brain & Creation) spoofs Miss Universe, with contestants caricaturing each country. However, Miss Tiffany Universe qualifies for America's global cross-dressing contest Miss Queen of the Universe, which Thai she-men won in 1999, 2000 and 2002. Come March, the media ponders who's prettier: Miss Thailand or Miss Tiffany? May the best man win.

top row from left: **Miss Mango 2002, Prachuab Khiri Khan. The 1960s movie star Petchara Chaowarat started out as Miss Hawaii in Lumphini Park. Miss Mobile IT's office girl chic.** *PJ*

bottom row from left: **One of 12 finalists in Miss Thailand 2003. Mr & Miss Photogenic at the Mon Songkran festival, Phra Pradaeng. Weerayudh Poonkum, crowned Mr Manhunt Thailand 2002.** *PJ*

Luuk Thung & Mor Lam
Thai country music delivers ancient song styles with Vegas glitz

In August 1997, life improved for Bangkok taxi drivers. Cherished cassettes of *luuk thung* folk music worn thin, they could suddenly tune in round the clock to Luuk Thung FM90. They haven't yet tuned out. While liquid petroleum gas powers the engine, *luuk thung* powers the driver. The car careens in harmony with accelerating beats, staccato refrains, melancholy meanders, brass swerves and verbal jousts. One wonders if Thai road manners would improve were drivers as fond of 'lounge music'. *Luuk thung* is music's answer to the energy drink. In fact, Loog Toong™ is an energy drink, the same way Carabao Daeng™ energy drink targets fans of Add Carabao's Songs For Life music.

To taxi-driving, labouring, factory-working, migrants from Buriram and Roi-et, *luuk thung* (children of the fields) folk music – and its regional Isaan counterpart *mor lam* – goes way beyond entertainment. Punctuating the pulsating vocal trills, acerbic lyrics draw on folklore and experience. While the state has at times used folk music to disseminate propaganda, their musical humour remains one of the few tolerated ways for the powerless to take swipes at authority.

"When they listen to *luuk thung* they feel they are experiencing their own lives through our music," says *luuk thung* singer Surachai Sombatcharoen of his rural and migrant audience. "Mostly our songs are about love, melancholy and grief, but they are not sentimental. They are too realistic for that. *Luuk thung* is not a music for escapism."

Bangkok's 1988-97 boom had been the time for escapism. Urbanites sought support and solace in the sweet balladeering of *luuk krung* (Children of the City) and its Westernised variants: bubblegum T-Pop and rockier *string* (early Thai guitar music). "*Luuk krung* is associated with Bangkok's ruling elite, and deals with romantic and idealistic issues," musicologist John Clewley observes. Chosen by producers for their looks, *Luuk krung* performers are invariably half-Western or Chinese-featured with a paleness implying affluence. But a dark complexion matters less in folk music than vocal skill and the ability to break the listener's heart.

The FM debut of *luuk thung* struck a chord, coming just a month after the economic bubble burst. It was a handy nostalgic vehicle to express the anguish roiling the nation. Extra mouths to feed at the farm – and fewer baht repatriated from returning migrants Bangkok salaries – provided fresh lyrics for fresh faces taking up the mike at temple fair singing contests. The sarcastic wit

of Boontone Khon-noom was typical in skewering the crisis in songs like 'Bpai Tham IMF' (Go Ask the IMF) and lines about a lover floating away like the baht.

From this heady moment, Jintara Poonlap and Siriporn Amphipong emerged to dominate, respectively, *luuk thung* and *mor lam*, writes music expert Tim Carr. "The genre's Dolly Parton, Jintara is more the sassy, sultry home-wrecker with a tiger's purr, a kitten's growl and a heart breaker's shattered heart just looking for some relief (in his rice ploughing arms). Siriporn has a sandpaper sob so sorrowful, so desperate, so eloquent, resistance is futile. Her *mor lam* feels like Aretha's soul or Loretta Lynn's country."

This new blood filled the vacuum left by the all-time great, Phomphuang Duangjan. An abused, illiterate farm girl who'd risen to be the first *luuk thung* performer at a *hi-so* function, she died aged just 31 in 1992. Her funeral was attended by 200,000 mourners including royalty, but her spirit still draws fans seeking lottery numbers to her shrine in Suphanburi, an ancient town that would be the Thai Nashville. Many stars still hail from 'Suphan', where the banter-like song style *isaew* emerged, and *luuk thung* gleaned some of its distinctive accent. Blessed with astonishing vocal range and articulation, Phomphuang urbanised a country art, airing grievance with goose-bump-raising grace:

"So lousy poor, I just have to risk my luck
Dozing on the bus, this guy starts chatting me up
Says he'll get me a good job, now he's feeling me up…"

Though risqué lyrics are banned, Clewley notes that folk songs are "one of the few public spaces where sexual pleasure can be discussed." That includes prostitution – a staple subject of both folk genres, along with life stories of truck drivers and buffalo herders, waitresses and maids. That's not the kind of reality breached in either T-Pop or polite company. The irony of *luuk thung*'s new FM radio respectability is epitomised in Phomphuang's song 'AM Girl', mocking city lothario tastes: "We are not compatible. You listen to FM radio!"

A term coined in 1964, *luuk thung* was not just reborn on radio, it was born *of* radio. AM broadcasts of foreign music gradually infused village songs with big band, swing, country & western, rock 'n' roll, and even the yodel of Gene Autrey. An injection of Latino ballroom dancing music sent rhythms sassy, brass surging, carnival costumes a-shimmy. As DJ and folk music historian Janepop Jobkrabuanwan explains, it began in the 1930s when rural adaptations of court music merged with the long, unaccompanied songs that central Thais sang together during and after work.

That communal singing impulse persists. Hence the success of karaoke. *Hi-so* gents croon ballads at parties. Salarymen pay hostesses to hold their mike in private rooms at KTV parlours. Teens record their renditions at karaoke booths in malls. Most sing pop, but folk often

rules the KTV jukebox at roadside bars, where videos depict nostalgic scenes of Thai culture. "Even if we're not good singers, we just enjoy singing," says theatre director Pradit Prasartthong, noting that *likay*, pop, country, or even Western standards get sung to simple stick-beating rhythms countrywide. Beats clacked on sticks and cans keep time for singalongs among workers, students and picnickers in parks, at waterfalls, on buses.

Thai vocals create some otherworldly aural textures. Tones and compound vowels veer into glissando warbles. Erupting out of a tremulous a cappella intro, *mor lam* takes its name (song doctor) from the eloquent vocalist, who dispenses quick-fire raps on rural and romantic travails, or plaintive homilies from *Jataka* scriptures. *Mor lam*'s dizzying collision of sounds is driven by pulsating rasps on the *khaen* bamboo pipes, whereas hurtling brass drives *luuk thung*. Though the two genres now mix, and singers slip between styles and dialects, the much older *mor lam* remains distinct whatever it appropriates: glitz from *luuk thung*, synthesisers and guitars from *luuk krung*, costumed theatricality from *likay*.

Nostalgia means there's still a sizeable market for old recordings and covers of songs by Surachai's late father, Suraphon Sombatcharoen, who pioneered the *luuk thung* sound and look. Killed by gangsters in 1967, the honey-tonsilled crooner in suit and bow tie still influences how male leads deport and dress. Only now the jackets reach towards the knees, with lapels flaring in a fruit cocktail palette of papaya, banana and lime.

This colour blast is largely owed to Phomphuang, who electrified the genre – literally with guitars and key-boards, visually with Broadway glamour – to combat the 1980s rise of *luuk krung*. In the wake of her glitter, mini-skirts and chorus lines, touring troupes took *luuk thung* to Las Vegas extremes: spangled leotard costumes, racy choreography, feathered plumes, comic routines, MC chatter, and high kicks to complement curl-fingered *ram wong* dance gestures. Come the end of the show, fans shower the singers with garlands, ribbons and banknotes.

Thai country music outgrew its roots, some say to its detriment. Awesome logistics push up costs and the clamour for sponsors and TV coverage. The stage at Sanam Luang on the King's Birthday night measures 100m across, the crowd 300m deep. A brightly jacketed singer magnifies his impact with dozens of dancing girls on multiple levels. The same goes for female stars and their ranks of dancing boys in spangled cuffs and luminous trousers. Even villages host productions nearly this big, filling temple grounds at festival time.

"Originally, *luuk thung* was pure art for entertainment only. The 1997 crash made it more commercial, just like other music," says DJ Janepop of the mixed blessings his radio station brings. Yet while country music goes pop, T-Pop is going country. Teenybop legend Thongchai 'Bird' McIntyre raided folk rhythms in 2002 for duets with female folk stars. The next year, sultry star Mai Charoenpura played Phomphuang in a TV drama and re-recorded her classics in pop style.

The marketing of *luuk thung* as an energy drink now posits the music as a lifestyle choice. As it overcomes class snobbery, there's no reason why Thai country music can't gain the same sway over middle class Thai ears as imported American country music does. Suphanburi isn't yet Nashville, temple fairs aren't yet the Grand Ole Opry, but *luuk thung* is evolving into a potent cultural force. While wannabe-Western T-Pop has struggled to gain a foreign audience, the brisk beats and fascinating vocals of Thai folk finds receptive ears and hips abroad, in the World Music footsteps of Griot and Bhangra, Soukous and Salsa. *Mor lam* is among the most insistent, infectious dance musics in the world.

"Many youngsters are turning away from their roots to Western music," laments Decha Suvinijit of country label Weyti Thai. "We can't stop that, but we can show them that Westerners are embracing our culture too." One of his *luuk thung* singers is blond Swede Jonas Anderson, who along with Briton Christy Gibson startle Thai audiences that foreigners can like the music as much as they do.

Comedy Cafés
What makes the Land of Smiles smile?

Laughter peals from behind a huge awning painted with zany faces. Inside, a spiky-haired man in farmer's garb pulls a rope between the legs of a shirtless man on all fours, playing a buffalo. Another man in a red rubber miniskirt and make-up pulls up the rope from the front. When his wig falls off he re-attaches it as a pubic wig and waves it at the squealing buffalo. The hall erupts in hoots of laughter. Labourers and office girls, shopkeepers and influential businessmen guffaw over their drinks and dinner. Welcome to Thai comedy: *talok*.

Freelance troupes of comedians tour their song-and-joke routines to play several venues a night on Bangkok's circuit of cafés – not coffee houses, but theatres with a bill of variety acts. In between the jesters, *luuk thung* folk crooners regale the crowd, backed by chorus lines called *hang khreuang* (tail pieces) for their frilly-tailed dresses that reveal plenty of leg and cleavage. Hostesses in Technicolor gowns (and serious plastic surgery) twitter ballads under strobe lights. Staff garland their necks with ribbons of plastic flowers stapled with banknotes ordered by an admirer to gain their company. Ladies do likewise for gigolos with a taste for clashing shirts and suits.

"Sex is part and parcel of the café scene," admits Somyot Suthangkoon, owner of Rama IX Café. With a reputation as bawdy as the punchlines – and alleged association with godfathers, the café scene has lost ground to television and movies. These offer a sanitised version of the same costumes, props and pratfalls of a humour that's often unsubtle.

"For a country proudly badged 'the land of smiles', we do not have a well-developed sense of humour," concedes columnist Salin Pinkayan. "Besides clever wordplays, most of the stuff that people find funny is no more sophisticated than slipping on banana skins." Visceral and visual, Thai humour is typically made by people with a 'funny' appearance. Most common are ugly, balding jokers with pronounced features and either toothless or goofy grins – dead-ringers for the faces-in-hell found on temple murals. The troupes are largely male. Some drag up in burlesque style, though genuine *kathoey* may jest, often in deliberately hideous make-up.

More upsetting to some are laughs aimed at disability, often viewed as payback for bad karma. With a voice like Darth Vader, the two-metre tall Yok Yek provides scope

for sizeist jokes, as does a disco-dancing midget in a sexy dress, popping out of a bag dragged on stage. Clowns with Down's Syndrome play the butt of more affectionate jokes. Most troupes employ people like Don Wide-Nose who have the sinister-looking genetic defect Anhidrotic Ectodermal Dysplasia, nicknamed *roke sangthong* after Sangthong Sisai, the first sufferer to become a *talok* star in the 1970s. Thinning an enlarged scalp and scrunching the features, the disease enables rubber-faced expressions that have café crowds in creases. Troupe leaders now defensively insert homilies about *talok* giving the disabled a chance to make a living and integrate.

Joking is always a group affair. Even when one comic launches into a shaggy dog story or song, his comrades interrupt with a funny walk or grimace. Often he simply slams the raconteur's head or bum with a dented metal tray. "The sense of humour is different here," says Wittawat Soontornvinate, who modelled his enduring TV chat format on Australia's Don Lane Show. "In English-speaking countries it's more subtle. Ours has to be obvious. Straight to the point. Bang!" You literally hear that 'bang'. In all comedy, variety and even concert banter and movies, every wisecrack gets greeted with a random cascade of musical notes. Drum flurries, bass strums and cymbal trills that went out with the ark in Western circus tradition, continue to announce jokes as being funny. This corny clatter is also performed on *phiphat* instruments in *likay*, an ancestor of *talok*.

Likay demands slick repartee and double-entendres of its multi-talented players, disguised under heavy make-up and spangled, Burmese-style costumes. This early Thai vaudeville features song, dance and soliloquy against a day-glo palace backdrop that's performed in markets, fairs and parties. Slowly losing craft and lineage

as appreciation of its subtleties wanes, *likay* comes to resemble café comedy. The core followers now are *mae yok*, 'women of a certain age' who indulge in fantasies away from domestic drudgery and unfaithful husbands. They garland ever-more-handsome *phra ek* (leading men) with banknotes, sometimes as inducements to sit with them for a while.

Court jesting ended up in the refined *lakhon nai* (palace plays), but *talok*'s direct origin is surprisingly serious: monks. Two centuries back, monks were banned from reciting the *phra malai* funeral chant using make-up and ribald mime, so professional *suad karuhat* (lay-man chanting) groups took the tradition into slapstick. The resulting *cham uad* (vaudeville) became a hit at fairs, then theatres, until *talok* emerged before World War II.

Talok's greatest star until his death in 2001, Lor Tok was the first comic to be awarded the title National Artist for six decades of wry ribbing. Nicknamed after his Chinese tycoon caricature, the hangdog, deadpan wit pioneered *talok* on TV in the 1960s and starred in over 100 films with his female sidekick Choosri Meesomon. Today the top bananas are Mum Jokmok, who ruffled censors with a nude streak for a 2004 film, and Thep Poe-ngam, best known for a spoof rock movie.

above: **Satirical modern likay by Makham Pom Theatre Group, led by Pradit Prasartthong, shown holding the spear.** *PCS*

left: **Tall stories in this comedy café skit at Rama IX Plaza. Drum rolls from the band are the cue for laughter.** *PCS*

top right: **A midget disco dances and tells jokes as light relief between singing acts at this *luuk thung* concert in Loei.** *PCS*

right: **Rubberfaced antics by a man with Anhidrotic Ectodermal Dysplasia disease. The troupe also contains someone with Down's Syndrome.** *PCS*

Though filmed *talok* lacks audience interaction, it can break new ground with sets, themes, video clips, editing and an emergent sophisticated wit. One show satirises public figures using puppets, while another programme pioneers a surreal 'intellectual comedy', drawing on skewed observations in the vein of Monty Python.

Thai language lends itself to legerdemain, but satire must tread a fine line in this face-conscious society. Wit can lead to dangerous repercussions if politicians feel mocked. Even on stage, comics pick on each other rather than humiliate people in the audience – unless they're foreign, which is more grist for group shenanigans. Given the intolerance for direct ridicule, the future for cutting-edge comedy can't lie in emulating confrontational Western wit, but perhaps in rediscovering roots. One retro vehicle for satire is *likay*. Its pastiches of classical tales have long been used to disseminate information to villagers, from anti-communist propaganda to safe-sex advice and grassroots protest. Now *likay* turns up at trendy events.

Playing Cyrano to today's 'indy' generation, Udom 'Note' Taephanich became Thailand's first solo stand-up comedian. His theatre shows sold-out among young, independent urbanites due to his Seinfeld-esque humour and gags on topical issues rather than sexual innuendo. However smart/funny shows rarely last that long. "Thai people prefer their jokes already prepared, easy to consume in small rib-tickling bits," Salin concludes. "Irony is not funny to Thai people. Maybe it is so much a part of our everyday life that it ceases to be funny."

Whisky Mixer Tables
Nightlife etiquette: shared drinks, themed clubs, and bars with no walls

Whisakee sodaa – the drink of choice among all Thai classes, all sexes, in all venues, from hotel to nightclub to roadside shack. Before the 1997 crash Thailand drank more Johnny Walker Black Label than all bar Japan and America. But order a glass and you may be refused. You might have to buy the bottle. At some suburban clubs that's the cost of admission. No sign states 'Groups Only', but solo drinkers are virtually pariahs. Even twosomes are troublesome with their potential for disagreement or silences that three or more friends would prevent.

Alcohol's famed for loosening social divisions, yet in Thailand it reinforces them. Drinking etiquette lubricates the hierarchy, while the urge to conform keeps the range of drinks remarkably narrow. Identity depends on rank within one's group. And status lies in the liquor brand that's ordered – plus the way its served.

Whisky reflects the wallet: from roughest rum-like Mekong to smoother Saeng Som laced with lime; from Spey Royal blended Scotch up to show-off Chivas Regal. Slaking a growing proportion of Thailand's thirst, beer comes in bottles and pitchers big enough for a gang to sup. That's the idea. Decanting lager into glasses – often on the rocks – distributes joy to all and roles to each.

Most Thais drink from a shared source, whether it be a bottle of Black, a pitcher of Singha beer, or a jug of kamikaze cocktail sprouting one straw per mouth. A Saeng Thip and Red Bull cocktail may get mixed in the ice bucket itself – a practical solution on dancefloors, for the hinged handle prevents spillage as you dance. By day,

street workers like motorcycle taxi drivers share the same communal technique. Whatever class the coterie, the most junior pours, the most senior pays, while extroverts propose relentless toasts of *chai yo!* – cheers!

Petite designer bottled beers aren't the epitome of 'face' Westerners might imagine, despite heavy marketing of small bottled beers and pre-mixed spirits. Individual drinks prevent the ritual of sharing, for hospitality is the happiest by-product of gaining face. Thus the constant companion to any boozing session is the whisky mixer table – a tiered tray on legs designed to hold each group's set: whisky bottle, ice bucket, sodas and limes. Waiters mark-off levels on a sticker and store part-drunk bottles for up to three months behind the bar – or in purpose-built storerooms. A host revels in beckoning for his whisky (or brandy) to be brought. *Phu yai* (big shots) don't even need to ask. Their bottle simply appears.

Throughout the session, deferential staff hover, refill, fetch, hover, refill. The pourer – often the youngest in a group – serves with the right hand, left fingers touching right elbow in the stance also seen when giving a business card, a gift or an offering. The host basks. Guests swoon under patronage. Everyone's content.

Everyone's even more content when the food arrives. Thais never let drinking interrupt eating and *kup klaem* (bar snacks) keep the palate oiled and salted. As well as popcorn come herbed peanuts in aromatic leaves, deep fried chicken knuckles, fermented sausages, a brace of astringent *yam* (salads) and deep-fried insects.

left: **A whisky-Red Bull cocktail served on Koh Samet in beach bar style – mixed inside the ice bucket and drunk from there direct through straws.** *PCS*

top right: **High-concept venues like this Neptune-themed night-club in Bangkok often focus more on food, karaoke, live music and other diversions than on DJs and dancing.** *PCS*

bottom right: **Royal City Avenue (RCA) became one of only three official nightlife zones in the capital, despite having declined from its mid-1990s heyday, when over 100 bars crowded the strip. The scene has long since moved elsewhere.** *PCS*

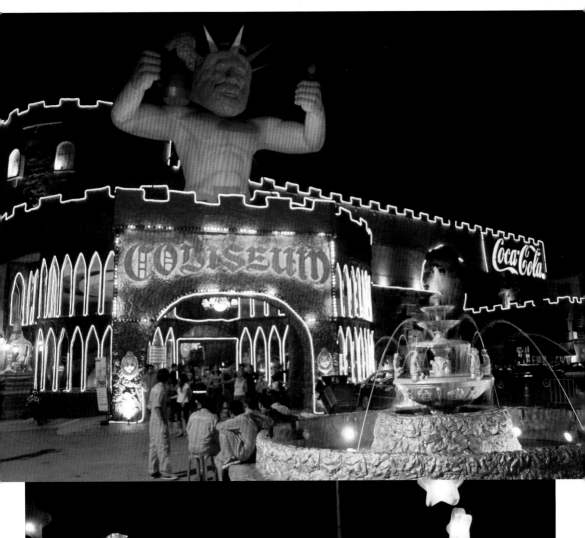

Just as Thais order more plates as needed, so alcohol's constantly topped up. "You leave drink-strength up to the server," says Lonely Planet's Joe Cummings. "Typically the *dek* [young waiter] goes light. This makes a shared bottle last longer and, according to locals, a light drink always tastes better." Blurring how much you've drunk, the constant flow ensures a ready supply when a newcomer joins. Even passers-by get proffered neat shots of *lao khao* (white rice liquor) at the street corner, where boisterous *kii lao* (boozers) swap tall tales over moonshine. Resisting a bamboo cup of their firewater is futile. Smile as it burns your throat and a night of slurred hilarity ensues. Violence is rare in Thai nightlife, though it may flare at upmarket venues when sons of *phu yai* imagine they've been slighted. If a *nakleng* (tough guy) commandeers your table for his entourage, well... you move!

Thai drinking habits impact not just the shape of a night out, but the shape of the venue: the furniture, the architecture, the streetscape. The archetypal Thai bar is simple and non-exclusive – partly since it has no walls! Open-air bars remain a staple in town and village. Night markets and roadside drink-ups install jukeboxes or folk karaoke-video, with food from nearby stalls. Fairy-lit cocktail carts erect tables and chairs on the sidewalk.

At tourist honeypots, alfresco *bar beer* counters enable lightly-dressed ladies and ladyboys to remain on their stools while touting at passing *farang* men to buy them a drink. Seemingly every Bangkok novelist records the experience. With music and neon signs competing as

brazenly as the girls, countless near-identical *bar beer* clog Pattaya, Patong Beach and Chiang Mai, plus the Bangkok a-go-go trio of Patpong, Soi Cowboy and Nana Plaza. In fact, exotic dancers didn't arrive with the 1960s GI-led boom in go-go bars, but in the saucy cabarets of 1920s Chinatown. In World War II, those early nightclubs then morphed into open-air dance halls, bars and cabarets. Air-conditioning then brought nightlife indoors – and led to revellers remaining in one venue all night.

It suits host culture that groups stay put, with friends coming and going. Since form follows nightlife function, the desire for varied entertainment led to venues offering multiple attractions. The clientele hangs out at shopping malls by day, so why not malls of nightlife? Thais call such places a 'pub' – not the traditional British/Irish style pub, though they're recreated here too. Huge 'pubs' offer a diverse menu: live music, karaoke, dancefloor, micro-brewery, restaurant, private rooms, VIP lounge. Not to mention valet parking of premium cars out front.

Bars tend to be tiny or gargantuan. *Rong beer* (beer houses) seat two thousand, 'party houses' span city blocks, and beer gardens colonise every forecourt in cool season. Since the 1988-97 boom, excesses like laser-powered discos designed like spaceships have economised into clubs with the acoustics, scale and décor of a barn. Possibly due to lacking a dance licence – yes, that needs official permission – dancefloors sprout a forest of little tables, with wallets and phones placed prominently on top, bags slung from the hooks underneath. Between stage acts, DJs talk over intros, MCs natter and the crowd sings along to requests.

With so much entertainment under one roof, the pub crawl is rendered redundant. Anyhow, the very idea of bar-hopping evaporates at the thought of traffic and the effort of galvanising a dozen comfortable people to move. Even on densely-packed strips of six-table shop-house bars, cliques settle into one neon nest for the night. The vast choice of venues was illusory during the late 1990s heydays of Khon Kaen's High Park, Chiang Mai's Ratwithi Road or the cacophonous kilometre of Bangkok's Royal City Avenue (RCA). Beneath the kooky themes – Baby Hang, Sensual Suan Plu, Black Cus, Shit Happens, Why Art?, School Bus – lurk pretty much the same shophouse, the same drinks, the same music.

Since the crowd defects en masse at whim, it's the bars that street-hop. Six months is a venerable lifespan for the archetypal bar-strip pub before the investors divide profits and regroup at the next happening *soi*. "Places last only a few months [because] nobody puts any feelings into the business," lamented Manuel Pinedo, late founder of Rome Club, which ruled Bangkok nightlife from the mid-1970s to early 1990s. "In RCA, 20 people invest 200,000 baht each and see how fast they can get that back using a music star or model. Sarasin Road has stayed because the owners don't have that fast-food thinking."

Each partner brings custom from their group until they collectively yawn "*na beua*" (boring), and the cycle restarts. Bangkok bar history has lots of short chapters. "It's amazing how these bar streets start the same way –

top left: **A side-table with a bottle of Saeng Som Thai whisky, an ice bucket, soda and Coke, plus limes (hidden) at the shophouse bar Larb-Jazz.** *PCS*

lower left: **Whisky bottles with customers' name tags, in the storage cabinet at Larb-Jazz.** *PCS*

right: **Mixing whisky, soda and** *sanuk* **at a Bangkok live music bar.** *PCS*

below: **Tables cover the dance-floor of Coliseum, a vast night-club with live bands and comic interludes between the pumping pop music. Across the wall is a Thai Mount Rushmore of recent prime ministers – Chuan Leekpai, Banharn Silpa-archa, Chavalit Yongchaiyudh and Chatchai Choonhavan – sculpted in fibre-glass.** *PCS*

fame for revelry. Drug use had become a scourge, notably of the methamphetamine *yaa baa*, but bar-goers proved an easier target than the big dealers and users like truck drivers or students. Officers would confine everyone in a venue for hours during forced urine tests, letting the media photograph the mostly innocent detainees. So what's the non-drug taking majority to do?

Until the crackdown, bored Singaporeans flew to Bangkok for weekend fun. Thereafter, wealthier bored Bangkokians sought their *sanuk* in newly-libertarian Singapore. While Thailand surrendered its cachet as the region's party capital, Singapore took on that title, having learned from research that its primness had stunted the wealth potential of creative industries.

Though investment in venues has declined, *sanuk* and entrepreneurial verve should ensure that trends continue to come, get copied instantly, then get replaced by the next fad. Sofas, dance podia, wine fridges, fibre-glass sculpted interiors have all had their moments. Early closing inevitably created a new unregulated maelstrom on the street, with police even raiding house parties. Whatever the pressures, wherever the venue, the Thai night out will continue to revolve around shared drinks, *kup klaem* and the whisky mixer table.

in developments designed to be something else," observes PR consultant Tom Van Blarcom. "Suddenly someone puts in a bar and... boom!"

That pattern is changing, with new zoning laws aiming to concentrate bars in fewer designated areas. Nightlife has since 2001 been the target of a 'Social Order Crusade'. Police raids and closing at first 2am, then 1am or mid-night, ruined the viability of many clubs, hitting millions of lifestyles and livelihoods. It also spoiled the country's

Red Bull
Energy drinks fuel the nation

The West drinks Red Bull to play harder; the Thai drink it to work harder. This Thai energy tonic gained fame abroad as vodka mixer and party-prolonging upper for nightclubbers, garnering 65%-90% of the market in 83 countries. Yet the caffeine-rich beverage began and continues as a labour-prolonging booster for the Thai working man. Energy tonics fuel modern Thailand, the drink equivalent of diesel.

Bottles of its local recipe Krating Daeng (translated as Red Bull) may be seen just about everywhere. Active ingredients like caffeine, taurine and sugar help truckers deliver, students revise, vendors pedal, drivers stave off fatigue, and factory workers reach production targets.

They need the energy. Observers marvel how Thais can doze off instantly, in the most awkward of positions. It's not unusual to catch guards nodding off while on duty, shop staff dozing forehead-on-counter, or workers kipping atop lumpy cargo on a speeding truck. This seeming narcolepsy isn't just down to the heat, nor does drowsiness mean laziness. Far from it. *Norn len* (play sleep, or napping) stems as much from the work ethic as from the relaxation ethic (*sabai*) or the fun ethic (*sanuk*).

For many low-paid Thais, work means long hours, lack of power and often a second job. An extra burden for migrants is the expectation to subsidise the extended family, which may account for half of a farm's income. Even in free time, many Thais end up assisting relatives and friends without complaint. Meanwhile in daily life, they must remain vigilant about status in all interactions.

Such unrelenting stress requires a pick-me-up. *Yaa dong* (herbal whisky) rouses some, *yaa baa* speeds others illegally. Caffeine's socially acceptable, though coffee's less convenient and tastes unpleasant to many Thai. Thus pocket-size bottled tonics keep Thailand awake.

One of few Thai products to go *inter* (international), Krating Daeng started as a local emulation of the Japanese energy drink Lipovitan D. Exported to Thailand for Japanese salarymen running local factories, Lipo (as it's nicknamed) also appealed to Thai workers. So in 1981, Chaleo Yoovidhaya cooked up a sweeter, stronger version branded with a bull icon meaningful to farmers and farm-raised urbanites.

Austrian Dietrich Masteschitz noticed the marketing potential. The two men became equal partners in 1984, making Chaleo's syrup fizzy and less sweet to suit European tastes. It became the 21st century answer to cola and made Chaleo one of only two Thais on the *Forbes* billionaire list. Red Bull become a case study at marketing colleges. Thus to Westerners it seems not Thai, but a global brand with a burly Austrian accent, like an extract of Schwarzenegger.

Perhaps due to taking several doses of Red Bull a day, Masteschitz exudes confidence: "If you *are* the category, others are imitations. Nobody wants the imitation." Despite a plethora of copyists, Red Bull shifts 1.5 billion cans a year. The tonic syrup has a taste, buzz and brand loyalty that even imitators launched by Coca-Cola and Pepsico can't match.

But in Thailand, Krating Daeng eventually lost market leadership to M100 and M150, while remaining ahead of Chalarm (shark) and Lipo. Rival brands also push macho values, with M150 for years being promoted by boxers. 'Red animal' symbols have proved popular among energy drinks with regional markets, like Mah Daeng (Red Horse), Singha Daeng (Red Lion) and Chang Daeng (Red Elephant). Other recipes exude bravado (Ranger, Salvo, Shogun) or militaristic numbers: 10mm, M16, .357 Magnum, Commando Bear 200.

left: **Some top energy drinks: Lipo, .350 Magnum, M-150, Krating Daeng, Carabao Daeng, Chalarm and the hangover tonic called Hang.** *PCS*

top right: **Extreme sports fans sparking with energy at the Red Bull X-Park in Bangkok.** *PCS*

right: **Get 'em young. A boy in Loei advertises the Carabao Daeng logo on his face.** *PCS*

Expanding the market required new drinkers to be found. In 2002, Songs For Life star Add Carabao drew on his legions of rock fans to snatch a huge chunk of the growing sector within just a year with yet another 'red animal' brand incorporating his own name, Carabao Daeng (Red Buffalo). In riposte, M150 recruited pop celebrity faces and Krating Daeng launched another energy drink, named Loog Thoong® to snare its folk music fans. Krating Daeng even re-imported carbonated Red Bull Extra cans to compete with its local brand and to grab the rave-going generation. Likewise, Chalarm launched its snazzily canned Shark version both here and abroad. Finally, Thai trendies could order the 'Vodka Red Bull' cocktail in Thailand.

While buzz-eyed workers had been taking high doses of caffeine for decades, it was only after middle class youths got hooked that the government queried the health impact. Taking caffeine with alcohol is notorious as a fast, cheap way to get smashed, however caffeine and taurine can actually help imbibers overcome mental and bodily stress. "We claim that we improve concentration, reaction time and physical endurance. We have the original taste and it is very important that our benefits have been clinically proven," Masteschitz retorts, citing

his Food and Drug Administration approvals. "We spent millions and years on research. We're the only ones who invested in the category. It is a New Age product, an 'efficient product'. We're not a soft drink."

Still, energy drinks keep the muscles active long after a sober brain would call a halt. Pushed to unsustainable limits, drivers may eventually fall asleep at the wheel and cause accidents. In 2003, the state suddenly classified energy drinks with alcohol and cigarettes, limiting the content, adding health warnings, and banning ads from prime time TV and from using celebrity or sporting spokesmen. Instead of claiming measurable attributes, ads must convey a brand's aspirational values. As a result, the competing campaigns practically define today's battle for Thai male self-image.

Red Bull has turned to sponsoring events, including Formula 1, X-treme sports and novelty outdoor pursuits. When X-treme sports took off in Thailand in the late 1990s, a brand-literate generation was ripe for a non-drug booster to keep them skating, biking and boarding. Red Bull opened a downtown skatepark and advocates the government's 'Just Say No' anti-drugs line.

Carabao Daeng appeals to different motivations. "I'd like to change society's image of energy drinks, which are looked down on as a product for blue-collar workers," says executive Kamoldist Samuthkochorn. The drink's sales vehicle is nationalism. To the rousing sounds of Carabao, TV viewers see righteous fighters walloping the Burmese. "Carabao has employed his world of visual arts and his pride at being Thai to serve commercial purposes," writer Pavin Chachawalpongpun observes. "He carefully crafted the Thai heroine and warriors as representatives of positive values and the Burmese and drugs as devilish elements that have sought to destabilise the nation. As a result, Thais are indoctrinated with the idea that by drinking Carabao Daeng, they are claiming their *khwam pen thai* (Thainess) and patriotism."

Krating Daeng countered by tapping another, more compassionate aspect of the national psyche, while still remaining macho. The company's 'Search for Real Men' campaign could more accurately be dubbed 'Search for New Men', for it got the public to nominate good works done by men. Their huge response was matched by sales of the drink, which soon rose 10 percent. With energy drink companies makers now diversifying into vitamin health drinks and 'enriched beverages' to get round the caffeine restrictions, ever more virtuous one-upmanship seems inevitable.

Yaa Dong
Herbal drugs, alcohol and sex – in a bottle

Thailand's recent traditional healing boom has seen Siamese herbs migrate into creams, scrubs, teas, oils and wraps. Yet perhaps their most effective agent rarely appears on the spa menu: alcohol. "There are two main ways the Thai get the goodness from herbs," says Khun Jirawan of pharmaceutical firm Osothspa. "One is to boil; another is to *dong lao* – preserve dried ingredients in liquor." *Yaa dong lao* (alcohol-pickled medicine; *yaa dong* for short) still gets supped from discreet stalls. Most offer at least four large jars of different recipes, each stoppered with red cloth. The tonic's hue – from amber to russet to ox-blood – depends on the stalks, tubers and wood chips inside. It tastes best taken with a chaser of sweet-yet-astringent fruit like star gooseberry or tamarind.

Herbalism, like most traditional healing, historically centred on the *wat*, where knowledge filtered down through apprenticeship and palm-leaf manuscripts. Mendicant and shamanic herbalists were often former monks who were now free to imbue their potions with magic and alcohol. Medicinal *waan* roots even count as amulets. "I think its origin had to do with the desire to drink whisky," says Dr Parinya Uthitchalanon from his apothecary in Tha Prachan Road, Bangkok's herbal hub. "Since taking medicine is different to drinking alcohol for intoxication, no rules were broken. It caught on. Thais of every era have always loved to drink."

Alcohol comes easiest and cheapest from distilling rice into *lao khao* (white spirit), though Thai whisky (actually sugar-cane rum) adds piquant flavour. "Forty-degree proof is better than 28-degree, because it extracts the medicine more," explains Parinya. "Low proof alcohol or *sura chae* (fermented liquor) dissolve it slower."

"Whisky raises body temperature and causes blood to circulate more quickly. In the right quantity, whisky itself is a kind of medicine," assures Santi Watthana of Queen Sirikit Botanical Garden, Chiang Mai. In a study covering just part of the North, he identified no fewer than 242 ingredients in 92 recipes of *yaa dong*. His study aims to help save the plants from neglect, over-collection or loss of biodiversity. But not all herbs can be traced. "They buy them already in pieces. There aren't many people who know what these plants actually look like."

The mystery adds to the allure. Variants of the tonic allegedly enhance appetite, enrich blood, salve aches, reduce fatigue, cure insomnia, restore digestion, nurture clear speech, balance 'wind energy', or prolong youth. "Most *yaa dong* formulae have similar ingredients, but in different proportions," says Parinya. "Women drink it to cure aches and pains; men for strength."

Workers knock back a shot of this Thai toddy for 20 baht. Like an early Red Bull, *yaa dong* boosts energy. Hence brew names like 7-Layer Wall, Rama Goes To War or Tribesman Carrying Buffalo. Others imply animal prowess by their name: Towering Dragon, Tiger Force, Male Elephant Power, Horse Bursts His Stable. But the most potent claims are aphrodisiac: Manly Man, Moaning Mistress, Never Flaccid, Murmuring Lady, Old Man Rapes Elephant. "It was said to produce unfailing, long-lasting erections so potent it could make a monk leap over the temple wall in search of romance," Parinya recounts. "But people who drink whisky can get pretty frisky, anyway." And as Anchana Wichit archly comments, "with such high alcohol content, a possible side-effect is *yaa dong* droop."

Collectively dubbed *yaa dope* (dope medicine), virility boosters often contain traces of auspicious animal: bear paw, deer antler, rhino horn, tiger penis. Venomous centipedes, scorpions or coiled snake counter poison with poison. Creatures lurking in the sediment betray Chinese influence, as does pickling herbs in alcohol. Animal parts may also be stewed into soups, while vendors peddle 'oil of goat' to enlarge the penis. Some folk prefer a fresh infusion, such as live gecko or a glass of cobra blood and gall from a disembowelled snake. The illicit wildlife trade (worth 185 million baht at a 2004 WWF survey of just 190 sites) continues at shops, hotels and restaurants near national parks, frequented by Northeast Asians.

No one's more interested in *yaa dong*'s cocktail of drink, drugs and sex than the authorities. Suppression of all three make *yaa dong* illegal, not that bureaucrats or ministers would ever partake themselves. Police harass vendors, raid rural stills and prevent pharmacists from diagnosis or doctors from prescribing herbs. Thus stalls

Schemes like 'One Tambon (Village) One Product' have brought distribution plus technical marketing know-how to small-time provincial producers, however they do risk cultural loss, particularly since ageing herbalists are dying out. "Many beliefs govern herbal medicine, such as the times and places for the collection of ingredients," writes spa pundit Chamsai Jotisalikorn of practical lore gleaned through trial and error that science has verified. Corporations eyeing the $50 billion herbal world market turn only profitable extracts like the 'national herb' *prai* into patented curatives, discarding the holistic, homespun culture from which they spring.

Local drinks face similar pressures. Laws 'liberalised' in 2000 have ushered in snazzily branded *sato* (fermented liquor) and wines made from mangosteen or lychee. Still, quality control remains critical; one fruit wine bottle exploded on the agriculture minister's desk. Given the liquor monopolies, commercialisation favours big firms, while 15° proof limits are too low for *yaa dong*.

Perhaps local wisdom thrives best underground. Take Thai herbal aphrodisiacs. These tend to involve love charms – that is the exciting of a man's partner rather than himself. As these black magic potions become more associated with the lower classes, they take on a dark quality. As Chamsai notes, "the rhizome *dok thong* (golden flower) was believed to make girls fall in love." It's now urban slang for 'slut'. *Mor phii* (shamans) imbue amulets and tattoos with women-luring spells, and sell a love philtre, *nam mun phrai*, made from the chin fat of the violently dead. Too many drops lacing a woman's food could lead beyond lust into lunacy. Women also self-administer herbal amatories, such as 'Maiden of Fighting Territory' for rejuvenation, and 'Tightening Heaven', which makes a matron 'like a virgin'.

Aphrodisiacs are likely to remain underground in our censorious, monitored future, because sex in Thailand remains private. In April 2004, legalisation of sex shops was discussed but shot down. Perhaps *yaa dong* vendors need to cast a love charm on lawmakers.

often sell legal, do-it-yourself jars of dry ingredients or sachets of powdered herbs – just add whisky.

Urban sophisticates add snobbery to the prejudice. "*Yaa dong* has always been associated with animism and folklore, which is still believed by labouring people," says vendor Nikhom. "It's a pity that *yaa dong* became a low class symbol, although it's a kind of traditional Thai medicine." Many doctors – like half the population – reportedly find herbalism at least partly effective.

Folk hooch and remedies come under *phoom panya* (local wisdom), a 1980s grassroots reaction to Western products and practices. Following the 1997 crash, *phoom panya* became a buzzword for self-reliance, sparking official 'Thai wisdom' trade fairs and traditional healing institutes. Things Thai gained a reprieve. "The law supports *samuun prai* (herbal medicine, literally 'servants of the forest') if scientifically analysed so people can feel confidence in it," says Parinya. The spa boom and the *cheewajit* macrobiotic movement have also helped restore herbalism's credibility among the middle class, though there's a fracture between local and standardised recipes.

Sanuk-on-Sea
Life at the beach

When the world thinks of Thailand, it often thinks beach. 'The Beach' to be precise, since Alex Garland's book and film located the world's most idyllic strand on a remote Thai islet. Increasingly more crowded than the perfect cove Leonardo di Caprio's character uncovered, Thai-oriented beaches have a popular culture distinct from resorts tailored to foreign tourists.

Farang prize Siamese strands not just for the coral, karsts and seafood, but for the surrounding incentives to tan. Thai skin is a walking advert for tourism. The hot climate – and genetic palette – has honed a luminous shade of golden brown for which white tourists would kill. Kill themselves, in fact, given melanoma rates among what Australians dub 'sunbakers'. There's karma to pay by roasting your exposed, oil-basted flesh on a bed of sand.

"The headman was somewhat shocked to find me basking in the sun," wrote anthropologist William Klausner of time spent in an Isaan village. "He asked me guardedly what the matter was… [concerned] that I would get sick or go crazy. Years later one of my village aunts remarked that my sunbathing was viewed as a morally commendable, though mentally aberrational, attempt to become as dark as my fellow villagers."

So why the stigma? A tan in the West proves the prestige of leisure earned. Not so in Thailand, where *piew dum* (black skin) is a put-down or self-disparaging term. Paleness implies outdoor work escaped, status accrued, merit earned. So for much the same reason, the white wish to be brown, and the brown to be white. Here sun tanning harms both your face and your 'face'.

Fearful of resembling lowly sunbaked fisherfolk, most Thais who holiday by the sea only venture into the brine as the sun sinks. They know it's safe when red-blotched farang remove their sunglasses and depart, panda-eyed, to slap on vitamin E recovery cream.

Often found in different kinds of resort on separate beaches, Thai and *farang* also pursue different seaside pastimes. *Farang* savour the shushing of waves as they quietly sizzle in solitude. There's rest to recoup, salads to nibble, Lycra to adjust so tan lines blur. Languid swims punctuate chapters in 'airport novels' with embossed, gilded covers. If Thais want a withdrawal from the world they don't go to the beach – they meditate. When their toes hit the sand they want *sanuk*, in the noisy, clothed company of friends and family. Hotels and guesthouses need to provide outsize rooms or bungalows to fit whole gangs of Thai holidaymakers, snuggling up to four to a mattress, plus others kipping on the floor. A double room invariably means two king-size beds.

Closely related to the scene at waterfalls on public holidays, *sanuk*-on-sea involves non-stop picnicking, whisky sharing, card dealing, guitar strumming, singing. The esplanade at Bangkokian weekending resorts like Bang Saen and Cha-am is a succession of game playing, with shuttlecocks to pat, *takraw* balls to tap, tandems (rather than bicycles) to pedal. Even ice cream is quite different, being scooped from wheeled steel drums into bread buns and slathered with peanuts. Inner tubes stack into Michelin Man sculptures ready for rent, since to float is more *sabai* than to swim.

While farang sunbakers may rouse for the occasional volleyball or Frisbee toss, group activity is the essence of Thai beach leisure. Raucous streetlife accompanies the revellers to the coast barely altered. Ear-splitting longtail boat motors apply traffic therapy to homesick urbanites. Few Thais even need to change footwear.

Thais can find fun anywhere, but many of the flip-flop wearing classes risk tanning because it shows aspiration. Seaside resorts originated as an elite retreat both in the West and here. King Rama VI adopted the Victorian passion for fortifying the health with bracing sea air by making Hua Hin his personal Brighton, England's pioneering royal resort. Ozone proved potent not just for

the constitution of the body, but of the body politic. In 1932, King Rama VII conceded the first Thai constitution while at the palace Klai Kangwon: 'Far From Worries'. King Bhumibol's long residence there since the late-1990s re-endorses the merits of coastal living.

High society's increasingly lured to the sea as part of a 'contemporary lifestyle' image promoted through local magazines and the boom in travel publications. This is made possible by the profusion of designer boutique resorts since around 2001. These attract monied young professionals, who regard the minimalist hotel as an extension of sophisticated, globalised, urban living.

Watersports provide another impetus bringing Thais to the sea. Diving, snorkelling and parascending have caught on big-time, but so has riding an inflatable banana. Hilarity ensues as the floating fruit ploughs between scattering swimmers, towed by a speedboat or jet-ski, a lucrative rental toy that defies repeated bans and has now colonised canals around Bangkok.

Serving the visitors, an army of hospitality staff are mostly new arrivals not born at the beach. Migrants swamp marginalised shore dwellers whose homes have transformed from somewhere commonplace into a purported paradise.

top left: **Ouch! The marks of a great seaside holiday for** *farang* **in tropical Phuket.**

above: **Tanned enough already, Thais wade into the waves only in late afternoon, and then while fully dressed in clothes.**

top: **Thais cover their sands with umbrellas, so they can keep out of the sun, while facing each other, not the sea. They frequent different beaches than** *farang*, **like the weekend retreat of Bang Saen, which is tailored to Thai-style** *sanuk*.

right: **Stacks of innertubes await rental for the day.**

below: **A dip in the sea is more *sanuk* when floating on tubes or riding 'banana boats' pulled by jetskis. On land, the attraction's not sand and sun, but Mekong rum and mixers, roast chicken, guitar strumming, and roving masseuses and manicurists – all under the breezy shade.**

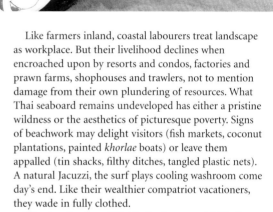

Like farmers inland, coastal labourers treat landscape as workplace. But their livelihood declines when encroached upon by resorts and condos, factories and prawn farms, shophouses and trawlers, not to mention damage from their own plundering of resources. What Thai seaboard remains undeveloped has either a pristine wildness or the aesthetics of picturesque poverty. Signs of beachwork may delight visitors (fish markets, coconut plantations, painted *khorlae* boats) or leave them appalled (tin shacks, filthy ditches, tangled plastic nets). A natural Jacuzzi, the surf plays cooling washroom come day's end. Like their wealthier compatriot vacationers, they wade in fully clothed.

Wearing shorts and T-shirt in the water shields the skin from both the sun's rays and, for women, men's gaze. Asian modesty prevails. Stripping down to bikini thongs offends many Thais. The pioneers of Koh Samui tourism – bohemian Western travellers – were wont to go naturist. It was the 1970s, and the affront to Thai values went barely noticed due to the thin population of remote coves. "It only became an issue when Scandinavians started wandering into [Samui's port] Nathon naked," recalled Samui native Kiat in 1996. "Though one nudist beach remains on Koh Pha-ngan, accessible only by boat." That particular full mooning party has since been eclipsed, though a Thai senator plans a discrete naturist resort. Tellingly, it's not in Thailand, but Burma.

Aside from topless European women, the only people stripping blatantly on Thai beaches are infants. Keeping kids amused is another reason that Thais run the UV gauntlet. From shade to shade they dash, crowding *sala*, promenading under casuarina pines, huddling under awnings that have the entire beach covered. Beneath this vast canvas, mats patchwork the sand and deckchairs line up. Not facing the sea – that's way too contemplative – but facing each other, in long rows, across tables laden with whisky bottles and *som tam* (papaya salad). In this netherworld of red and blue striped half-light, the only oil-basted flesh getting roasted belongs to a chicken.

Multi-Purpose Celebrities
How to get famous in fashion, pop and acting – all at the same time

Tour through Thai pop culture – magazines, movies, CDs, billboards, catwalks, soap operas, websites, product launches – and the same faces follow you around. Thai stars exploit their 15 minutes of fame by appearing in multiple media at once. In the West, personalities who grab several slices of life's cake draw suspicion, even derision. With quality so equated with specialisation, few stars jump genres successfully. Here, career-collecting is the norm, and expected of anyone famous.

Some multi-purpose celebrities started as mere faces on advertisements. Sornram Theppitak became a model, then soap star then pop singer; Pornchita na Songkhla went from model to actress, folk singer and cosmetics businesswoman. In different order, Mai Charoenpura and Marsha Watthanapanit both soared via film acting to TV to advertising, modeling then pop supremacy. Repeatedly topping 'handsomeness' polls, Jetsadaporn Pondee dominates film, TV and advertising.

The Thai jack-of-all-trades tendency echoes in Gilda Cordero-Fernando's take on the Filipino personality: "To save time the Westerner maximises technology. To save time the Pinoy maximises his time. No specialisation." That's true in Thailand, where historically each villager had to fish, hunt, invent and mend, weave, carve and build, as well as meditate, massage and box. Everyone made work *sanuk* by entertaining each other. And at the temple fair, each performer still needs to sing, jest, dance, banter, act, look beautiful and charm both sexes. *Dara* (stars) continue that variety tradition.

They may diversify in myriad directions, yet a pattern emerges. First come looks (modeling, advertising), with paler Chinese or part-Western *luuk khreung* complexions favoured over golden indigenous skin. The next phase is

above: **Hairdresser-to-the-stars Somsak Chalachol holds court like a Thai Elton John, with fun fashions and outrageous parties that are the talk of the town.** *TT*

right: **Tata Young is the first Thai star to go** *inter*, **with a string of number ones across Asia. Over a decade, the half-American singer went from cute teen sensation to vampy siren with lyrics like "sexy, naughty, bitchy me" that miff prudes but delight millions.** *SMP*

far right: **Reality TV arrived via UBC's** *Academy Fantasia*, **with the daily life of talent contestants viewable on cable 24/7. In polite Thai style, SMS votes were cast** *for* **rather than** *against* **anyone, with all joining the finale group concert. The victor, Vit, stands left in the hat.** *UBC*

scripting the voice (soaps, movies), then speaking ad lib (MC, VJ, DJ, gameshows). Ultimately, few resist the urge to sing, though some really should. Carrying a note matters less than carrying an audience. Hence politicians reap votes by crooning 'My Way' at hustings and dinners. One boy band singer, Vasu Sangsingkaeo, became a diplomat who moonlights as an Elvis impersonator. Having amassed cash and cachet, stars go into business. Many favour ventures – cafés, bars, clubs – where fans can 'touch' their idols.

Among the masses, Thai entertaining has always meant sharing, community, no barriers. Hence MCs and stars chatter casually at length, stages sound-blast each other, actors dissolve plays into a private party. Celebs remain very accessible. Since Thai entertainments evolved from overlapping sideshows lasting hours, no star (of film, or show) is too precious for the public to devote its full attention. Thai audiences don't sit in rapt silence; as the show goes on, so must life: gossiping, eating, greeting. Hence the talking on cellphones in cinemas.

Polls rank 'fame' high among youth aspirations. Aside from exposure though music, sport or high society, many ways have emerged to gain recognition. Since fickle tastes bore fast, an industry arose to recruit fresh faces. Being Miss Something is a passport to credibility, so agents scour provincial beauty pageants and temple fair talent contests; malls attract kids and teens into promotions; producers spot Cinderellas in service jobs. While some academics have graduated into showbiz, cheerleaders can

end up reporting the news. Perhaps Thailand's unlikeliest celebrity is a middle-aged forensic pathologist, Porntip Rojanasunan, who writes books and does the TV rounds in between autopsies, all the while wearing Goth make up, studded belts and punky, skin-tight tops. When presented the title *khunying* in the official white suit, she kept her trademark dyed spiky hair.

Natural fashion leaders, *dara* play clotheshorse for brand names. Many do fashion sets in demure women's magazines or more daring shoots in *Lips* or *Image*. A few stars strip for solo portfolio books, and now for lads' mags like *GM* or the Thai version of *FHM* that raise the flesh quotient on newsstands. With sex semi-taboo, porn models haven't gone mainstream as in the West.

Despite the Thai regard for beauty, the catwalk didn't capture the media spotlight until Elle Bangkok Fashion Week presented local designers and models en masse in 1998. Now models from magazines have turned into supermodels, many with their own diversified activities: half-French Florence Faivre went into acting, half-English Sonia Couling launched a perfume Sonia.

As in Hollywood, the celebrity machine evolved from a studio system. Only here, it's music studios that nurtured a stable of singing models to supply other media that the labels expanded into. Thailand and India are the only big music markets where multinational labels struggle. The local giants Grammy and RS have the clout to steer their stable into tailored roles. If *dara* seem to receive some-what less leverage and creative control than their Western

counterparts, that's partly because media empires often double up as agents. And in line with Thai social mores, young discoveries defer to their social seniors.

Dara whispered to be 'difficult' often turn out simply to have said "no" sometimes, or exerted creative will. Tata Young, the first Thai popster to succeed overseas, inspires both huge sales and the ire of puritans for her ambition and independence. Her self-mocking lyric "sexy, naughty, bitchy me" earned censure from the Culture Ministry – and number one hits. "You can't be too independent," says Areeya 'Pop' Sirisopha, a journalist-turned-Miss Thailand who joined the army. "If a job is against my principles I have to question who's asking me, and if I say no, what's the damage? You have to know who to please, be flexible and always have someone fight for you."

While *dara* may have skills, they're picked more for looks and charm since their 'brand' matters more than the formats they skip between. What *Vanity Fair*'s Maureen Orth calls the "celebrity-industrial complex"

knows no limit here. Advertisements plaster everything, from record covers and train tickets to the sets of concerts, talkshows and especially gameshows, in which contestants tend to be celebrities rather than Joe Public. With so much money at stake, *dara* need to be controlled. So private lives get as airbrushed as publicity shots.

Just like political secrecy fuels the rumour mill, this control causes gossip to swirl. While glossy magazines fill their fronts with respectful society photos, tabloids like *Daily News*, *Khao Sod* and *Thai Rath* report whatever they can. Wielding clout among both the powerful and the powerless, the bestselling *Thai Rath* barely censors bodily images, whether glamorous or gory (one random 1990s issue showed 22 corpses), amid ads for amulets and *National Enquirer* style exposés that no other media either gets to hear or would print. However, the wildest gossip circulates in an anonymous online column of the *Phujatgarn* (Manager) newspaper.

Despite all the cooing, Thais recognise the flimsiness of showbiz, calling it *maya* – Sanskrit for 'illusion'. One celebrity paper is called *Maya Channel*. Lamenting the lack of substance, columnist Alongkorn Parivudhiphongs writes that those raised on idolatry of fame try to copy artistic successes rather than emulate the commitment behind that artistry. "It's not surprising that many actors, singers and *hi-so* personalities become celebrity writers in the blink of an eye. Many from upper echelons become 'artists' simply because they went to study arts overseas." As Thailand's top international painter Tawan Dutchanee quipped on – where else? – a TV chat show: "I'm not an artist, because I don't have a singing album." Perhaps for art to have an audience – as the portraits of famous Thais by Greyhound fashion designer Jitsing Somboon show – it helps if the subject of art is celebrity.

Soap Operas
Formula TV drama reveals the secret life of Thailand

Soap is the new *Ramayana*. Mass addiction to Thai soap operas seems a phenomenon of the past few decades, and a generic international product. Yet these frothy prime-time sagas update the mythic essence of ancient drama. Thai soaps differ from those abroad in the way their very fixed characters still conform to traditional moral roles.

Adopted from India into every Thai classical art, the *Ramayana* epic is cast with eternal archetypes, good, bad and ugly. Now similar caricatures recur in designer guise on every TV channel. A loveable-rogue, the handsome *phra ek* (leading man) ends up as righteous as the hero Rama, while his humble *nang ek* (leading lady) plays Sita, who must prove her sacrificial devotion and, crucially, her virginity. Her domineering parents pose like gods, buddies frolic like angels, and loyal siblings combat the villain, a manipulative *nang rai* (bitchy aunt or ex) who injects wicked glamour. The brew is leavened by slapstick cameos from the obligatory uppity servant, fat hanger-on and screaming queen.

All human life is here. Plus non-human life – supernatural stories occur not just in *lakhon* (traditional plays) but as fodder for *lakhon tee-wee* (TV plays). Other genres include the historical romance, the teen romance, the rural romance, the nouveau riche romance. The power behind these materialist tales is not a Hindu god, but advertising. Soap operas get their nickname from the product sponsors, and Thai soaps take commercialism to extremes. Multi-purpose celebrities lead the cast, the theme song tops the charts, newspapers carry updates, magazines focus on each soap, talk shows hype must-see moments, and the credits display more logos than a mall.

Instead of lasting for decades like soaps do in the West, Thai soaps have a distant but definite end. Just as the entire *Ramayana* story takes literally days for dancers to perform and fills dozens of mural panels, soaps unfold thrice weekly for 30-50 episodes. Eventually they reach breaking point, stop, change set, cast and costume, then restart the tale in new guise.

The handful of production companies often reshoot the exact same stories within just a few years, with over half a dozen remakes of perennials like the nationalistic *Sai Lohit* (Bloodlines), the classic ghost tale *Mae Nak Phrakhanong* and *Khoo Kam* (Fated Couple). In the latter wartime weepie, an occupying Japanese lover once took six episodes of heightened ratings to die. The audience apparently loves to weep over familiar love triangles, reunitings and revenges. Among practical reasons for repeats, sponsors like predictability and few modern scripts or novels inspire such responses. However, reworked Hollywood plots like *The Bodyguard* and *Ghost* may be spread thinly over months of airtime.

One can see soaps in several lights: an exaggeration of reality, a denial of Thai values, or the Siamese underbelly exposed. Or they're a template in whose image society is being remade. Official moral guardians think so. They've threatened to cut production contracts if soaps don't adhere to the Victorian values they graft onto their own definition of Thainess.

Most of the public see soaps for what they are, calling them *nam nao* (murky waters) due to their stagnant plots and unsavory behaviour. Restrained in life by politeness and hierarchy, viewers can sublimate their suppressed feelings through the unrestrained on-screen antics: face slaps, hair pulling, screaming fits, mockery. Oh, the release! Yet Thai censors are far more effective than America's religious right at ruling airtime. Hand-holding and smoldering gazes from a pillow are as far as love scenes dare push. A kiss is pure porn.

While soaps revel in dynastic intrigues and wring every last drop of emotion from envy to infidelity, they avoid social controversy. "People in television know that they must portray life truthfully, but must not venture too far beyond social norms," admits scriptwriter Chanintorn Prasertprasart, citing the rarity of positive gay characters in *lakhon tee-wee*. "If they miscalculate, homosexuals might be confronted with severe social sanctions. This is why the image of *kathoey* is usually so one-dimensional and stylised." Though pirate DVDs of UK/US gay soap *Queer as Folk* sell from stalls, the authorities baulk at screening anything so provocative.

Similarly, storylines about corruption get mysteriously cut short. Producers avoid political issues for fear of taking sides. Sub-plots daring to mention oft-seen *mia noi* elicit condemnations for "destroying the marriage institution." Only *kathoey* get to utter the ripe innuendo typically bantered in office and farm. No trace either of the wife-beating, drugs, teen abortions, murders or rapes that are daily grist to Western soaps – and indeed to the Thai press. Any scandal or skimpy clothing gets confined to early episodes to whip up publicity in the indignant-yet-salivating tabloids and entertainment rags. They soon settle into bland routine. "Although we no longer have the TV censorship board, we still stick to the rules," admits Channel 7 producer Surang Prempri. "There is nothing for the government to get worried about, because self-censorship is at work."

Of course it would be; all of the channels are owned the state, the Army, or ministers' companies. With soap in service of ideology, even costume drama dialogue often sounds like it's scripted by the National Identity Board. Then in 2007, the coup regime initiated 'family'

ratings to make all bar late night TV suitable for children, to the dismay of producers and those wanting soaps to be more, not less, adult.

Like myths, the Thai soap helps people make sense of their lives by revealing eternal truths while peddling a fantasy. "It's the Thai people's desire to watch the upper class act out their roles. The hero drags himself up from poverty so that the viewers get a good feeling," explains Supatra Suparb of Chulalongkorn University. Soap unites the nation. From those murky waters emerge fashion trends and shared experience, whether they experienced it or not. While few Thais live like the label-touting *hi-so* inhabitants of many family dramas, that dream lifestyle encourages ordinary folk. Rural soaps often follow the initiative of *Mon Rak Luuk Thung* (The Spell of Country Music), which rekindled interest in folk songs, as had the film version in the early 1970s.

For decades, Channel 7 dominated the drama ratings by catering to working class viewers. "Soap operas are the sole source of entertainment that is convenient and affordable to them," explains scriptwriter 'Salaya', who's won several Mekhala and Golden TV awards. "So I use maids or labourers to colour the story and write stories they can relate to." Reflecting rural respect for hierarchy and virtue, Channel 7 adheres closest to the moral role-playing formulas, though the hero may be poor rather than *hi-so*, the heroine may be merely pretty rather than gorgeous. Ex-beauty queens instead play the bitch.

With a huge urban female following, Channel 3 makes their beautiful *nang ek* sassily modern, while keeping her virginity in a bank vault requiring a perfect combination to open. Her born-rich, *hi-so phra ek* gets to swagger as a dandy playboy until ultimately tamed. Their playground is a neo-classical mansion, their tears dripping on Versace

above: **A dutiful *nang ek* seeks forgiveness from her wounded mother in the aftermath of a soap trauma.** *EX*

right: **A wronged woman with hair extensions gets the support of her *hi-so* parents: *mae* in beige frills and 'swan flick' hair, *phor* in the *phra ratchathan* silk jacket national costume.** *EX*

rugs, their fights unheard beyond gilded electric gates. Echoing a desire for social freedoms, yuppy soaps are increasingly set abroad, where Thai mores needn't apply. Meanwhile Channel 5 has concentrated on dramas with a teen appeal. Real hi-so people even get to act, as with eco-aware aristo Chulachak 'Hugo' Chakrabongse, actor-politician Danuporn 'Brook' Punnakan, and Theerapat 'Tui' Sajjakul, the son of Thailand's football manager.

Soaps invariably show upward mobility. Tales like *Nuan Nang Khang Khiang* (Pork Vendor's Daughter) reflected the changing roles of women, the soaps' key demographic. *Luad Lai Mongkhon* (Pattern of the Dragon) became a coming-out of Sino-Thai pride, being the first of many soaps to trumpet the swift ascent of immigrant Chinese. "These historical dramas created a past for the new city that had just sprung into existence," suggests pundit Pasuk Phongpaichit. "*La-ong Dao* [1990-1991] was a modern Cinderella. The theme said: it's alright to become rich, even instantly. It focused only partly on the story, and more on the setting: grandiose houses, luxury cars, fancy Frenchified décor."

The finishing – lights, camera, acting – may not be so fancy. Some channels film whole series before broadcast, whereas others may air episodes within days of being shot, in pandering to ratings and media hype. Continuity errors thus creep in: mikes hove into view, wires thread through period sets, loinclothed warriors sport watches.

Many soap directors leave actors standing around chatting or staring too long into camera. This saves costs, stretches the plot and helps fill extended two-hour slots, but blame also lies in actors being paid by the scene. Staring and chatter build into frequent histrionics. Arms flail, voices shriek, faces grimace. Meanwhile, an over-dramatised soundtrack tries to drum-up suspense or hint when a scene is funny.

"But Thais like it that way," concedes director Kasidin Saengwong. "They want to be able to cry. That's why we spend 30 minutes on a farewell scene." The production standards have changed, but the generic format, honed over centuries, remains. Viewers might regard Thai soaps as *The Days of Our Past Lives*.

top left: **Slapstick humour keeps the soap format bubbling, with drum clatters and 'boing' sounds to herald every pratfall.** *EX*

top right: **The obligatory *kathoey* hanger-on in a light interlude at the beach.** *EX*

above: **A bemused dad wakes to a domestic confrontation in a rural soap. Note the village home décor of window grilles, vivid curtains, floor mattress and bright fleecy blanket.** *EX*

Songs For Life

The soundtrack to 1970s rebellion, Thai folk-blues keeps relevant

Between the fifth reign's waxed moustache and the hip-hop era goatee, the little facial hair cultivated in Thailand has bristled mostly on fans of Songs for Life. A musical offshoot of the left-leaning Art For Life movement, 1970s-style *pleng peuer cheewit* (Songs for Life) remains the soundtrack of disaffected middle-aged Thai males with a penchant for radical chic.

You can instantly spot these democracy pioneers, growing old grungily with their wispy beards, straggly long hair, and rumpled khaki fatigues, the ironic badge of anti-war theology. Yet the blood and sacrifice of which they sing was for real. Unlike the bleating peaceniks of corporate-sponsored T-Pop, the For Lifers actually fought. Hence their respect among a general public who'd otherwise consider their behaviour déclassé.

Grooming proves decisive in a culture of social and intellectual conformity where looking different implies thinking different, a trait not always thought desirable. Driven by politeness and non-confrontation, the instinct

to be *riab roi* (conservatively tidy) turned oppressively knee-jerk under decades of strict military autocrats. Originated by Marxist academic Jit Bhumisak in 1957, Art For Life evolved over the next decade to challenge the abuses of dictatorship in a very sixties way: happenings. Poetry, painting, literature, music – all got the egalitarian, "peace, man" treatment. Like the slovenly grooming, the questioning attitude affronted the old, but that was partly the point. Starting anew looked attractive then. With revolutions overthrowing nearby regimes, radicalised students and workers manned the Bangkok barricades in a reprise of Paris, 1968. Amazingly, it worked.

In an 'incident' that seared the national consciousness (although glossed over by school books), the military strongmen were driven into exile after shooting those protesting the arrest of constitution advocates. That was October 14, 1973, a date hallowed by the so-called 'October Generation', who were suppressed after another military-led massacre on October 6, 1976. During the sequence of theorising, protest, liberation, defeat, exile, amnesty, and then social work, 'For Life' activists found a distinctive look, lyric and music to suit the moment.

The two Octobers typify a globally rebellious era. Among its hirsute icons: hippies, Woodstock, Vietnam vets. Faced with such overwhelming facial hair and guitar strumming, earnest young Thais adopted the sartorial aspects of the politics along with the music. The potent combination of plaintive vocals, campaigning lyrics and bluesy guitar was then called progressive, though it now sounds rather dated. "The protest rock style is suffering from… the fact that the music, still rooted in Western styles of folk-rock, has changed little," says musicologist John Clewley. Its enduring popularity comes from the genre acting as a communal catharsis.

Songs For Life seem just that: for life. Veterans still gather with like-minded look-alikes in music bars lined with posters, flags and photographs of struggles past and present. With Thailand having one of the world's most liberal constitutions (though its spirit's rarely followed), the battle turns to the environment, poverty and public consultation, with demos usually held in a good-natured spirit. Personalities and imagery from the glorious '70s still make their appearance at disputes over the Pak Moon Dam, the Malaysian Gas Pipeline, the filming of *The Beach* in a national park.

Some have grown dreadlocks and enact protest art with surprising freedom, since the authorities daren't go too far in muzzling the October martyrs. At many demonstrations and gallery openings some of them

insult bigwigs with a lewdness the media would be scared to convey. His exhibition censored by Chulalongkorn University, Art For Life veteran Vasan Sitthiket invited attendees of the opening to hang effigies of the cabinet. Everyone there joined in. They got away with it.

Other sons of October have shaved and entered the government, prompting a paradigm shift in a state that increasingly accepts meritocracy and welfare. When their voice is expected to counter reactionary policy, however, they go curiously mute. Though the state conceded the designation of 'October 14 Democracy Day' on its 30th anniversary, Bangkok Governor Samak Sundaravej (who was involved in the post-1976 clampdown) banned the festivities from their historic site, supposedly to beautify grass on Sanam Luang for the looming APEC summit. Simultaneously honoured and marginalised, the veterans camped on the sidewalk, screening uncensored footage of the massacres of '73, '76 and '92. Intruding onto Sanam Luang, dozens of huge paintings by Vasan defied the ban with images like generals defecating on the people.

While Art For Life continues to stimulate the culture, musical references have shifted from quotes of theories by Karl Marx to covers of ballads by Richard Marx. In fact, Marxism proved skin-deep among the activists who faced no other option in 1976 but to take their guitars to the jungle hideouts of Communist insurgents. "None of Caravan [the pioneer For Life band] had been members of the Communist Party before joining the guerillas and they found the rigid discipline stifling," Craig Lockhard

left: **Thailand's greatest rock star, Add Carabao, is a Songs For Life legend. Note his trademark gear: facial hair, buffalo horn logo, bandanna, long hair, earrings, and a fighting cock.** *AC*

top: **Art for Life continues today, with an Art Vote campaign, in the Bangkok governor election of 2004, to build an art centre.** *PCS*

above: **One of many paintings by Vasan Sitthiket displayed on Sanam Luang on the 30th anniversary of the massacre of 14 October 1973.** *PCS*

writes. Disillusioned by the Maoist cadres' petty rules, inflexible rhetoric and contempt for Thai culture – not to mention the jungle discomforts – they reintegrated with society after a 1981 amnesty.

The heroic romance of their outlaw life lent itself to sentiment, nostalgia and mythologising. Camaraderie and an undaunted national taste for American soft rock thus turned *pleng peuer cheewit* into an entertainment genre. Where country-rock meets the mainstream, you get requests for songs by The Eagles in cowboy-themed log cabins with wagon-wheel windows. No hyperbole conveys how often 'Hotel California' gets played. Purist devotees flock to reunion concerts of Caravan, says Lockhard, even though "their music was and remains too controversial for most Thai elites, even liberal ones." Born too young to have fought, the latest star Pongsit Kampee projects credibility despite have a smooth chin.

In the 1980s shift of Songs For Life from niche appeal to mass popularity, the key figure was Add Carabao, a household name thanks to immense talent, eloquence and courage. Named after his veteran band Carabao ('buffalo' in the Philippines, where the band had sought refuge after 1976 crackdown), Add resembles an Asian Willie Nelson. He dons a bandanna emblazoned with the buffalo-skull logo that brands his own lines of clothing, pubs and energy drink. "But for the language disconnect, he'd be an international superstar," says music executive Tim Carr. "The most prolific, prodigious and, possibly, profligate musician/artist/personality in Thailand… Add channels not only Nelson and Santana, but Dylan, Springsteen and 1,000 years of Thai folk."

Most iconic is Add's 1980s anthem against consumer imports, 'Made in Thailand'. Such strident nationalism – bolstered by anti-globalisation reflexes and his daring advocacy of independence from Burma of the (ethnically Tai) Shan – rather jars with some of the 'Art For Life' intent. However dubious his rousing soundtrack for the Burma-bashing move *Bangrajan*, Add injects Thai music with a wit, edge and relevance that few can match.

When Thailand's various counter-cultures found their social lives the target of a morals campaign in 2001, only Add dared confront the prudes. His song 'Purachai Curfew' assailed the then Interior Minister for nightlife harassment that did real cultural damage to Thailand – in addition to lowering a million incomes.

Though the non-politicised youth of today don't listen to rock riffs of revolution, their current favoured genre, hip-hop, does still feed off grievance. With ever-stricter efforts to force adults to stop partying till late, limiting computer gaming communities and threatening to put a 10pm curfew on under-18s, it remains to be seen if music will again challenge the authorities' recurring fetish for discipline. Perhaps the next wave of reform will be spurred by the *indy* generation, following up Songs For Life with Songs For Lifestyle.

T-Pop Goes Indy

How mass entertainment went pop, spawned subcultures and now aspires to art

What *wairoon* (teens) want increasingly determines what the rest of the culture gets. Formally, elders were always right, tradition dictated taste, and fashions filtered down from above. Now much of mainstream culture rises up from below and from the young, whether conventional pop or maverick *indy* (independent). In a land revering elders, that's a paradigm shift. This reversal of seniority plays out in magazines, products, advertising, broadcasts, websites, clothing and thoughts. Eventually, *indy* thinking may impact many things in this book. As always in pop culture, music provides the spark and sets the tone of each youth tribe's identity.

Business has conspired in Western pop since the 1950s, but wasn't until the 1980s that local companies could mould Thai pop. Imported fads influenced folk music like *luuk thung* more through instrumentation, than structure or substance. For a Thai pop style – and a Thai pop industry – to emerge required the tricky task of marrying tonal Thai singing with Western song structure. Languorous Siamese balladeering doesn't suit a slogan-like chorus. Thai vocals emphasise showpiece mono-logues or jousting interplay, not harmonies. Even rhyming differs, here echoing the end of one line with words at the start of the next.

Eventually, Caravan managed to craft plaintive folk warbling onto blues in the early 1970s and birthed Songs For Life, which evolved into Thai rock. Then in the 1980s, male guitar duo Asanee and Wasan mastered the trick in pop. Ever since, T-Pop songs have sounded much alike, partly because lyricists so need the stock phrases that can fit the short-line format in tone and rhyme whilst making sense. Thus no breathy T-ballad is complete without "*chun rak ter*", the most melodic way to sing "I love you". Sentimental T-pop tunes have become the urban soundtrack: chimed by pals in the street, belted out in private karaoke room, recorded by school friends in a KTV booth, lip-synched by stars to singalong crowds at Sunday lunchtime concerts held in malls.

Bubblegum pop cuteness spread throughout *wairoon* lifestyle and became the norm for adults too. The film industry focused on teen melodramas and the fine arts struggled to find an audience. Generally, Thais adopt a music style for the look and sound over its original meaning, whether it be British punk, American hip-hop or heavily made-up Japanese boy bands. Twice, however, Thai youth rebelled against dictatorship and forged not just political change, but creative pop subcultures. Protests in 1973 and 1976 rallied to the Art For Life movement of earthy, communal idealism. The middle

class that manned the barricades in 1992 pursued more individualist goals. From this emerged a generation with the urge to be *indy*.

The word came from Britain's non-corporate 'indy' music broadcast by DJs Wasana and Bee to an alt crowd that read the magazine *Hyper* and frequented *indy* pubs like Redwood. From a surge of new labels, Bakery Music packaged innovative music in fresh ways. It distributed Thailand's first indy hit for Modern Dog, a trio named for their lack of boy-band looks. With a now-proven market, Bakery championed alternative acts like rock siren Ornaree, bewitching Goth vamp Rik, funk jester Yokee Playboy and the founder of *rap thai*, Joey Boy.

Rap proved more suited than any Western music to Thai ways of singing. Quickfire rap boasts a long local heritage, from *mor lam* banter in Isaan and the central styles of *lamtad* and *isaew*, in which teams of men and women trade repartee with saucy, ingenious wit. Joey Boy – followed more caustically by Da-jim then Thaitanium – expressed the new mindset through explicit lyrics on taboo topics: sex, drugs, corruption. To avoid censors, Da-jim had to hand-distribute his early cassette *Hip-hop Above the Law*. Since going mainstream they've toned

down the controversy, but the Rubicon was crossed. Lunchtime mall concerts now throb to hip-hop, and rap-style nu metal. Tens of thousands tune into the indy Fat Radio and throng its annual Fat Festival, which features almost 200 bands. A parallel thrash metal scene arose into such a following that since 2004 the biennial Demonic gathering shakes the genteel Thailand Cultural Centre.

The *indy* generation embraced the foreign film festivals that started in the mid-1990s. In the film zine *Nang Thai* they wistfully read about the new and classic quality films never shown in Thai cinemas. Soon art films gained regular screenings and film festivals appeared most months, some also showing upcountry. World stars now attend Bangkok International Film Festival, partly as Thailand's a set for so many foreign films.

Movie content went indy, too, as screens and film production both improved and multiplied. Nonzee Nimibutr directed fine films like *Nang Nark* and *OK Baytong*, while Wisit Sasanatieng's retro Siamese cowboy art movie *Tears of the Black Tiger* earned a fraction at home of its global box office. Previously, Thai films weren't subtitled due to no expectation of interest abroad. Pen-ek Rattanruang likewise dissects pop culture to acclaim, as in *Mon Rak Transistor*, about a would-be singer, and his paean to Thai-Japanese alienation, *Last Life in the Universe*. Apichatphong Weerasethakul burst from the experimental film scene to win successive awards at Cannes for *Blissfully Yours* and *Tropical Malady*. But in 2007 he withdrew *Syndromes and a Century* from

Thailand, to prevent censors cutting scences milder than equivalent scenes they'd allowed in mainstream movies. This sparked a 'Free Thai Cinema' campaign, which also protested that a law to establish film ratings actually increased censorship, not decreased it.

Aside from words, music and film, *indy* thinking has transformed visual design. Dowdy magazine layouts have been infused since the 1990s by a crop of stylish, more stimulating monthlies. Many copy international formats, but the difference lies in the *indy* attitude to be original. Again things started small, and Thammasat University played a pivotal role. Formerly its students demonstrated for democracy, now its graduates open bars showing art on Phra Arthit Road. This old riverside district of court dancers became the *indy* HQ. At fairs in the road's park, *indy* fairs sold hand-made books, fanzines, artworks, self-designed clothing and home-recorded music.

The typical Thai gallery opening is no haughty affair, but a party, where the art may act as a backdrop to socialising. *Indy* art being exhibited in bars enhances this feeling of art being part of a shared experience along with food, drink and laughter. Often indy exhibits have a quirky, observational quality. This personalised, diary-like aesthetic has spread throughout youth products and publishing. While mild as art movements go, this indi-vidualist seed has grown.

Indy painter Thaweesak 'Lolay' Thongdee progressed from cartoon strips to international exhibitions within a couple of years. Meanwhile, Bangkok's H Gallery brought fine art by young talents into bar spaces, creating a new market for art among the monied young. This influx is changing an art scene dominated by Buddhist modernism, 'Art For Life' activism and conceptual installations. Artists have also created a visual identity for protests, and one art zine carried the title *Defy*.

Just as in the 1960s, Western art schools added imagination to the commercial pop revolution, alumni of Silpakorn art university infuse Thai creative industries. Though the community of bohemians is tight and could be considered elite, their impact can be felt on the street. Art venues like About Café actively involve the street, utilising shop windows, rock gigs, parties, fashion shows, rooftop markets, graffiti and customised transport and buildings to make art more accessible and relevant to the public. Often held in parks with temple fair informality, theatre festivals tap a fresh interest in plays tackling pertinent themes, like homosexuality, current affairs or family breakdown.

Out of the handmade book craze came *a day*. An arts and issues magazine founded by enthusiasts, it depends less on advertising, than small investors and loyal readers. *A day*'s circulation exceeds that of many glossy monthlies. Alternately whimsical and serious, it warps conventions, spots trends and profiles *indy* role models like comedian Udom 'Nose' Taephanich and Prabda Yoon, a young writer who miffed some literary traditionalists in 2002 by winning the SEAwrite literary prize for mostmodern musings that toyed with Thai grammar. In 2004, *a day* launched a news weekly aimed at *wairoon*, laying down a graphical and editorial challenge to news magazines like *Matichon* and the freewheeling tabloid dailies.

left: **Hand-made book fairs have helped turn reading into a trendy pursuit. Starting in the art-bar strip Phra Arthit Road, they have spread since the late 1990s. The annual** *indy* **musical gathering Fat Festival has dozens of hand-made book stalls, all displayed at ground level as pictured.** *PCS*

above: **A star of Thai rap, Da-jim rhymes about issues that T-Pop lyrics never discuss.** *GMM*

left: **Bakery Music has led the** *indy* **music scene. Here are some of the label's stars (from left): Anuwat Sanguansakphakdee (Boy); Krissada Sukosol Clapp (Noi from Pru); songwriter and animator Boyd Kosiyabong; Nop Ponchamni; Burin Boonvisut (from Groove Riders); Thanachai Ujjin (Pod from the first hit indy band Modern Dog); Chalatit Tantiwut (Ben); and Piya 'Poe' Sastrawaha (aka Yokee Playboy), shot on Bakery's 10th anniversary in 2004.** *BM*

a day 1

Volume 1 number 1
september 2000
80 baht

COLLECTOR ISSUE
TRIBUTE TO THE READER

NEW AGE!

Like all subcultures, *indy* boosts group identity, while resisting conventions. The state now urges new thinking in business, but not in new thinking about society. Since 2001, a moral clampdown restricted fashion and nightlife, and imposed a curfew on *Ragnarok*, the online role-playing game that keeps over 700,000 young Thais in Internet cafés for several hours a day. "In Thailand it is almost exclusively a social place; a glorified chatroom," writes Don Sambandaraksa, noting that foreign players focus more on the game details. "Players from Thailand now have a bad reputation. If you see an avatar [created character] begging for money and just chatting, chances are they will be Thai." Thai gamers have even sought to buy avatar skills or offered high-level characters for sale.

While some regard *Ragnarok* – here called *rak narok* (love hell) – as akin to loitering in malls or bars, studies suggest gamers aren't anti-social slackers, but modern, if alienated multi-taskers with good computer and thinking skills. However, as Singapore found, creative industries can't flourish without individual free expression, so the city-state reversed course and let the youth party all night, so they can create by day.

Perhaps *indy* can't be stopped. Business is addicted, with youth marketing agencies like the Filter Group out to target every *indy* niche from X-treme sports and DJs to bohemian art scenesters. So many fans of indy music and arts attend Fat Festival that they're called the '*dek naew indy* (indy trend kids) generation'. "It's a person who reads *a day*, listens to Fat, watches short films and shops at Chatuchak Weekend Market," says Ohn of ska-punk outfit Adulterer. As a subculture goes mainstream, though, it changes the norm. Pop barometer Thongchai 'Bird' McIntyre went from cute T-pop to mine house, rap, folk and then indy by duetting with Sek Lo-So.

The most blatant form of artistic dissent is graffiti. It arrived late onto Bangkok walls, through the hip-hop wave, placing what Norman Mailer calls "your presence on their presence… hanging your alias on their scene."

Like Art for Life, *indy* fits Dick Hebidge's subculture definition: "The process begins with a crime against the natural order… but it ends in the construction of a style, in a gesture of defiance or contempt. It signals a refusal." Many dismiss a Thai dressed in punk style as being unconscious of punk's rebellious spirit. Still, Thai punks do break norms. Each fad chips away at the consensus.

Indy is not exactly an import. Many things in Thai life have a surface conformity yet happily go their own way. This book is full of such idiosyncratic subcultures. By being interested in the popular culture itself, the *indy* mindset might perhaps have an ability to cross the boundaries between high and low culture, elite and pop, folk and fashion, past and future. *Indy* happenings aren't homogenous; the *dek naew indy* that they attract can be *hi-so*, middle class, provincial migrants, foreigners or the simply curious. *Indy*-ness often gives a modern spin to indigenous things, rather than equating modernity with something foreign or hi-tech. In its eclectic, improvising attitude to life, *indy* is in many ways very Thai.

far left top: **Thai graffiti tends to be tidy and limited to derelict buildings or special sites like the Red Bull X-Park, where an extreme sports tyke in top-knots rides a turbo-charged traditional hobby-horse.** *PCS*

far left below: **The cover stars of** *a day* **magazine's first issue were the new generation businessman Thanakorn Huntrakul, quirky actor/MC Ray Macdonald (half-Scot), model Florence Faivre (half-French) and Prabda Yoon, free-thinking author and winner of the SEA Write Award.** *ADM*

above: **The artist Thaweesak 'Lolay' Srithongdee took his anatomically gifted figures from magazine cartoon strips into fine art exhibited by H Gallery.** *HG*

left: **An indy hero and art film favourite, director Apichatpong Weerasethakul, stands outside the mainstream of censors, film makers and cinema-goers. Yet he was the first Thai to win awards at Cannes, for** *Blissfully Yours*, **a love story about an illegal immigrant, and the surreal** *Tropical Malady*, **about an Isaan gay romance and possession by a tiger spirit. It remains to be seen if he'll spark a new wave of indy filmmaking.** *AW*

Acknowledgements & Sources
Including bibliography and picture credits

Philip Cornwel-Smith would like to thank:

John Goss for his images, friendship, technical wizardry and appreciation of things Thai; Alex Kerr for his insight and mentoring since the start, sharing many research travels, writing the preface, editing the text, providing some punchlines and being a soulmate; MR Narisa Chakrabongse, Paisarn Piemmattawat and the staff of River Books for publishing the book I had started writing in 1999; and Holger Jacobs for ingeniously balancing so many words and pictures in the design.

I'm also indebted to: Chatchai Ngoenprakairat for his research and assistance; Navamintr Vitayakul for his advice; the ajahns Vithi Phanichphant, Paothong Thongchua, Phiriya Krairaksh and Anucha Thirakanont for their incredible knowledge; Pradit Prasartthong of Makhampom Theatre Group; and all the interviewees, from *hi-so* to vendors. I'm also grateful to my parents for their support and Surachai Pinthong for his kindness.

One spark for this book was my exposure to the diverse content of *Bangkok Metro* magazine during my eight years as founding editor. So I offer thanks to past colleagues and contributors at *Metro*, especially John Twigg, Ian Crawshaw and Howard Richardson.

For supplying information, pictures and other help, I thank: Irwin Cruz; Zulkifli Mohamad; Kathareeya Jumroonsiri; Chamsai Jotisalikorn; Saa; Phatarawadee Phatarawanik of *The Nation*; the *Bangkok Post*; Vitsanu Riewseng; Rungsaeng Sripaoraya at TAT; Bakery Music; Naphalai Areesorn at *Thailand Tatler* magazine; Inthira Thanavisuth, Patpong Thanavisuth and Preyamon Thanavisuth at *HiSoParty.com*; Prasert Jermjuthitham; GMM Grammy; Ekachai Uekrongtham; Apichartpong Weerasethakul; Waraluk Wisitwattanakul at Exact Co Ltd; Virapoj Asavajan; H Ernest Lee at H Gallery; Tim Young; Eric Booth, Beverly Jangkamonkulchai and Nicky at Jim Thompson Silk Company; Add Carabao; Hugo Chakrabongse, Payom Valaiphatchra at Syllable; Phimphimon Phim-ngam; Nat Prakobsantisuk, Manod Soising; Tom Kerr; Norachai Boonsom; *a day* magazine; *Elle* (Thailand) magazine; Sonida at Sony Music Pictures; *Thai Rath*; Prapit Jai-ngam of Lumphini Stadium; Sarinya Tatthong at Red Bull X Park; Krisda Sodprasert of Baan Chang Thai; Direk Thaworn & Mard Bangtalad at *Tumniab Kai Chon* magazine; Fantasia Wedding Center; and Click Radio (104.5 Fat Radio/Fat Festival).

I wish to recognise and celebrate all those who share my interest in the subject and have ventured to report it. Finally, I'd like to thank the Thai people for providing such wonderful material.

John Goss would like to thank:

Philip for his vision, encouragement, and sense of humor even in the midst of childbirth; our dream publishers, MR Narisa Chakrabongse and Paisarn Piemmatawat at River Books; our dedicated designer, Holger Jacobs; Alex Kerr for kind words always; Amarin Ratanarat for his patient support, artistic eye, and driving beyond the call of duty; Joe Moe; Robert Hori; Robert McLeod; Toshie and Takaki Urabe; Mai; William Meyer; Eric Allyn; Saksit; Supot and Mian; Asana; Tawan; Tor; Ajarn Saji; everyone at Emerald Thai and Sunshine; and Tom Coughlin.

Notes on Sources

Printed sources veer between the plentiful, the rare and the impossible-to-find. The best records of contemporary folk and pop culture are probably the archives of the *Bangkok Post* and *The Nation* daily newspapers.

For a quoted author, check first the bibliography, which includes other titles of interest. If an author has more than one book, reference to the relevant volume is made under the chapter headings, where I also credit articles from newspapers and magazines. Where I've cited quotes obtained by an author, I've listed them under the speaker's name and given the author's credit. A few quotes have been slightly compacted for clarity, brevity and avoidance of word repetition, while seeking to preserve their meaning, nuance and style. I apologise for any errors or omissions.

Quotes without a credit are drawn from interviews by myself or Chatchai Ngoenprakairat. In addition to the sources listed, statistics and facts are drawn from published interviews or reports. All sources were published in Thailand unless otherwise stated. Thai authors are sorted by first name, all others by surname.

BIBLIOGRAPHY

Allyn, Eric, *Trees in the Same Forest* (Bua Luang, 1991).
Askew, Marc, *Bangkok: Place, Practice & Representation* (Routledge, 2002).

Bangkok Metro Magazine, issues 1-122 (City Media, 1994-2004).
Barmé, Scot, *Woman, Man, Bangkok: Love, Sex & Popular Culture in Thailand* (Rowman & Littlefield, 2002, USA).
Bell, Barry, *Bangkok: Angelic Allusions* (Reaktion Books, 2003, UK).
Beurdeley, Jean-Michel, *Thai Forms* (Weatherhill, New York & Tokyo, 1980).
Blenkinsop, Philip, *The Cars That Ate Bangkok* (White Lotus, 1996).

Chaleo Manilerd, Dr, *Thai Customs & Beliefs* (Office of the National Culture Commissioin, 1988).
Chamsai Jotisalikorn, *Classic Thai* (Periplus, 2002); *Thai Spa Book* (Periplus, 2003).
Chaturachinda, Gwyneth, Sunanda Krishnamurty & Pauline W Tabtiang, *Dictionary of South & Southeast Asian Art* (Silkworm Books, 2000).
Clewley, John, *World Music: The Rough Guide* (Rough Guides, 2000).
Cohen, Erik, *The Commercialized Crafts of Thailand* (Curzon, 2000).
Cummings, Joe & Martin, Steven, *Thailand* (Lonely Planet, 2003).
Cummings, Joe, *World Food: Thailand* (Lonely Planet, 2000).

Graham, Mark, *Thai Wood* (Finance One, 1997).
Guelden, Marlane, *Thailand: Into the Spirit World* (Asia Books, 1996).

Hargreave, Oliver, *Exploring Chiang Mai: City, Valley & Mountains* (Within Books, 3rd edn, 2002).
Harris, Andrew, *Bangkok After Dark* (McFadden Books, 1968).
Hebdige, Dick, *Subculture: The Meaning of Style* (Methuen, 1979, London).
Holmes, Henry & Suchada Tangtongtavee, *Working with the Thais* (White Lotus, 1995).
Hopkins, Jerry, *Strange Food* (Periplus, 1999).
Hoskin, John, *Bangkok by Design: Architectural Diversity in the City of Angels* (Post Books, 1995); *The Super-natural in Thai Life* (Tamarind Press, 1993).

Ingersoll, Jasper, 'Merit and Identity in Village Thailand', *in Change and Persistence in Thai Society*, ed G William Skinner & A Thomas Kirsch (Cornell University Press, 1975).

Jackson, Peter A & Cook, Nerida M, *Genders & Sexualities in Modern Thailand* (Silkworm, 1999); with Sullivan, Gerard, ed Ladyboys, Tom Boys, Rent Boys (Silkworm, 2000).

Klausner, William J, *Reflections: One Year in an Isaan Village Circa 1955* (Siam Reflections, 2000); *Thai Culture in Transition* (Siam Society, 1997); *Reflections on Thai Culture* (Siam Society, 1993).

Kukrit Pramoj: His Wit & Wisdom compiled by Vilas Manivat, edited by Steve Van Beek (DK, 1983).

Lai, Richard C, *Gone Astray: The Care and Management of the Asian Elephant in Domesticity* (FAO/RAP, 1997).
Lockard, Craig A, *Dance of Life: Popular Music & Politics in SE Asia* (Silkworm, 2001).

Majupuria, Trilok Chandra, *Erawan Shrine & Brahma Worship in Thailand* (Tecpress Service, 1993).
Manit Sriwanichphoom, introduction by Ing K, *Bangkok in Black & White* (Chang Phuak Nga Dum, 1999).
Melly, George, *Revolt into Style: The Pop Arts* (Oxford University Press, 1970 & 1989, Oxford).
Montri Umavijani, *Facets of Thai Cultural Life* (PR Dept, 1984).
Muang Boran, *Guide to Muang Boran* (Viriah Business, 4th edn, 2001); *Old Market Town* (Muang Boran, 1992).
Mulder, Neils, *Everyday Life in Thailand* (DK, 1985); *Thai Images: The culture of the Public World* (Silkworm, 1997).
Navin Rawanchaikul, *COMM…* (S&S Co, 1999, Tokyo).
Nostitz, Nick, *Patpong: Bangkok's Twilight Zone* (Westzone, 2000, UK).

Origibet, Jorges, *From Siam to Thailand* (Kofco, 1982).

Pasuk Phongpaichit & Baker, Chris, *Thailand's Boom* (Silkworm, 1996).
Phillips, Herbert P, *The Integrative Art of Modern Thailand* (Lowie Museum of Anthropology, 1991, USA).
Phuket: A Traveller's Guide (Sarakadee Press, 2002).
Phya Anuman Rajadhon, *Essay on Thai Folklore* (DK, 1969); *Popular Buddhism in Siam* (Sathirakoses Nagapradipa Foundation, 1986).
Pimsai Amranand & Warren, William, *Gardening in Bangkok* (1970, 1996).
Pittaya Homkrailas, *Ta Klang: The Elephant Valley of Mool River Basin* (Pittaya Homkrailas, 2002).

Quaritch Wales, HG, *Divination in Thailand* (Curzon Press, 1983).

Redmond, Mont, *Wondering Into Thai Culture* (Redmondian Insight Enterprises, 1998).
Reynolds, Craig J, *National Identity and its Defenders* (Silkworm, 2002).
Ridout, Lucy & Gray, Paul, *Rough Guide to Thailand* (Rough Guides, 2001).
Ruethai Chaichongrak, *The Thai House* (River Books, 2003).

Sangsidh Piriyarangsan, Pasuk Phongpaichit, & Nuannoi Treerat, *Guns, Girls, Gambling and Ganja* (Silkworm, 1999).
Sanitsuda Ekachai, *Keeping the Faith* (Post Books, 2001).
Segaller, Denis, *Thai Ways* (Asia Books, 1989).
Somkid Chaijitvanit *Rare Breed* (Post Books, 2002).
Sulak Sivaraksa, *Siam in Crisis* (Thai Inter-Religious Commission for Development, 1990).

Sumet Jumsai with R Buckminster Fuller, *Naga* (Chalermnit Press, 1997).
Suthorn Sukphisit, *The Vanishing Face of Thailand: Folk Arts & Folk Culture* (Post Books, 1997).

Thailand Arts Directory (Visiting Arts, 2002, UK).
Thongchua, Paothong, *Karn Taeng Kaai Thai* (Thai Costume) (National Identity Board, 1999).
Time Out Bangkok Guide (2003).
Totman, Richard *The Third Sex: Kathoey* (Silkworm, 2004).

Van Beek, Steve, *Bangkok Then & Now* (AB Publications, 1999); *Thailand Reflected in a River* (Wind & Water, 2004).

Warren, William, *Bangkok* (Talisman, 2002, London).
Wyatt, David K, *Siam in Mind* (Silkworm, 2002).

SOURCES BY CHAPTER

INTRODUCTION
Chai-anan Samudavanija, in Reynolds.
Gilda Cordero-Fernando, *Pinoy Pop Culture* (Bench, 2001).
Phya Anuman Rajadhon, *Essay on Thai Folklore* (DK, 1969).
National Cultural Maintenance Act, cited by Reynolds.

SUGAR
Mallika Khuansathaworanit, 'A Menu of Nostalgia' (*BK magazine*, 21/05/2004).

INSECT TREATS
Pairath Disthabamrung, cited by Chompoo Trakullertsathien in *Rare Breed* (Post Books, 2002).
Thongchart & Rotjana Nusu, cited by Chompoo Trakullertsathien in 'Bugs on the Menu' (*BP*, 22/05/2003).
Uamdao Noikorn, 'Insects gain gourmet acceptance' (*BP*, 17/10/1999).

VENDORS
Sawong Srimongkhol, cited by Supoj Wancharoen in 'Vendors to return Apec food carts' (*BP*, 30 October 2003).
Suthorn Sukphisit, 'Classic Dish' (*BP*, 3/05/2003).

LONGTAIL BOATS AND BARGES
Pin-Fat, Olivier, 'River Gypsies' (*Metro*, 09/1994).

MOTORCYCLE TAXI JACKETS
Bangkok Post letter by 'BA', 'Motorbike races still there en masse' (*BP*, 13/10/2004).
'Insurance for the future' (*TN*, 12/09/2003).
Kosin Hinthao, Pol Maj Gen, 'Register by Friday, drivers told' (*TN*, 28/05/2003).
Piak, cited in 'Bribes, bribes, bribes' (*BP*, 4/08/2003).
Samak Sundaravej, 'Motorcycle-taxi drivers liberated: Samak' (*TN*, 24/05/2003).
Sopon Ongkrara & Preecha Sa-adsorn, 'Perils of life in the fast lane' (*TN*, 1/04/1999).
Wassayos Ngamkham and Manop Thiposod, 'Motorcycle taxi jackets symbol of mafia control' (*BP*, 26/05/2003).
Wirawat Watanakul, 'Cracking Down on motorcyclists' (*BP*, 13/09/2003).

TUK-TUK
Surakiart Sathirathai, cited by Rungrawee Pinyorat, 'Fog threatens view

of Royal barges' (*TN*, 22/07/2003).
Maekawa Ken-ichi, *Three Wheeled Vehicles of SE Asia* (Ryokonin, 1999, Japan).

FAIRY LIGHTS
Loubère, Simon de la, cited in *Thailand: A Traveller's Companion* (Archipelago Guides, 1994).
Neale, Frederick Arthur, cited by Sumet.

SECURITY GUARDS
Klausner, William, 'Power & Hooliganism' in *Reflections*.

BLIND BANDS
Amorn Samakkarn, cited by Karnchariya Sukrung, 'Daddy's Home' (*BP*, 4/03/2003).
Chetana Nagavajara, cited by Atiya Achakulwisut, 'Tale of blind busker a real eye-opener' (*BP*, 18/01/2003).
Jerawat Laowang, cited by Kultida Samabuddhi, 'Almost all career options for blind' (*TN*, 23/11/2003).
Napanisa Kaewmorakot, 'Blind Street bands find new stage' (*TN*, 8/05/2003).
Nareupol Inkaew, cited by Nitida Asawanipont, 'Breaking down the arts boundaries' (*TN*, 12/02/2003).

SOI ANIMALS
Bangkok Post staff, 'Snake Problem keeps staff busy' (*BP*, 31/05/2004).
Clutterbuck, Martin R, *The Legend of Siamese Cats* (White Lotus Press, 1998).

TRASH RECYCLERS
Anon Nakornthab, 'Shopping & Services' in *Time Out Bangkok*.
Suwandee Chaiwarut, cited by Ranjana Wangvipula, 'Shoppers don't like the idea of using cloth bags' (*BP*, 24/08/2003).
Urban Community Development Office, 'Housing People in Asia' (*UCDO*, issue 12/04/1999).

UNIFORMS
Nation staff, 'Tighter the shirt, better the look' (*TN*, 21/12/2002).
Nation staff, 'We're being sexually harassed, say police' (*TN*, 12/03/2003).

HI-SO
Apiradee Pinthong, cited by Pratchaya Pruedthapol, 'High Society' (*BP*, 06/06/1997).
Sanitsuda Ekachai, 'It's not just money for most women' (*BP*, 04/03/2004).

NICKNAMES & NAMECARDS
Somchai Khemklad, cited by Penchan Phoborisut 'Tao grows up' (*BP*, 23/4/2003).
Jumsai name, reported by Theeranuch Pusaksrikit, 'No hard feelings says Sumet' (*TN*, 27/04/2003).
Thomas Fuller, 'Thais ask: 'What's in a nickname'?' (*International Herald Tribune, 23/08/2007*).

MALE GROOMING
Chetana Nagavajara, 'Unsex Me Here' (*Warasan Mahawitthayalai Silpakorn* 12).
Vasu, cited by Kreangsak Suwanpantakul, 'Still Macho' (28/09/2003).
Onsiri Pravattiyagul, 'Men: The New Women' (*BP*, 16/11/2003).

KATOEY & TOM-DEE
Bunmi Methangkun, 'How can people be kathoey?' (Abhidhamma Fdn, 1986).
Chanintorn Prasertprasart, cited by Alongkron Parivudhiphongs, 'The Katoey Connection' (*BP*, 13/03/1997).
Ornapa Krissadee & Dr Seri Wongmontha, cited by Alongkorn Parivudhiphongs, 'Absolutely Fabulous' (*BP*, 19/10/2002).

Prempreeda Pramoj na Ayutthaya, cited by Aree Chaisatien, 'Always here' (*TN*, 27/06/2004).

Thanyaporn Anyasiri, cited in 'The Next PM?' (*TN*, 13/11/2002).

Yuan Pumeekiatisak, cited by Daniel Gawthrop, 'Becoming Visible' (*TN*, 17/11/2002).

Sinott, Megan, 'Masculinity & Tom Identity in Thailand' in Jackson, Peter A & Sullivan, Gerard, ed *Ladyboys, Tom Boys, Rent Boys: Male & Female Homosexualities in Contemporary Thailand* (Silkworm Books, 2000).

INHALERS
'Kat's Window on Thailand: Personal Hygiene' (*TN*, 28/05/2001).

Chamsai Jotisalikorn, *Thai Spa Book*.

FURNITURE FOR FUN
Saiyaat Sema-ngoen, cited by Suthorn Sukphisit, 'Sit on this!' (*BP*, 19/07/2004).

Chamsai Jotisalikorn, *Classic Thai*.

THE ALPHABET TABLE
Klausner, William J, 'Thai Personal Pronouns: A Linguistic Labyrinth' in 'Transition' (*Journal of the Siam Society*, 1997).

Phya Anuman Rajadhon, 'Thai Language' in *Essay*.

Pracha Suveeranont, *Kae Roy Tua Pim Thai* (Tracing Thai Letter Printing), (*SC* Matchbox, 2002).

POTTED GARDENS
Nithinand Yorsaengrat, 'Thais, trees & the history of gardening' (*TN*, 30/03/1998).

Phya Anuman Rajadhon, 'Some Siamese Superstitions about Trees & Plants' in *Essay*.

THE POODLE BUSH
Alongkorn Parivudhiphongs, 'Balancing nature and artifice' (*BP*, 8/12/1995).

Pimsai Amranand & Warren, William, *Gardening in Bangkok* (Siam Society, 1970, 1996).

CUTE
Geraci, Massimiliano, 'Shattered Childhood' (*Cyberzone magazine*, Italy, issue 17, 2003).

Gomorasca, Alessandro 'Under the Sign of Kawaii' in *The Fourth Sex: Adolescent Extremes* (Edizioni Charta, 2003).

Richie, Donald, *The Image Factory: Fads & Fashions in Japan* (Reaktion, 2003).

GARUDA
Nidhi Eoseewong, cited by Sanitsuda Ekachai, *Keeping the Faith* (Post Books, 2001).

Wisut Busayakul, *Garuda* (Prime Minister's Office, 2000).

DAY THEMES
Brown, Richard S, *Ancient Astrological Gemstones & Talismans* (AGT, 1995).

Phya Anuman Rajadhon, 'Sawasdi Raksa' in *Essay*.

MONK BASKETS
Sunee Tuampuemphol, article on Pithee Kong Khao spirit appeasing ceremony in Sri Racha (*BP*, 26/04/2001).

AMULET COLLECTORS
Chamlong Krutkhunthod, cited by Nauvarat Suksamran, 'Revered monk made unwitting canvasser' (*BP*, 9/12/2000).

Choochart Marksamphan, cited by Krisna Chaiyarat, 'Luck in the Box' (*TN*, 27/02/1999) and Pongpet Mekloy, 'This Charming Man' (*BP*, 9/08/1999).

Kamol Sukin, 'Losing its Charm' (*TN*, 26/08/2007).

Sanitsuda Ekachai, 'Sale of amulets not so charming' (*BP*, 26/11/1997).

Wasan Potipimpanon, cited by Montira Narkvichien, 'Wasan barters Benzes for Buddha amulets' (*TN*, 12/05/2003).

TAXI ALTARS
Suwit Thongthim, cited by Ramona Bohwongprasert, 'Drivin' Disco' (*Metro*, 10/1999).

MAGICAL TATTOOS
Phya Anuman Rajadhon, 'Thai Charms & Amulets' in *Essay*.

PALAD KHIK
Freidman, Bruno, 'Thai Phallic Amulets' (*Journal of the Siam Society, vol 65 part 2*, 1977).

Phya Anuman Rajadhon, 'Thai Charms & Amulets' in *Essay*.

Terwiel, BJ, 'The Origin & Meaning of the Thai city pillar' (*Journal of the Siam Society, vol 66 part 2*, 1978).

TRADE TALISMANS
Phya Anuman Rajadhon, 'Thai Charms & Amulets' in *Essay*.

Thanapon Chadchaidee, 'Essays on Thailand' (*DT Today*, 1994).

'Superstore zoning extended' (*TN*, 5/02/2003).

NANG KWAK
Bornoff, Nicholas, 'Things Japanese' (*Periplus*, 2002).

Phya Anuman Rajadhon, 'Thai Charms & Amulets' in 'Essay'.

Sombat Plainoi, *Thai Customs and Beliefs* (Office of the National Culture Commission, 1988).

Thanapon Chadchaidee, 'Essays on Thailand' (*DT Today*, 1994).

FORTUNE TELLERS
Bangkokian, 'If it's a Pulitzer, I'll toss fortune cookies' (*BP*, 16/08/2003).

Sungkorn Horharin, cited by Karchariya Sukrung in 'The Art of Tarot' (*BP*, 9/10/2003).

Nidhi Eoseewong, cited by Sanitsuda Ekachai, *Keeping the Faith* (Post Books, 2001).

Phra Dhammapitaka, cited by Sanitsuda Ekachai, *Keeping the Faith* (Post Books, 2001).

Vorapan Lauhawilai, cited by Tabitha Phillips, 'Revelations' (*Metro*, 01/1995).

Figures on fortune telling spending, Kasikorn Bank research

MEDIUMS AND SHAMANS
Brecelic, Tom, 'Some Enchanted Evening' (*Metro*, 06/2001).

Han Raksajit, cited by Tom Brecelic, 'Serial Griller' (*Metro*, October 2001), and Benjawan Somsin 'Into the world of black magic' (*TN*, 21/08/2002).

Nidhi Eoseewong, cited by Sanitsuda Ekachai, *Keeping the Faith* (Post Books, 2001).

GHOST STORIES
Phya Anuman Rajadhon, *Essay & Buddhism*.

Undon Thani monk cited by Sumet Suwanapruek, 'Ghost busters hunt entrail-eating bogies' (*BP*, 4/06/2003).

MODERN SHRINES
Nidhi Eoseewong, cited by Sanitsuda Ekachai, *Keeping the Faith* (Post Books, 2001).

Nopadol Thithipongpanich, cited by

Chompoo Trakullertsathien, 'A new home for the spirits' (*BP*, 05/23/1996).

Nuttamon, cited by Karnjariya Sukrung, 'Looking for love in all the old places' (*BP*, 06/06/2004).

Suluck Visavapattamawong, cited by Chompoo Trakullertsathien, 'A new home for the spirits' (*BP*, 05/23/1996).

TEMPLE FAIRS
Subhatra Bhumiprabhas 'All the fun of the fair' (*TN*, 17/04/1997).

Suthorn Sukphisit 'Let's go to the fair!' (*BP*, 23/09/2002); 'Magnificent Spirit Calling Ceremony in the North' in *The Vanishing Face of Thailand* (Post Books, 1997).

GAMBLING
Anchalee Kongrut 'Lizard on its last legs' (*BP*, 30/06/2001).

Chaiwat Pasokpuckdee, cited by Theeranuch Pusaksrikit 'You've got to be in it to win it!' (*TN*, 20/04/2003).

Karuna Buakhamsir & Bussarawan Teerawichitainan 'The gambling game' (*BP*, 24/06/1996).

Preeyanat Panayanggoor 'Lottery "a way of life", not just gambling' (*BP*, 5/06/2003).

'70% of Thais gamble' figures from Thai Farmers Research Centre.

Sangsidh Piriyarangsan & Santhana Prayoonrat, cited in Supradit Kanwanich & Surath Jinakul, 'An open secret is revealed' (*BP*, 17/11/2002).

Theeranuch Pusaksrikit 'You've got to be in it to win it!' (*TN*, 20 April 2003).

Theeranuch Pusaksrikit & Kanniga Buraphatanin 'Soccer betting - how to score' (*TN*, 9/11/2002).

Wichit Chantanusornsiri 'Turning the Table on Punters' (*BP*, 21 April 2003).

ANIMAL CONTESTS
Fang, Sam, 'The Cockfight' in *Bangkok's Chatuchak Weekend Market* (Sam Fang, Singapore 1988).

Police Colonel Wichit Nanthawong, 'Fears dealers released piranhas into canals' (*BP*, 30/05/2004).

MUAY THAI
Amornrit Pramorn, cited by Tatpachuen Thaiprasithiporn, 'Fighting for a vanishing art' (*TN*, 25/08/2003).

Junlakan, Lesley, *Muay Thai: A Living Legacy* (Spry Books, 2001).

BEAUTY QUEENS
Anjira Assavananda, 'Trees engaged in Thai-style ceremony to promote nature' (*BP*, 28/02/2003).

Prof Dr Nongpa-nga Limsuwan, cited by Sukanya Sae-Lim, Prapasri Osathanon & Tulsathit Taptim, 'Dual ambitions or double standards?' (*TN*, 4/06/1999).

Prasert Joemjutithum, 'Eye of the Beholder' (*TN*, 9/06/2002).

LUUK THUNG & MOR LAM
Carr, Tim 'Music' in *Time Out Bangkok* (2003).

Decha Suvinijit, cited by Rob Few in 'Blue Suede Shoes' (*Bangkok Metro*, 09/2000).

Surachai Sombatcharoen, cited by Lockard, Craig A in *Dance of Life: Popular Music & Politics in SE Asia* (Silkworm, 2001).

COMEDY CAFÉS
Somyot Suthangkoon, cited by Boonlert Siakim, 'The Café King' (*TN*, 23/07/1988).

Salin Pinkayan, 'We're famous for smiles, not humour' (*TN*, 25/04/2004).

Tawee Peungboon na Ayutthaya, 'Playing for Laughs' (*Caravan*, 07/1994).

Wittawat Soontornvinate, cited by Richard Ehrlich 'Talk of the Town' (*Metro*, 05/1996).

THE WHISKY MIXER TABLE
Blarcom, Tom Van, cited by Philip Cornwel-Smith 'Strip Search' (*Metro*, 03/1999).

Cummings, Joe, *World Food Thailand*. Pinedo, Manuel, cited by Philip Cornwel-Smith 'Strip Search' (*Metro*, 03/1999).

RED BULL
Mastechitz, Dietrich, cited by Veena Thoopkrajae, 'Mr Red Bull shares secrets of his success' (*TN*, 29/08/2003).

Kamoldist Samuthkochorn, cited by Kwanchai Rungfapaisarn, 'Carabao exec looks to boost energy drinks' (*TN*, 20/05/2003).

Manit Rattanasuwan, cited by Kwanchai Rungfapaisarn, 'Two new brands in fiercest market' (*TN*, 20/12/2002).

Pavin Chachawalpongpun, 'When nationalism becomes self-serving' (*TN*, 11/06/2003).

YA DONG
Anchana Wichit, 'Spice of Life?' (*Metro*, 09/1995).

Dr Parinya Utitchalanon, from interviews and cited by Suthon Sukphisit, 'Healthy Spirits' (*BP*, 22/02/2000).

Santi Watthana, cited by Suthorn Sukphisit, 'Healthy Spirits' (*BP*, 22/02/2000).

MULTI-PURPOSE CELEBRITIES
Alongkorn Parivudhiphongs, 'On Reflection: Fame' (*BP*, 3/05/2004).

Areeya 'Nong Pop' Sirisopha, cited by Philip Cornwel-Smith, 'Girl Uninterrupted' (*Metro*, 03/2002).

Gilda Cordero-Fernando, *Pinoy Pop Culture* (Bench, 2001).

SOAP OPERAS
Chanintorn Prasertprasart, cited by Alongkorn Parivudhiphongs, 'The Katoey Connection' (*BP*, 13/03/1997).

Kasidin Siengworapong, cited by Peter Beckett 'Murky Waters' (*Metro*, 05/1996).

Peter Beckett 'Murky Waters' (*Metro*, 05/1996).

Salaya, cited by Alongkorn Parivudhiphongs, 'Made for TV' (*BP*, 23/06/2004).

Supatra Suparb, cited by Peter Beckett 'Murky Waters' (*Metro*, 05/1996).

Surang Prempri, 'Storm in a tea cup' (*BP*, 14/08/2003).

SONGS FOR LIFE
Carr, Tim, 'Music' in *Time Out Bangkok* (Time Out, 2003).

T-POP GOES INDY
Don Sambandaraksa, 'Ragnarok Online' (*BP*, 6/08/2003).

Mailer, Norman, cited by Dick Hebdige, Subculture.

Manond Apanich, 'Bigger, Fatter', (*TN*, 05/11/04).

Nation staff, 'Ragnarok: Friend or Fore?' (*TN*, 13/02/2003).

Newspaper research, Dr Anucha Thirakanont, Communications Faculty, Thammasat University.

Swartzentruber, David, 'Bureaucrats once again out of touch' (13/07/2003).

Index

Incorporating glossary, picture index and historical eras

Bold numbers indicate the pictures accompanying text. Thais are listed under first names, as per convention.